PREPARING FOR POWER

PREPARING FOR POWER

AMERICA'S ELITE BOARDING SCHOOLS

Peter W. Cookson, Jr.

Caroline Hodges Persell

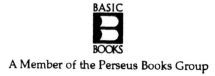

A Member of the Perseus Books Group

Library of Congress Cataloging-in-Publication Data

Cookson, Peter W.
  Preparing for power.

  References: p. 240
  Includes index.
    1. Preparatory schools—United States.   2. Upper
classes—Education (Secondary)—United States.
I. Persell, Caroline Hodges. II. Title.
LC58.4.C66 1985   373.2'22'0973   85–22989
ISBN   0–465–06268–7   (cloth)
ISBN   0–465–06269–5   (paper)

Basic Books is a Member of the Perseus Books Group.
Visit us on the World Wide Web at www.basicbooks.com

To Susan, Sasha, and Aram, with love and pride.

PWC, Jr.

and to

Charlie, Patty, and Steve, with love and gratitude.

CHP

Contents

CONTENTS

PART III

THE WORLD BEYOND

Acknowledgments

THE STUDY of boarding schools has been an exciting and rewarding challenge. One of the most gratifying aspects of our research has been the many supportive people who have helped us through each part of our work. We are deeply indebted to them. To express our appreciation of them publicly is one small way of acknowledging their varied and crucial contributions. They deserve special recognition for sharing with us their time, energy, and knowledge.

A number of individuals helped us with data gathering and management, coding, keypunching, computer analysis, and typing. They include: Daniel Cohen, Lisa Eig, Charlotte Fischer, Annie Geo, Nancy Harris, Patricia Hartman, Karen Helsing, Kathleen Helsing, Bert Holland, Nilma Maichin, Kathleen Montgomery, Pam Pozarny, Sheri Prupis, Michael Putnam, Yolanda Romero, Martin Rouse, George Sharrard, SoHo Typing, and Martha Wolf.

It has been our good fortune to share our work with many colleagues at New York University and elsewhere. We have benefited greatly from their constructive suggestions and encouragement. Needless to say, they cannot be held responsible for the way we have or have not utilized their comments. In particular, we want to thank Philip Altbach, Mordecai Arieli, Christopher F. Armstrong, E. Digby Baltzell, Lloyd Barenblatt, Basil Bernstein, Steven Brint, Roger Bullock, Randall Collins, Paul Cullinan, Kevin

Dougherty, Edgar Epps, Mary Frank Fox, Eliot Freidson, Kathleen Gerson, Joseph Giacquinta, David Greenberg, Bruce Hare, Wolf Heydebrand, Barbara Heyns, Robert Jackson, Yitzhak Kashti, Jerome Karabel, Hope Klapper, Edward W. Lehman, Richard Maisel, David Mallory, Herbert Menzel, John Meyer, Karen Miller, Spencer Millham, Henry Perkinson, Richard R. Peterson, Edwin Schur, Patricia Cayo Sexton, Rina Shapira, Susan Shapiro, Malcolm Spector, Beth Stevens, Michael Useem, Dennis Wrong, and a number of anonymous journal reviewers. We would especially like to thank Floyd Morgan Hammack of New York University for sharing with us his wide scholarship and enthusiasm in the early phase of this research. For nearly a decade we have collaborated on a number of research and writing projects, which we feel have benefited greatly from our combined efforts. Both of us have contributed equally to this research study and this book, and the order of our names should not be interpreted otherwise.

James Oliver Brown helped us to find a happy home with Basic Books, where we benefited from the considerable editorial sagacity of Jo Ann Miller, the careful production supervision of Maureen Bischoff, the astute copy editing of Erin Clermont, the thorough indexing of Ruth Elwell, and the able assistance of Amy Ellis.

Our fieldwork was greatly aided by the generous hospitality and support of many friends, including Maurice and Ruth Ash, Peter and Beatrice Cookson, Evelyn Edson and the Springtree Community, David and Sandy Edwards, Sue and Bob Fletcher, Dan and Mary Frank Fox, Carl and Henrietta Hartman, Karen and Tom Louis, Anne and Barry Mahoney, Sue and Malcolm Martin, and Leslie and Florence Share. They fed us, often invited us to stay overnight with them, and generally nurtured us in the course of our work.

We are grateful for the direct or indirect support of various funding agencies including the Elmgrant Trust, the National Istitute of Education, New York University Challenge Fund, the Spencer Foundation, and Tel-Aviv University, which contributed in various ways to one or another strand of our overall research project. The views reflected in this book are those of the authors alone and should not in any way be taken as official policies of any of the funding sources.

Lastly, and most important, we want to thank the many boarding school students, teachers, administrators, and alumni for generously and graciously sharing with us their time, thoughts, and feelings. We are indebted to them for their willingness to tell us what life was like for them; without their participation this book would not have been possible. The heads of the schools, in particular, deserve special recognition for their commitment to independent research and for facilitating this study in many practical ways.

PREPARING FOR POWER

Prologue: Seeking the Prep School Perspective

IF ONE were to think of American education in terms of a landscape, boarding schools would occupy a tiny corner of the topography. Accustomed as we are to equating size with importance, the relatively small number of boarding schools nationwide might suggest that the serious study of these schools will not substantially increase our understanding of how education shapes young people, or how education affects the larger society. In the public mind, boarding schools cater to the rich on the one hand, or are imposed on the weak and deviant on the other. The fact that less than 10 percent of American high school students attend private school and only 20 to 30 percent of those are enrolled in private residential schools suggests that boarding schools are marginal to the main contours of American life. If we were to reduce our sample even further to include only elite preparatory, or "prep," schools, then the number of students attending those schools is less than one percent of the total high-school population. The one percent who attend the elite schools are not randomly selected from the population at large. They are overwhelmingly the children of the privileged classes. At one elite school, 40 percent of the 1982 graduating class was drawn from families listed in the *Social Register*. Tuition at the elite schools hovers around $10,000 per year. Given that the pre-tax median income of the American family is about $21,000 a year, arithmetic alone can provide a clue to the economic backgrounds of most boarding school students. The maintenance of this privilege, we will argue, requires much more than money alone; it requires a philosophy, a way of living, and a justification.

In this book we document how the philosophies, programs, and life-styles of boarding schools help transmit power and privilege and how elite families use the schools to maintain their social class. We believe that this study is the most comprehensive examination of elite schools to date; our observations are based on hundreds of hours of interviews and conversations with prep school heads, teachers, students, and alumni, as well as on thousands of student questionnaires and hundreds of teacher questionnaires. We visited more than sixty boarding schools in the United States and England. Wherever possible we have used the participants' own words to tell the prep school story so that the inner lives of the schools can be revealed.

We begin with a preliminary observation that much of the importance of boarding school lies in the eye of the beholder. To many people, residential schools are commonly associated with juvenile reform, whether in the form of an actual reform school or a military academy. Boarding school is where the student who could not make it in public school is sent. On the East Coast, knowledge about boarding schools is largely confined to the upper class, the upper-middle class, and a small proportion of the middle class. This is not to say that knowledge about boarding schools beyond the eastern seaboard or south of the upwardly mobile middle class is entirely absent. There are a number of regional schools, such as the Cranbrook School in Michigan and the Hockaday School in Texas that have strong, loyal constituents; on the West Coast, Thacher and the Cate School.

Yet, the idea of sending a child away to school has distinctly European —especially British—overtones, and it is on the East Coast where the British influence is most strongly felt. One of the hallmarks of the American upper class is its Anglophilia, and a good many prep schools were founded on the British model. Like most cultural imitations, American Anglophilia is heavily influenced by national behaviors and attitudes and compared to Eton or Harrow, even the most venerable of American schools seems very young indeed.

This Anglicism is part of the snobbery that is associated with prep schools. As schools that train the children of such illustrious American families as the Rockefellers, Kennedys, and Vanderbilts, prep schools have gained the reputation of being educational country clubs where children of wealthy families are sent to get socially polished and prepared for admission to acceptable colleges. Writers such as David Halberstam cultivated this perception when he described McGeorge Bundy, a prep school alumnus, in larger-than-life terms:

> He attended Groton, the greatest "Prep" school in the nation, where the American upper class sends its sons to instill the classic values: discipline, honor, a belief in the existing values and the rightness of them. Coincidentally, it's at Groton that one starts to meet the right people, and where connections which will serve well later on—be it at Wall Street or Washington—are first forged; one learns, at Groton, above all, the rules of the Game and even a special language: what washes and does not wash. (Halberstam 1969, 51)

This sense of prep power and privilege is reinforced by such magazines as *Town & Country,* which publishes articles with titles like, "New England Prep Schools—Are They Still the ULTIMATE?" (Strong 1980, 65–72) and the *Atlantic Monthly,* which published Nelson W. Aldrich, Jr.'s witty satire "Preppies—The Last Upper Class?" (1979, 56–66).

Of course, for those on the inside, the public image of a prep school education is taken with a few grains of salt. The recent marketing of "preppiness" through *The Official Preppy Handbook* (Birnbach 1980) and other "preppy" paraphernalia contains more than an element of mockery. In true prep fashion, however, it is difficult to know precisely who is mocking whom.

The schools themselves do a great deal to cultivate the public image of intellectual rigor and social responsibility. For instance, we were told by several heads that their schools represented "the best of western civilization," and in more than a few cases, it was implied that boarding schools were one of the last hopes of western civilization. When asked what quality was most important for the development of an outstanding head, those heads we questioned in an earlier study chose morality over all other choices by a wide margin (Cookson 1980).

How paradoxical it is, then, to see the *New York Post* headline, "COKE SCANDAL RIPS POSH PREP SCHOOL" (5 May 1984). Or to read in the more sedate *New York Times* that, "The school would not give additional details. Reporters were denied interviews with school officials, and security guards tried to keep reporters and the expelled students off the school grounds" (5 May 1984). Why would young people who are the recipients of the very best education available spend time in the drug trade? The glare of negative publicity casts the schools in a new and somewhat strange light. Is the gap between the ideal and reality as great as it appears? Is there an underlying explanation for this apparent paradox?

We believe that the answers to these questions lie deep within the prep mystique. Part of this is the purported inaccessibility of the elite schools. Because most of the schools are physically remote and socially exclusive, social scientists have assumed that their ivy-covered walls could not be scaled by outsiders. Ian Weinberg, the English sociologist, stressed this idea in his 1968 paper, "Some Methodological and Field Problems of Social Research in Elite Secondary Schools."

Yet, by and large, we found the schools we visited to be quite receptive to our study. With a few exceptions, access was not difficult; most of the schools were very generous with their time and allowed us considerable freedom in the data collection process. Our strategy for gaining access was direct; we wrote to the heads of the schools we wanted to study and requested permission to visit their campuses and interview various members of their community. At some schools we asked permission to administer a student questionnaire to freshmen and seniors. Our letter was followed up with a telephone conversation with the head. In all but one case, each school we approached immediately or subsequently agreed to have us visit. We know of only one case where the school "checked up" on us. We did happen to come across one intraschool memo at another elite school that noted in reference to us, "They don't appear to be hostile." A few schools wanted to meet us in person before agreeing to join the study, but no school set down any conditions prior to our arrival. We pulled no strings, nor did we need to. After being forewarned by colleagues, "You'll never get into those schools," the graciousness of our reception was gratifying and a little perplexing. Had Weinberg and others exaggerated the aloofness of the schools, or had they recently changed their attitude toward research?

If one were feeling cynical it might appear that the schools were willing to participate because they hoped the study would put them in the best light. Most heads probably hoped that this study would highlight the positive aspects of boarding school life, but as they had no control over how the results of the study were reported it is somewhat difficult to believe that they saw it as a public relations exercise. We had no official status within the private school world but we did assure the heads that we would treat the material we gathered with confidentiality and integrity.

Some heads will not like everything we have to say about the schools, and some may disagree with us, but we hope that in remaining true to the data we have gathered we have managed to capture the real importance of these schools. Thus, while we don't in any way feel coopted by the schools, we have gained a genuine respect for their willingness to share themselves with outsiders.

The open-door policy of the elite schools was not limited to our study. Other authors have been admitted to the elite schools (see, for example, Armstrong 1974, and Baird 1977). In two other research efforts we have found private boarding schools to be generous with their time and data (Cookson 1980, 1981). In an irony that might have confounded Weinberg, access to American public schools can be more difficult than to private schools because in the public sector authority to make decisions is often complicated by competing interest groups, including unions and administrators. In part we believe we were able to study the elite schools because we demonstrated a serious approach to the subject. We tried to see as many schools as possible, and we sampled a range of schools. We gathered hard data, as well as listened with our inner ears, because facts unconnected by understanding can add to the collective ignorance rather than dispel it. Measurement without empathy is empty, and we tried to sensitize ourselves to the prep school perspective.

Our primary, but by no means only, source of information is firsthand field visits to fifty-five American boarding schools, ten English boarding schools, two Cuban boarding schools, and one Israeli boarding school. The fifty-five American schools include eleven boarding schools that we visited in 1978–79 as part of a study of teacher evaluation in private schools.[1] We visited schools in fifteen states, including New Hampshire, North Carolina, Michigan, Texas, Colorado, Arizona, and California (see appendix for a complete list of the English and American schools). Between us, we traveled more than 60,000 miles. The statements we make in this book are based primarily on the visits we made to schools between 1981 and 1983, and on questionnaires given during those years at a subsample of the schools.

The days we spent in American schools were long ones; we arose as early as 4 A.M. to witness students mucking out the cow barn at a progressive school, and we stood dorm duty with teachers until students settled in for the night. We stayed anywhere from one to five days at each school, and observed classes, assemblies, chapel services, sports contests, cultural events, discipline committee meetings, and student and faculty parties. We shared innumerable meals and saw dorms, libraries, laboratories, gymnasiums, and other facilities in operation. We interviewed heads, teachers, directors of admission, college advisors, deans of students, deans of faculty, dorm supervisors, school psychologists and doctors—and students— alone or in small groups.

---

1. See appendix for a copy of the teacher questionnaire completed by 382 teachers in that study.

While 50 out of 55 of the American schools we visited are college preparatory secondary schools, we also visited schools for special populations such as deaf and blind children, "pre-prep" schools for junior high-school children, military schools, and a publicly financed boarding school for high school juniors and seniors gifted in science and mathematics.

It should be clear, however, that when we speak of America's elite boarding schools we are referring to private secondary boarding schools. As part of the background for this study, we surveyed the American prep school world by recording the number of schools and their most important attributes. We used the definitive *Handbook of Private Schools* (Porter Sargent 1981) as our guide, and in general when we speak of the elite schools we are referring to the 289 schools the handbook defines as "leading" secondary boarding schools.

The schools we visited between 1981–83 gave us a full complement of their printed materials, including catalogues, curricular listings, school newspapers, alumni magazines, application forms, and brochures. Friends who knew of our interest in boarding schools provided us with school directories, reunion class surveys, speeches by heads, and similar materials.

At twenty of the schools we administered anonymous questionnaires to 2,475 freshmen and senior students,[2] exploring their family backgrounds, views about the academic climates of their schools, what they like best and least about boarding school, why they came, whether they think it has changed them and if so, how, and what their educational, occupational, and life goals are. Some of the items included in our questionnaire were identical to those used by Coleman, Hoffer, and Kilgore in their study of public and private school students (1982, 250–77). The inclusion of these items enabled us to compare boarding school students with a national sample of public and private school students. In addition, we asked students to write an open-ended essay about their futures. This information enabled us to do extensive statistical and qualitative analyses of the students' experiences and thoughts.[3]

2. In most cases we administered the anonymous questionnaires to all freshmen and seniors ourselves. In three schools a random sample of half of those students were selected to answer the questionnaires and in two small schools a non-random sample of students answered the questionnaires. Two schools administered the questionnaires for us, either before or after our visit.

3. Table A–1 in the appendix indicates how our student questionnaire sample and our field sample compare with the national population of leading boarding schools. Our sample of schools, including those where we administered the questionnaires, was not drawn randomly from the national population of boarding schools, but was instead chosen because it was representative of the types of boarding schools we were interested in studying. In particular, our sample includes more socially elite schools than is found in the population of boarding schools in general.

There were 1,345 seniors who completed questionnaires. Schools provided us with complete academic information for 1,035 seniors, including Scholastic Aptitude Test scores, grade point averages, academic, athletic, social, or other honors received at graduation, names of the colleges to which they applied, where they were accepted, and which ones they would attend.

We also tabulated data on 289 leading secondary boarding schools from the Porter Sargent directory, including date of founding, male or female enrollments, location, faculty size, characteristics of school heads, number of advanced courses, endowment, facilities, and religious affiliation.

Finally we conducted formal and informal interviews with more than one hundred boarding school alumni, exploring their feelings about the experience, friendship ties, and school influences. The integrated use of field visits, observations, interviews, school publications, survey questionnaires, school record data, directory data, and statistical analysis has afforded us a rare opportunity to examine the richness and complexity of boarding school life.

True complexity is extremely difficult to measure, however, because paradox and contradiction characterize so much of human behavior. We might collect perfect data and still fail to understand the subject because a culture is too deep and pervasive to be understood out of context. Often our most important insights occurred when we least expected them, or when heads or students inadvertently let their guards down. A chance remark is often more likely to reveal a person's real feelings or thoughts than an answer to a formal question; points of view are best observed in action rather than in words alone. What is hidden from public inspection must be discovered by indirection and subtlety. There were times during this study when we felt as though we were visiting a series of remote and small tribes. Much of this work was ethnographic, in that we tried to sensitize ourselves to our subjects' personal attitudes, feelings, and vocabularies. We wanted to understand the real folkways of the prep school world, not simply measure inputs and outcomes.

As a rule of thumb, we found that the greater a school's social prestige, the more complex the access, though there were exceptions to this rule. In fact, several of the most elite schools were among the first to join the sample and many of these were very generous in their support of our efforts. Small, lesser known schools provided us with many key insights into the boarding experience, and, as another rule of thumb, we found that as we left the East Coast our relations with the schools were easier and more informal.

Many heads and other administrators tried to evaluate us, as well. How much did we really know about boarding schools? What could they tell us in confidence and what should remain hidden? Most heads are adroit at assessing people and most often they tried to direct our attention with wit, subtlety, and style. One vice rector at a very socially elite school asked, "And who will buy this book?"—as though interest in prep schools certainly must be limited. We hope that this is not true. The story of how America's most elite secondary schools train their students for academic success and social position is one that should be told, in large part because it reveals the price of privilege and the inner sacrifices that children are expected to make on the road to power. It is an intriguing and illuminating tale.

We begin our examination of boarding schools in part 1, The World of Boarding Schools, by examining their importance vis-à-vis privilege in the first chapter. Chapter 2 provides an overview of elite total institutions around the world and the varieties of American boarding schools. In chapter 3 we discuss who actually goes to boarding school. Part 2, The Prep Rite of Passage, deals with life within the schools. Chapter 4 is about boarding school curricula and the life-styles of boarding school teachers. Chapter 5 describes boarding school teaching styles and how the pressured academic atmospheres of the schools affect students. Chapter 6 examines the careers of school heads and power relationships within boarding schools. Chapter 7 analyzes the prep crucible in detail and Chapter 8 describes how students react to life in the total institution. Part 3, The World Beyond, looks at what happens to preps after they leave school. Chapter 9 is a full discussion of how prep school students get into college and where they go, and chapter 10 is about prep life after boarding school, at play, in the power structure, and the problems of maintaining power in the face of a growing culture of narcissism.

PART

I

THE WORLD OF BOARDING SCHOOLS

1

Privilege and the Importance of Elite Education

I N 1946 a young, politically ambitious Choate graduate was asked to make some remarks on the occasion of Choate's fiftieth anniversary. "I think," John F. Kennedy said, "the success of any school can be measured by the contribution the alumni make to our national life." Chastising private schools for not producing men or women who contribute to political life, he added with his characteristic directness, "In America, politics are regarded with great contempt; and politicians themselves are looked down upon because of their free and easy compromises . . . [but] we must recognize that if we do not take an interest in our political life we can easily lose at home what so many young men have so bloodily won abroad. I don't think this will happen. But it is the great challenge of our times" (McLachlan 1970, 298).

Kennedy's call for "prep power" was not altogether original. Endicott Peabody, the first rector of the Groton School, was explicit on the importance of preps in high places when he wrote in 1901 to Vice President Theodore Roosevelt (who had two sons at Groton), "There are great possibilities latent in our body so that you might legitimately look upon it as not entirely apart from your great work of the development of the nation" (McLachlan 1970, 243).

The frequency with which both Kennedy and Peabody used the word "great" was not by chance. Peabody's hope that "prepness" and greatness would become synonymous was at least partly fulfilled; President Franklin D. Roosevelt and Secretary of State Dean Acheson were both Grotonians. The rector's grandson, also named Endicott Peabody, became governor of Massachusetts and his granddaughter, Marietta Endicott Peabody Tree, played a key role in New York City politics as a member of the Lexington Democratic Club. Adlai Stevenson was a Choate man and Kennedy, of course, became president in 1960.

Certainly there was much in John Kennedy's style that was prep, including his ability to enunciate high ideals while simultaneously practicing *realpolitik* with a certain refined vengeance. The New Frontier was in some ways the product of the first truly prep government, but not the last. Curiously, Ronald Reagan's "sagebrush" rebellion against the Eastern Establishment includes a number of preps, as well as Westerners with Ivy League degrees. Vice President George Bush is a Phillips Andover alumnus, and Secretary of the Treasury James Baker III is a Hill School graduate. Secretary of Commerce Malcolm Baldrige graduated from the Hotchkiss School. In a political irony that might not have appealed to the liberal Kennedy, prep school graduates of a more politically conservative orientation have answered the "great challenge" to serve the republic in growing numbers.

Power and privilege are not usually central issues in discussions of education. After all, part of the tradition of democracy is that individuals should be allowed to succeed according to their abilities; barriers to mobility are an affront to the frontier spirit in American life. Of course, we recognize that barriers do exist; demonstrating that education does little to reduce social inequalities has become something of a growth industry in academic circles. To the general public, however, the purpose of education goes largely unquestioned. Schools are places where students learn to read, write, and do their sums, and because students are evaluated according to their abilities, the great status race starts off fairly if not exactly evenly. If some students excel while others fall behind it is a personal, not a social, problem. Like the Statue of Liberty, education should be blind to race, religion, sex, or national origin.

Thus Kennedy's and Peabody's attitude about the role of education in a democracy is something of a puzzlement because they imply that elitism in the public service, far from being a social embarrassment, is in fact a kind of national treasure. From their power point of view, it seems almost naive to argue that education should be the great equalizer. Implicit in the prep call to greatness is the unexpressed assumption that equality of educational opportunity is a fine idea as far as it goes—it just should not go too far. For those like themselves, who are destined for greatness, a different kind of education is needed.

Privilege and the Proper Study of Education

Opinions about the importance of elite secondary schools in American education and society are varied, but if silence can be interpreted as an opinion then it is fair to say that most observers of the educational scene either consider the schools too specialized or snobbish to be relevant in the larger context. There is virtually no systematic research on the specific topic of elite boarding schools, although private schools in general have recently been the focus of some public and scholarly attention (Coleman, Hoffer, Kilgore 1981).

One of the reasons there is so little research on the topic of elite schools is that the mere assertion that elite schools exist, especially socially elite schools, goes against the American grain—democracy is supposed to begin at the schoolhouse door. One has to be somewhat blinded by this glowing image of equality, however, not to see that private schools, in general, represent an elite alternative to the public educational system in much the same way that private cars are alternatives to public transportation. Private transport is easier, cleaner, often safer, and a good deal quicker. Yet it may also be more expensive and wasteful of resources.

The lack of information about what the elite schools actually do has led to some intriguing but not completely satisfying theorizing. Sociologist Ralph H. Turner minimized the importance of elite schools when he argued that unlike Great Britain, where "upward mobility is like entry into a private club where each candidate must be 'sponsored' by one or more of the members," upward mobility in the United States is more like a "contest," where elite status can be achieved "by the aspirant's own efforts" (1966, 450). Turner continues: "American studies of social mobility usually omit information on private versus tax supported secondary school attendance. Under contest mobility, the private schools presumably should have little or no mobility function" (Turner 1966, 456). Another sociologist, John Meyer, has argued in a similar vein that "Since for many personnel assignment purposes all American schools have similar 'status rights,' variations in their effects should be small" (1977, 60).

THE WORLD OF BOARDING SCHOOLS

Is it reasonable to suppose that a private school that has a carefully selected student body composed of the privileged children of the rich and famous has the same "status rights" as the average public high school, not to mention urban public school? Such a hypothesis certainly is counter-intuitive. Both authors are implying that where a person goes to school is of little or no consequence in later life. Is this the way life really works?

The educational sociologist Earl Hopper (1971) has pointed out that there is an important difference between "educational amount" and "educational route." Where one goes to school can be very important in determining his or her life-styles and life chances. Along these same lines, sociologist Randall Collins (1979) has argued that the most fundamental purpose of education is to prepare students for social and cultural positions within society. Thus, where a person goes to school may have little to do with his or her technical abilities, but it may have a lot to do with social abilities.

Learning certain social roles and behaviors is a central—and perhaps the only—purpose of education. Because we know that *where* individuals go to school determines *with whom* they associate, and we also know that the social characteristics of schools' student bodies have powerful effects on a number of "student outcomes," then the study of the most socially elite schools might provide important evidence of how schools shape students' life-styles and life chances.

Support for the view that where people go to school affects them and society in general most often comes from scholars and nonscholars who diverge from the mainstream of educational research by insisting that the issues of privilege and power are basic to discussions of who gets ahead and why. Unlike Turner, they do not see life in America as one big open contest. To the contrary, they think mobility in the United States is not too dissimilar to Great Britain, where class and hierarchy determine in large measure who stays on top and who stays at the bottom.

To propose that American society is almost as class-based as British society pushes one to the fringes of social respectability. The "advancement through merit" argument has become so dominant in public discussions of schooling that the "advancement through privilege" critique seems a trifle un-American. It is ironic, therefore, to discover that the first serious discussion of elite boarding schools and their place in American society was undertaken by E. Digby Baltzell, who has written extensively on the importance of the upper class and their values. Like most conservatives, he has devoted much intellectual energy to the search for "legitimate" authority. Baltzell (1958, 1964) has argued that the elite boarding schools are important because they prepare students for their places within what he calls the "Protestant Establishment." In discussing "Aristocracy and the Private School," he argues that not only do prep schools pass on class position, they also act as aristocratic assimilators in that they cream off the best and brightest of the non-WASP students and help forge a new "ethnic aristocracy of talented and ambitious young people" (Baltzell 1964, 344). He contrasts this true aristocrat with the old degenerate aristocrat "whose ancestors have intermarried for generations, there is often very little to talk about except sports and the market, child rearing and the mild extramarital affairs of the overly-bred-bored or how so-and-so, who was president of his class at St. Grottlesex [and who] is now quietly drinking himself to death" (Baltzell 1964, 303).

The candor with which Baltzell embraces class privilege is refreshingly honest, but unfortunately his romanticism leads into a certain sociological lyricism that rings false when, for instance, he writes that prep schools provide "dramatic witness to the staying power of the American Dream of equality of opportunity" (1964, 344). His curious inversion of the obvious is perhaps a result of having not actually studied the schools himself. Although in fairness to Baltzell, we will see in chapter 9 that prep schools do serve as sponsoring agencies for some students of lower social class backgrounds.

The historian James McLachlan, in partial response to Baltzell's romantic upper classness, has argued that the elite schools are victims of the press. Far from being bastions of snobbery, the elite schools were set up "to preserve the innocence of childhood into a pure and responsible maturity" (McLachlan 1970, 13). "Innocent" is not a likely adjective to describe Kennedy or Peabody, and one wonders if perhaps McLachlan's utopian romanticism springs from a historical illusion based on the pronouncements of the schools' headmasters and founders, who, after all, may have cloaked privilege in the mantle of innocence. What better way to diffuse criticism than to present a public face of rectitude and service?

At the other end of the political spectrum are the left-wing academics and writers who often have a love-hate attitude toward the elite schools or, more properly, find them the schools they love to hate. Their indignation at inequality has a tendency to shade their claims in dramatic contrasts of black or white. Inequality is bad; ergo elite schools are bad. Marxist scholar Paul M. Sweezy has written that prep schools undermine the revolutionary ardor of the working class by "sucking upwards the ablest elements of the lower classes, and thus performing the double function of infusing new brains into the ruling class and weakening the political leadership of the working class" (quoted in Baltzell 1964, 344).

One hesitates to argue with Sweezy because, as an Exeter and Harvard graduate, his assertions are underpinned by firsthand knowledge. With all due deference to Sweezy's elite credentials, however, the melodramatic image he creates about boarding schools seems arch, and even comical. For instance, it must be a bit of a letdown to pick up an Exeter school alumni bulletin and read such prosaic items as "Many Exies also turned up in New York in October for the Simon and Garfunkel concert in the park," or "I married my Hometown Honey . . . he's a plumber . . . and I'm a keypunch operator" (*The Bulletin of the Phillips Exeter Academy* January/February 1982, 45). Can one really say that such illustrious Exies as Gore Vidal and George Plimpton were working-class heroes nipped in the bud because they went to Exeter?

C. Wright Mills, whose interest in the "power elite" led him to believe that in the calculus of class, prep schools are essential for the preservation of privilege, wrote:

> As a selection and training place of the upper classes, both old and new, the private school is a unifying influence, a force for the nationalization of the upper classes. The less important the pedigreed family becomes in the careful transmission of moral and cultural traits, the more important the private school. The school—rather than the upper-class family—is the most important agency for transmitting the traditions of the upper social classes, and regulating the admission of new wealth and talent. It is the characterizing point in the upper-class experience. (Mills 1959, 64–65)

With such sociological *sturm und drang* one would anticipate a full exposure of exactly how the elite schools manage their upper-class responsibilities, yet discussions have been limited by a lack of evidence. As part of a larger ideological jig saw puzzle, the elite schools have been assumed to fulfill the purpose that authors have assigned to them. This nonempirical orientation is, paradoxically, compatible with the general style of modern educational research, which is to begin with "inputs" (that is, teachers, resources, facilities) and end with "outputs" (that is, achievement scores, college attendance rates, drop-out rates).

What all too often is missing from the study of schooling is what happens in the "black box" of the school itself. Schools are the object of study, but seldom the real subject. We became increasingly aware that the problem of studying the elite schools wasn't *if* they contributed to educational and social inequality, but how? The inner life of the schools became more absorbing to us, at the same time that the standard opinions about the schools seemed progressively too simplistic. Thus, while the topic of elite schools and the problem of educational and social inequality informed our perspective, it was only after hundreds of hours of data collection that the real subject of this book came into focus.

What Is Taught and What Is Learned

Fatigue is not usually considered one of the high roads to knowledge, but in our case the state of exhaustion that we felt after a day in boarding school was one of our first clues that life in elite schools was not all that it seemed. What we discovered was that the calm and beauty of most boarding school campuses is, as it were, only skin deep. Prep schools generate the pressures of a society in which everyone lives in close proximity and from which there is almost no escape. The external gentility of the schools often masks an incredibly demanding and sometimes unforgiving life-style.

Boarding school students, we began to see, are taught that they should be moral and treat life as an exciting challenge, but what they often learn is that life is hard, and that winning is essential for survival. The "muscular Christianity" that so well describes the essence of prep pride is exactly right: speak like a man or woman of God, but act like a man or woman who knows the score and can settle a score without flinching. Preps are taught that right should prevail, but they learn that often it does not.

The struggle to reconcile right and might, however, is only one of many paradoxes that characterize the prep school world. We wondered why it is that parents who want to "broaden" their children's outlooks enroll them in schools where the outlook seldom stretches beyond the school's boundaries. Why would parents who want to protect their children from the temptations of society send their children to environments where the temptations are so close at hand?

It took us some time to realize that many of the paradoxes about the schools were more apparent than real and that what appeared to be contradictory was actually complementary. Part of the preparation for power is learning to live in a world of seeming contradictions. By learning to reconcile the difference between what the schools teach and what is learned, students discover that power and pain are inseparable and that to a large degree the price of privilege is the loss of autonomy and individuality.

The popular image of prep schools as oases of learning and/or schools for snobbery is naive; prep schools are hard places, where literally from dawn to dusk each person's life is so regulated that freedom must be won by stealth. Moreover, most boarding school students come from homes where achievement is highly valued, even venerated. There are few mercies for the weak or inept. From the cradle, most prep school students are told to "be somebody"; few are told "just be yourself." Pressure on these students is relentless. From the moment they jump over (or stumble through) the hurdles of admission to an elite school, they must prove their worth by mastering the curriculum, the student culture, and their own vulnerability. The pressure to get into the right college can be excruciating for many of these young people. While they are taught cooperation, they learn competition. And they also have to grow up quickly: "Adolescent problems aren't real," one dean said with chilling finality. We began to see boarding schools as crucibles, from which some students emerged as tempered steel and others were simply burnt to a crisp. Life in the "total institution" is demanding, even a little frightening to some students, and there is, in the words of one student, "no place to hide."

Boarding school students are pressured from three different directions, in a triangle of tension. Families are anxious that their children succeed, which often runs counter to the school's public insistence on "morality," which is usually in direct opposition to the student culture's message of eat, drink, and be merry for tomorrow you graduate. These competing values create a psychic gauntlet through which the elite student must pass —the prep rite of passage. The difference between what is taught and what is learned is what creates the dynamic tension that permeates the campuses of the most elite schools.

By isolating students from their natural environment of family and community, the schools are also able to intervene in the adolescent growth process, the end result of which the schools hope will be intellectual and psychic transformation of their students. By stripping away the students' private selves, they are more easily able to socialize them. Yet when the self is exposed, increased vulnerability is created, making students ripe not only for the healthy influences of the school but also for the less healthy influences of the student underlife. The inner capital that a prep school graduate accumulates is not all fourteen-carat gold; some of it is brass.

Too often in the study of schools there is a kind of scholarly lip service paid to socialization without demonstrating its processes, without evaluating its manifest and latent effects, or without acknowledging that most socialization creates intended and unintended consequences. The prep rite of passage is designed to forge a certain type of elite consciousness, but not without a price. The elite boarding schools were not founded to "liberate" young adults. Quite the opposite, they were created to mold and shape adolescents in a particular way. In one sense, the prep rite of passage is unencumbering, if not liberating, because it is constructed to foster the belief that preps have earned their status by surviving the rigors of the total institution, and thus guilt is transformed into service. The belief that privilege is justified is essential to the upper-class outlook. Yet ironically, collective illusion is often less liberating than imprisoning.

What holds the upper class together is not only wealth and power, but shared beliefs and shared lives. A sense of collective identity, however, does not develop naturally; it must be forged out of actual encounters. Sociologist Randall Collins, who has offered a number of perceptive insights into the relation between the individual and society, has written:

> Everything we have hitherto referred to as "structure," insofar as it really occurs and is not just one of those myths people fabricate, can be found in the real behavior of everyday life, primarily in repetitive encounters . . . . Instead of trying to place individuals as members of certain groups, I should look for a set of influences on how each individual behaves, including what will make him associate with others in particular ways. (Collins 1975, 53–54)

Certainly boarding schools are designed to increase opportunities for "repetitive encounters." One of the consequences of the intensity of the prep crucible is that the usual adolescent behavior of seeking peer group support and approval is heightened. Friendships in prep schools can be deep and lasting, carrying over into adult life. Thus the web of affiliation that begins in the dormitories, playing fields, classrooms, and dining halls of elite schools does not end on the day of graduation but continues to grow, becoming more interwoven, entangled, and in the end, the basis of status group and class solidarity.

As Baltzell has pointed out, "The character of American upper-class institutions has usually been more a product of interpersonal networks than of ideological affinities" (1979, 278). Thus the intensity of the prep rite of passage has implications for social structure. We may not ignore *how* people think if we want to understand what they do—to themselves and to others. The "resonating relationships," as one head termed them, initiated at boarding schools may have vibrations that echo far beyond the boundaries of the elite cloisters.

The "Status Seminary" and Socialization for Power

The difference between a public school and an elite private school is, in one sense, the difference between a factory and a club. Public schools are evaluated on how good a product they turn out, and the measure of quality control is inevitably an achievement score of some kind. Public schools are not expected to educate the "whole child"— that is primarily the parents' responsibility. Education for participation in public life is usually confined to civics classes and the daily Pledge of Allegiance. Most high-school principals probably feel that their students do too much "resonating" and not enough studying. Who knows how a school board would respond to a principal who suggested that the real mission of the school was to "build character," or who proposed a faculty committee to study school "tone."

There is nothing intrinsic to private education that makes it superior to public education; on the contrary, many private schools turn out products that would make a public high-school principal blush. There is a lot of salvage work that goes on in the private sector and not all of it is successful. So to compare public and private schools in terms of their output really misses the point. To be accepted into a private school is to be accepted into a social club, or more generally speaking, a status group that is defined as a group of people who feel a sense of social similarity. People sharing the same status have similar life-styles, common educational backgrounds, and pursue similar types of occupations. Like a pyramid, the higher one goes the smaller and more elite the status group. Toward the top of the pyramid, status becomes reinforced by great wealth, and an upper class begins to emerge. Thus, the higher the social status of the students attending a school, the more elite the school is perceived. Because the most exclusive boarding schools have traditionally educated many upper-class children and a large number of children from high status families, they have become what we call "status seminaries."

A seminary, *Webster's Dictionary* tells us, is an environment producing a "specified class of persons." In a seminary, novitiates learn the norms, values, and mores of their particular group, but whereas the religious novitiate pursues a spiritual vocation, the prep novitiate has what might be called a "status" calling. Interestingly, "seminary" and "seedbed" have similar linguistic origins, and it is commonplace to compare elite boarding schools with hothouses. In the elite hothouse temperature, moisture and light are all regulated to produce healthy, standard, manageable products

—at least that's the ideal. In the seminary, the individual is submerged in the collective, and consciousness is molded by an unquestioned faith.

Of course, not all hothouses raise the same kind of plants, and not all boarding schools are equally elite. The vast wealth of the benefactors of the most exclusive schools is an indication, however, that the intention of many of the school founders was to create schools that were socially and culturally homogeneous, even though a key function of boarding schools was to integrate parvenus and patricians.

Yet, we wonder why the upper class and other high status families chose to create total institutions for the education of their adolescent children. After all, there were and still are socially elite day schools in Boston, Philadelphia, New York, and other cities. There is nothing natural about sending children away to school and there is nothing intrinsically elite in residential education. In fact, to some, the idea of sending a child away to school might seem an extreme solution to the problems of bringing up young people. Of course any cultural product that was stamped "Made in England" was snapped up by the American upper class in the latter part of the nineteenth century to legitimate and stylize their new wealth and extravagant life styles. If total institutions were good enough for the English upper class, why not for the American upper class?

Here one must distinguish reasons from rationalizations. McLachlan's argument that boarding schools were founded to create "bourgeois gentlemen" and to preserve adolescent innocence leaves unexplained why it was that the upper class was attracted to such a radical educational solution as that of exiling their children. Certainly an exclusive day school can be just as "gentlemanly" as a boarding school. Other explanations, such as congested cities and poor public schools, are not without some plausibility but still don't explain the need for a total institution.

The founding of boarding schools in the United States was part of an upper-class "enclosure movement"[1] that took place in the late nineteenth century. In order to insulate themselves from the rest of society, the American upper class established their own neighborhoods, churches, suburban and rural recreational retreats, and a number of social and sporting clubs. It was during this period that the *Social Register* was first published and, in lavish displays of conspicuous consumption, the social season was highlighted by debutante balls and charity benefits. The rugged individu-

---

1. The enclosure movement in England during the fifteenth century referred to the process of fencing in formerly common land for sheep herding.

alism of the robber barons had become civilized and regulated; winning was now not enough, credentials had to be formalized and bloodlines identified and protected. By insulating themselves, the upper class could get on with the business of creating an American aristocracy without too many prying eyes.

According to Baltzell (1958) the exclusive prep school played an important role in the formation and maintenance of an American upper class because the schools enrolled both Eastern patricians and parvenus.[2] By putting a Boston patrician under the same roof with a New York parvenu, the schools ensured that blood and money would recognize their class interests were the same and that they should act in concert. The shared ordeal of the prep rite of passage would create bonds of loyalty that differences in background could not unravel. The collective identity forged in prep schools would become the basis of upper-class solidarity and consciousness.

Ultimately, however, sharing alone will not preserve or enhance a class's interest; as a group, the members must be willing to exercise their power against others. The very definition of power is to impose one's will on another, and to be effective power must be exercised collectively. As the character O'Brien points out to Winston Smith in George Orwell's *1984*:

> The first thing you must realize is that power is collective. The individual only has power in so far as he ceases to be an individual. (1949, 218)

The preservation of privilege requires the exercise of power, and those who exercise it cannot be too squeamish about the injuries that any ensuing conflict imposes on the losers. The people who founded American boarding schools during the time of the robber barons were far from innocent or naive about how the world worked, and deliberately chose heads who were adept at portraying the world in moral terms. The founders of the schools recognized that unless their sons and grandsons were willing to take up the struggle for the preservation of their class interests, privilege would slip from the hands of the elite and eventually power would pass to either a competing elite or to a rising underclass.

Thus, the idea of taking boys, in particular, away from their mothers and placing them in barracks where their personal identities were stripped away begins to make sense. These boys were meant to become soldiers for

2. The question of whether this was the intent of the schools or simply a result is examined by Levine (1980).

their class and to become "combat ready." They had to be made tough, loyal to each other, and ready to take command without self-doubt. Boarding schools were not founded to produce Hamlets, but Dukes of Wellington who could stand above the carnage with a clear head and an unflinching will to win. It was, after all, the Iron Duke who said that the Battle of Waterloo was won on the playing fields of Eton. McLachlan was on to something important when he saw a relationship between boarding schools and innocence; only he was off course, as it is the *destruction* of innocence that occurs in the status seminary, not its preservation.

From the power perspective, it becomes clearer why the girls' schools were not built like barracks, but more like homes. Their rites of passage were considerably softened by better food, more gracious living, and less overt pressure for academic success. They were not being socialized for power, but to be the helpmates of the powerful. For girls to compete against boys would only weaken class solidarity, although girls could compete against girls for boys. Unlike the boys' schools, where status was objectified by combat (real or symbolic), girls were taught to avoid open combat, because it was unladylike, and were encouraged to learn the fine art of persuasion through suggestion.

When we think of power and the exercise of social control we are apt to think of a higher person or group imposing themselves on a lower person or group. We are less apt to think of how those in power must exercise social control over themselves and their children. Sacrifices must be made, and upper-class fathers, in particular, have been willing to sacrifice their sons' inner lives for the sake of their class. The stripping away of the private self that is essential for the prep rite of passage is but the first step in a lifetime of personal denial and the denial of the person. Impersonal regulation becomes a substitute for personal decision making, ensuring that the troops will stand firm in a crisis.

Only in a controlled environment can the self not escape. One cannot physically or psychologically escape from the residential school. The group claims the individual self, and the value of victory is pressed home with relentless regularity. To compensate for the loss of self, students acquire "character." To have character is to be strong, self-disciplined, and fair, at least to one's equals. To keep a stiff upper lip under difficult circumstances is the mark of a properly educated man or woman.

Not every prep school student, however, takes to the power treatment, and schools vary considerably in terms of how much privilege they can or want to transmit. The regimentation of boarding school life has different effects on different students; a true loner, for example, would quite likely find life in the status seminary difficult and frustrating. In the process of molding their students, some raw material is lost or discarded. Thus while some students say they love boarding schools, others are angry or sad at being sent away. The interplay between the individual and the school gives rise to a number of responses, not all of which the schools find desirable. Certainly not every prep school student becomes a gentleman or lady, and not every graduate is a responsible soldier for his or her class; some become playboys and playgirls more intent on squandering the family fortune than increasing it. There is no foolproof method for ensuring that preps will shoulder the burden of responsibility placed on them.

Moreover, schools vary in their ability to socialize their students for power. All status seminaries are not equally elite; in general, the further socially and geographically a school is from the most elite schools the less its ability to maintain high status. Some progressive boarding schools were founded as antidotes to the regimentation found at both public high schools and elite boarding schools. In these schools cooperation is more valued than competition, and their curricula are almost always less constraining than are the curricula at the more socially elite schools. Progressive schools are generally more interested in individuality than the formation of a collective identity, which may be one of the reasons why they have fallen on hard times. Group loyalty maximizes long-term support, including financial support.

Power without authority, however, is fragile. To justify inequality requires the powerful to acquire a style of behavior that legitimates unequal relationships. The "habit of command," which Randall Collins has called the essence of upper-class style, is a learned behavior. In Great Britain, public school graduates often became literal soldiers for their class, either by serving in the officer corps of the British army or by becoming civilian administrators somewhere in the British empire. Being able to command respect could mean the difference between life and death to public school boys in "Her Majesty's service."

The aristocratic and military traditions of the British upper class, however, are quite different from those of the American upper class (Cookson and Persell 1985b). The American upper class is primarily a business elite, and in the economic marketplace inherited titles and battle flags count for little. The founders of American boarding schools imitated the British in many ways, but stopped short of trying to create a military and administrative elite, even though many of the schools' founders dreamed of an American empire to rival the British. To legitimate their privilege, the American upper class developed a different style of behavior from that of the British.

Life in the Status Seminary

If the ghost of Endicott Peabody were to happen into a big city bookstore and discover the best-selling *Official Preppy Handbook* (Birnbach 1980) how would he react? Leafing through it, even that august rector might not be able to contain a few chuckles. The cleverness with which the authors poke fun at prep snobbery and insularity is genuinely funny. Topics include "The Virtues of Pink and Green," "Regulating the Cash Flow," and "Prep Sex: A Contradiction in Terms". Aspiring preps can learn what to wear, where to go to college, and the "20 Ways to Express Drunkennes̖s." Breathless in style, the handbook has become a kind of comic bible to the country club set. Along with J. D. Salinger's *Catcher in the Rye* (1951), it epitomizes prep.

It might be something of an exaggeration to say that the great headmasters of yesterday would turn over in their graves if they knew how completely the parvenu has conquered their campuses, but it is safe to say that they would be dismayed to discover that the prep rite of passage has been softened by conspicuous consumption. As one head put it, "It has something to do with the sense of entitlement that many of our youngsters have today." Gone are the spartan living standards, the cold showers, and the pride of deprivation. The "culture of narcissism" threatens to swamp today's schools in floods of new wealth. The *Preppy Handbook* devotes many pages to "dressing the part" and includes an analysis of the "politics of monogramming." The inverse snobbery of the true patrician is jeopardized by a store-bought preppiness that treats an elite education as a consumer item. The country club atmosphere of some prep schools is the product of parvenu culture and is a far cry from the patrician ideal of the schools' founders.

In the evolution of prep school cultures, however, certain traditions have remained strong. The upper-class love of hunting, for instance, is still apparent in the prep duck motif and the presence of hunting dogs on most campuses (retrievers and setters are the most popular). Certainly one difference between a public school principal and the prep school head is that while the former would almost never think of bringing a dog to school, it is almost *de rigueur* for the latter to have a pedigreed pup by his or her side, even in the office. In the cultural history of the British upper class the master and his dog is an enduring image of benevolent authority, and American heads have retained this aristocratic custom.

The presence of a large, almost invisible, staff is also a useful vestige from a different era. The physical operation of a prep school is a complex process involving all the problems of maintaining a small town and feeding a small army. Building maintenance alone requires carpenters, plumbers, painters, and electricians. The extensive grounds of the schools need care-taking, and the miles of private roadways need plowing in the winter. Janitors pick up the litter of the elite students and the dogs, and young "townies" mow the lawn as the prep athletes improve their golf strokes. Each afternoon the schools quite literally resemble playgrounds as the students and faculty hone their athletic skills in the gym, on the field, or at the rink. Cooks, assistant cooks, and dishwashers arise early and go to bed late so that meals in the status seminary are ample, tasty, and on time.

Of course, not every boarding school is run like a five-star deluxe hotel; many of the lesser schools are similar to one- or two-star hotels and many of the western and progressive schools require students to do most of the real work of maintaining the school. The true eastern prep school, how-ever, has many amenities.

Part of a prep school education is the acquisition of taste, and at the most elite schools it is on display. Wood paneled rooms are graced with antique furniture, oil paintings, and china bowls brimming with fresh-cut flowers. Prep school students grow up in splendor as part of learning the intricacies of high culture. Despite the quick cadence of the prep daily schedule there is an aura of timelessness that permeates the schools, as though a more mechanized age had not quite caught up with them. There is almost never the sound of machinery, and the walls generally echo with the voices of students as they hurry to their next activity. At the church schools, the chapel bell rings each hour or sometimes each quarter hour.

Because everything is provided for the elite student there is no need to carry much cash, and a consequence of a cashless society is that nobody talks directly about money. According to the *Preppy Handbook,* "The thing about money is that it's nice that you have it. You're not excited to get it. You don't talk about it. It's like the golden retriever by the chair—when you reach out for it, it's there. You find this comforting" (32). Part of the socialization for power is learning how to conceal wealth, or at least mini-mize its importance by never openly referring to it, something that the schools have to teach the parvenus, who like to flaunt theirs.

The utopic element of aristocratic elegance in boarding school life con-tributes to the romanticism about the schools. Even though the schools have had to accommodate themselves to the parvenus by allowing stu-dents to bring on campus the stereos and trunks of clothes that represent the paraphernalia of consumerism, the schools have retained much of their hauteur. To adjust, the parvenus must learn that privilege has a cost, and that while physically life in the total institution may have softened over the years, emotionally and intellectually the prep rite of passage is still meant to inflict a certain amount of pain—for without pain there can be no transformation and legitimation.

Prep Style and Cultural Capital

The primary difference between British public school graduates and American prep school graduates is that while the former are trained to parade their eliteness publicly, the latter are trained to disguise their eliteness. The English public school student, for example, is almost always required to dress in a highly specialized manner, whether it is the black morning coats worn by Eton boys or the blue jackets ("bluers") and boaters worn by the Harrow boys. In England a man or woman is what he or she wears and the aristocratic origins of the English upper class have traditionally mandated dress that was beyond the grasp of commoners.

The American elite, in contrast to the English, have generally frowned on flamboyant dress, especially for men. Part of the explanation for this is the Puritan streak that pervades the Protestant Establishment. Fittingly, the uniform of choice among American elites is the business suit, and the prep uniform of choice has generally been jackets and ties. Until very recently most prep school students dressed like respectable country squires rather than flamboyant aristocrats. The prep style has not been starchy or stiff for a long time, and even then respectability was often undermined by small rebellions like a torn shirt, or a jacket missing a button. Today, when many dress codes have been relaxed, the prep style of dress may sometimes border on the sloppy. Some schools prohibit the wearing of blue jeans as a last stand against teen culture.

By camouflaging eliteness in the cloth of common dress, American prep school students generally deflect attention from their privilege. Privilege publicly worn is an affront to democracy, and the American elite discovered that inverse snobbery is more effective in masking social class difference and weeding out patricians from parvenus than flagrant snobbery and public displays of financial superiority. Thus, at the most socially elite schools the dress is often the most casual. In fact, affectations of poverty can be carried to such extremes that respectability is mocked. In some schools, a ratty and battered pair of shoes just barely patched by masking tape and string is a prized possession. To see America's most elite students struggle through snow in footwear more fit for a defeated army is to witness the power of calculated self-denial in the face of affluence. In a curious way, the inverse snobbery of the prep school world is faintly aristocratic—it tweaks the nose of middle-class propriety and rises above crass materialism.

Understatement, then, is generally the prep style. The habit of disguising wealth is carried over into adulthood where a Ford is often more preferable to a Mercedes Benz, and crew neck sweaters and chinos are considered more tasteful than tailor-made suits and shined shoes.

Learning how to dress and act properly are not the only skills taught in prep schools. Boarding school curricula are demanding and students are required to work hard at their studies. Although there is no requirement that they be intellectually curious, part of entitlement to privilege is proving one's merit by mastering a difficult curriculum. The academic skills that boarding school students acquire may help them to get into a select college and master the technical and social intricacies of the business, political, and financial worlds. Being comfortable in the world of ideas and being able to express thoughts in a concise and logical manner are not only the mark of a well-educated person, but are essential skills in the struggle for power today.

The cultural capital that prep school students accumulate in boarding schools is a treasure trove of skills and status symbols that can be used in later life. Armed, as it were, by the classical curriculum, the prep school graduate is prepared to do battle in the marketplace of ideas, competently, if not necessarily brilliantly.

The study of boarding schools, then, touches a number of elements in American life. The maintenance and transmission of privilege is a complex process that affects us all. Knowing how the elite schools prepare students for power illuminates one corner of the social fabric within which we are all enmeshed. The story of the elite schools is a tale told in many parts, each worthy of investigation and intriguing in its own right. Each chapter in this book examines an element in the prep school story, the end result of which, it is hoped, is a unified narrative about how the children of the American elite are prepared to assume the privileges and burdens of power.

2

Rousseau's Children: Total Educational Environments

THE ORIGINATOR of the boarding school idea was not a proper Bostonian, an English gentleman, or even a right-thinking clergyman, but the radical philosopher Jean Jacques Rousseau (1712–1778). He was among the first critical thinkers to identify adolescence as a special period between childhood and adulthood. Rousseau's conception of adolescent malleability predated Erik Erikson's description of adolescent turmoil by almost two hundred years, but they are nonetheless similar. Both Rousseau and Erikson make much of the adolescent identity crisis and the need for a "moratorium" period. Much like the French prime minister Georges Clemenceau, who believed that war was too important to leave to the generals, Rousseau believed that adolescent development was too important to leave to mothers and fathers.

In *Emile,* Rousseau sketched out what he believed would constitute an ideal education. The young student should be plucked from his parents and the contamination of the city and placed in a rural environment (isolation) to be tutored by a knowledgeable and sensitive mentor (intervention) in order to produce a natural man (transformation). Rousseau advocated an education where adolescents could develop free from the tyranny of unreasonable discipline, adult vice, and, perhaps, even the printed word.

Overview of Total Institutions

Rousseau's belief in individuality and his advocacy of a developmental perspective on human growth sparked a number of educational experiments in Europe that in turn influenced the founders of America's boarding schools. In particular, the schools established by Emmanuel Von Fellenberg and Johann Heinrich Pestalozzi in Switzerland in the early nineteenth century, had a profound impact on two Harvard-trained school teachers, Joseph Green Cogswell and George Bancroft, founders of the Roundhill School in Northhampton, Massachusetts in 1823 (McLachlan 1970, 71).

Von Fellenberg wrote, "The great art of educating consists of knowing how to occupy every moment of life in well-directed and useful activity of the youthful powers, in order that, so far as possible, nothing evil may find room to develop itself" (McLachlan 1970, 60). The French historian of childhood, Philippe Ariès, points out that a boarding school was "substituted for society in which all the ages were mingled together; it was called upon to mold children on the pattern of an ideal human type" (1962, 285).

Perhaps because of its heavy emphasis on socialization and development, the idea of sending children away to school has appealed to groups who, for political, social, and economic reasons, have wanted to leave little to chance in the education of their children. These groups have been quite disparate, but, in the main, they have fallen into two camps. At one end of the social spectrum, elite schools have been established for the children of the upper class and upwardly mobile parvenus; at the other, schools have been established to serve special groups of children.

The schools of the wealthy are nearly always private, conservative, and offer a classical curriculum. Napoleon I established several boarding schools in France and various Roman Catholic religious orders have founded elite boarding schools, especially throughout Europe and South America. But the relish with which the British founded "little Etons" around the globe makes other European powers seem like dabblers in the field.

Boarding schools were established in most Commonwealth countries, particularly in Canada and Australia. Not content just to send adolescents away for an education, the British upper class had learned by the nineteenth century the convenience of sending even their smallest children away to school. It is not uncommon to meet an Englishman who began his boarding school education at the age of seven. St. Paul's School of Darjeeling in the foothills of the Himalayas is but one example of where the sons of local elites learn to rise at dawn, take cold showers, sleep communally, and study Latin and Greek, thereby transforming "the sons of Brahmins into brown sahibs" (Alexander 1982, 36). Since 1981 Kamuzu Academy in Lilongwe, Malawi, has been training some 360 young Malawians (two-thirds boys and one-third girls) to be a "future ruling class of superior but incorruptible administrators" (*London Times,* 2 July 1983, 8).

Socialists have also experimented with residential schools. In the Soviet Union, Anton Makerenko (1880–1939) set up residential schools for the "wild children" who roamed Russia in the chaos that followed World War I. However in times of tranquility, Russian parents are not keen on parting with their children (Jacoby 1975). It is only in the rural areas of the Soviet Union that children attend residential schools in any numbers, and then only because no other schools are available to them.

Nikita Krushchev made the last serious effort to use residential schools as part of a larger plan to reform Soviet education. He was deeply offended by the elitism of the top party officials who monopolized certain state schools in order to forward their children's educational careers (similar to how certain Americans use private schools). This elitism had also bred an unsavory corruption where admission could be bought by "blat," that is, bribery. But with Khrushchev's ouster, the impetus to found boarding schools dwindled.

In Cuba, the government has established a number of schools in the countryside, where particularly bright and politically correct youngsters are sent to work and study. These schools have as their specific objective the development of the "New Socialist Man and Woman" and are considered by Cuban educational authorities to be quite successful, compatibly combining the disparate ideals of collective behavior and individual effort. What seems to unite both capitalists and socialists in founding residential schools is their emphasis on elitism.

At the other end of the social spectrum are the schools that serve special populations of children—those who are deaf, blind, or otherwise disabled, such as dyslexic, emotionally disturbed, or delinquent. There are also schools with special mandates, such as the Church Farm School in Pennsylvania which admits boys who come from homes "where the natural mother and father no longer live together." The Bureau of Indian Affairs runs eight boarding schools for Native Americans. The Riverside Indian School in Oklahoma is a good example of how residential schools can be used to educate the non-elite as well as the elite. At Riverside, a former student reported, "We were conditioned to work with our hands, not with our minds" (McBeth 1984, 4–13).

The students at these schools are defined as in need of protection and rehabilitation and generally undertake vocational or remedial curricula. A variant of this tradition is the use of boarding schools by some developing countries to socialize and prepare recent immigrants for citizenship. Israel, for instance, has a network of residential schools designed to teach the children of immigrants basic language skills and to prepare them for Israeli citizenship. *Save the Children Federation, Inc.*, and a number of other international agencies support schools for children displaced by war and political turmoil.

Any discussion of boarding schools, no matter how brief, should mention the small but brave group of schools that are truly Rousseau's heirs. Beginning in the 1920s, there were a number of educators in Europe and the United States who repudiated repressive education in favor of a child-centered educational philosophy. They believed strongly that youthful goodness was soured only when contaminated by adult manipulation. A. S. Neill, who along with his wife Ena founded the Summerhill School in England, was among the more radical of these progressives. Taking a Freudian approach to child development, he believed that any repression causes neurosis and education's most important objective was to produce "happy" people, not driven competitors.

In its historical evolution, the boarding school has taken on a number of specific characteristics which Ian Weinberg (1967) delineated for England, and which we have adapted here for the contemporary American scene:

1. The private secondary boarding school is one in which at least half the students live during the year. Most of the schools are situated in rural or semirural settings. While the students are at school it is responsible for their welfare— *in loco parentis,* or in place of the parents.
2. The school is independent from state and local authorities, although schools must meet certain minimal state standards and be open for health and safety inspections by state officials.[1]

1. Even in cases where the schools may receive funds from the state for specific educational services rendered, the schools are subjected to a minimum of regulatory activity. In a series of Supreme Court decisions, the private schools have been protected from public dismemberment or encroachment. The most important decision was *Pierce v. Society of Sisters* in 1925,

3. The school is usually organized as a nonprofit corporation, although some proprietary (that is, possibly profit making) schools do exist.
4. The school charges fees. Fees range widely, but as of 1985 most boarding schools charged between nine and eleven thousand dollars a year. This does not include other charges and expenses that may cost several thousand dollars more per pupil per year. Most boarding schools offer scholarships.
5. The school was often founded on religious principles. The chapel is still an important part of life in many schools, though many eschew heavy-handed religious training. Seven percent of today's heads hold a divinity degree (*The Handbook of Private Schools* 1981).
6. The school's ultimate policy decisions are made by a self-perpetuating board of trustees that appoints the head, who in turn appoints the teachers and other staff and administrators.
7. The school is organized for college-bound students, although there are some state-supported residential schools, such as those for exceptional children, which are not.
8. The school, is part of an informal hierarchy, with the older eastern schools often setting the standards.

According to sociologist Erving Goffman there are four central aspects of life in what he and others consider a "total institution": (1) all activities are conducted in the same place under a single authority; (2) daily life is carried out in the immediate company of others; (3) life is tightly scheduled and fixed by a set of formal rules; and (4) all activities are designed purportedly to fulfill the official aims of the institution (Goffman 1961, 314).

The following is an example of a typical schedule for an American total institution. Add to this that most schools conduct Saturday morning classes, and the picture that emerges is demanding.

DAILY SCHEDULE

Weekdays

A.M.

7:00	Rising Bell
7:15	Breakfast
7:55–8:10	Work Period
8:20–9:55	Class Periods
10:00–10:10	Chapel
10:15–10:40	Recess
10:45–12:20	Class Periods

commonly known as the Oregon Decision. It ruled unconstitutional an Oregon law requiring all children to attend public school.

P.M.

12:30	Luncheon
1:20–3:15	Class Periods
3:15–5:20	Athletics
6:15	Dinner
7:15–10:30	Study Period
10:00–12:00	Lights Out (time varies with age)

Sundays

A.M.

8:30–9:15	Breakfast

P.M.

12:00 Noon	Chapel
1:00	Dinner
6:00	Supper
7:15–10:30	Study Period
10:00–12:00	Lights Out

Boarding schools vary in terms of their totality. Small, rural schools that have few or no day students are environmentally quite different than large suburban schools that have many day students and provide ample opportunities to visit nearby towns and cities. The degree to which a school is "open" or "closed" is an important consideration when assessing the impact of the school on its students, teachers, and administrators. Most boarding schools in any case are semi-total institutions because they have their "inmates" only half of the year. Yet the powerful experience of going to a boarding school is partly due to its total characteristics.[2]

The Varieties of Prep Schools

It is a cliché in the boarding school world that "each school is different," and like most clichés, it both captures and caricatures some truth. One of our findings was that this sense of uniqueness develops in part because

2. Several books about boarding school life help illustrate Goffman's observations: *A World Apart* (Rae 1983), *A World of Our Own* (Prescott 1970), *The Hothouse Society* (Lambert 1974), and *The Cloistered Elite* (Wakeford 1969).

most boarding school people know relatively little about schools other than their own. With the exception of the heads, who through meetings of the Headmasters' Association and other such gatherings, exchange information regularly, most teachers and students are surprisingly hazy in their knowledge of other schools, even those in close geographic and social proximity.

This lack of information about America's most elite schools, even among those who should know them the best, is because they are often isolated from public view and from each other by distance and sometimes tradition. Of the 289 leading American prep schools, 69 percent are located along the eastern seaboard; 34 percent of those are in New England. Since World War II, twenty-three new schools have been founded in New England. Massachusetts is the state with the largest number of boarding schools—twenty-nine—in the entire United States. Nearly 20 percent of boarding schools are in the western portion of the United States, and more than half of those are on the Pacific Coast.

Most of these schools are small by public secondary school standards. Thirty-seven percent have less than 200 students, and 40 percent have between 200 and 400 students. Only a few schools have over 600 students.

While most of the schools do not have formal religious affiliations, more than one-third do, and of those, nearly half are Episcopalian, despite the fact that only 3 percent of the national population is Episcopalian. Nine percent of all boarding schools are Roman Catholic, compared to 27 percent of the national population, and 5 percent are Quaker schools. It is worth noting that many of the nondenominational schools are distinctly Protestant in their ethos and religious orientation.[3]

We identified nine distinct traditional types of American prep schools: Academy, Episcopal, entrepreneurial, all-girls, Catholic, western, progressive, military, and Quaker.[4] Some types overlap, for instance all-girls and Catholic schools. In such a case, we decided that one of those characteristics was the dominant one, in this instance, that of being all girls. We have not designated an all-boys category because so many of the schools were founded for boys only. Instead, boys schools will be discussed within their specific type of school, and their current status as either single sex or coeducational will be indicated.

3. See Ravitch (1974, chap. 5) on how non-denominational public schools in New York City were perceived as hostile by Catholics.

4. We visited one of two public American boarding schools, the North Carolina School of Science and Mathematics. Because it is not private, however, it is not considered a prep school in the traditional sense.

THE WORLD OF BOARDING SCHOOLS

We will see that while these varieties of prep schools share similar organizational and curricular features, they differ in their ability to socialize their students for power due to varied connections with America's most powerful families and varied philosophical and cultural orientations.

ACADEMIES

Originally established to prepare boys for college, the New England academy is the oldest type of boarding school in the United States. The origin of the academy is obscure, although it is believed that Benjamin Franklin may have suggested the idea (McLachlan 1970, 35). That it was intended to be a place of intellectual inquiry is evident from the word *academy*, which was the name of the school where Plato taught in ancient Greece. The early American academies, however, combined scholarship with more than a little Puritan hellfire. Samuel Phillips, Jr., the founder of Phillips Andover, advised his first headmaster to teach his students of "the fall of Man—the Depravity of Human Nature—the Necessity of Atonement," (McLachlan 1970, 40).

Academies often had close ties with their surrounding communities, and it was a common practice to assign the name of the town to the academy (Sizer 1964, 21). Although academies spread south and west from New England in the nineteenth century, three-quarters of the forty-one academies listed in the *Handbook of Private Schools* (1981) are in New England or the Middle Atlantic states. There are almost none west of the Mississippi. The most prestigious academies such as Phillips Andover and Phillips Exeter have, since Revolutionary War times, attracted the children of many of America's most powerful or illustrious families. With their classical colonial architecture, spacious grounds, and taste for understatement, these academies represent the epitome of the "great" New England boarding school.

EPISCOPAL SCHOOLS

Usually founded before the turn of the century and located in New England, the early Episcopal prep schools epitomize the ethos of the elite tradition, because they modeled themselves after British public schools. The central feature of the public school was the idea of using total institutions for the creation of a collective identity and the development of a leadership cadre. From their inception their American counterparts attracted many of the children of the Episcopal Establishment.

While the founders of the American Episcopal schools did not replicate all the features of the British schools (their schools were smaller, for example), they adopted similar architecture, sports such as cricket and crew, the use of prefects for enforcing discipline, and some terminology, such as "form" for grade.[5]

Because the development of a collective identity is so highly stressed in these schools, the students are brought together on a frequent basis. Groton, for example, has daily roll calls and chapel is still a central part of school life. At St. Paul's, the chapel is designed so that students face each other, fortifying their sense of collective identity.

ENTREPRENEURIAL SCHOOLS

In addition to the Episcopal schools that were founded in the late nineteenth century, a number of nondenominational, or what we term entrepreneurial, schools were founded around the turn of the century by wealthy non-Episcopalians. They also adopted some of the features of the British schools. More than four-fifths of the seventy-seven schools we call entrepreneurial are in New England or along the Atlantic seaboard. The oldest and best endowed of these schools traditionally attract large numbers of children of successful business leaders, for example, the Hotchkiss School (founded in 1891) in Lakeville, Connecticut, and the Choate School (founded in 1896) in Wallingford, Connecticut.

In their curiculum the entrepreneurial schools reflected a pragmatic blend of the needs of a rising capitalist class and a growing university system. Their discipline reflected an effort "to strike a balance between the freedom of the academies and the heavily paternalistic discipline of the church schools" (McLachlan 1970, 216). The schools were nonsectarian in their theological orientation, but were predominantly Christian and Protestant.

GIRLS SCHOOLS

Girls schools were generally founded by strong, independent, unmarried women, most of whom had close ties with higher education, often with the leading women's colleges. Except for Emma Willard (founded 1814) and Miss Porter's (founded 1843), they tend to have been founded in the years between 1880 and 1920. Often begun as proprietary schools, only recently did they become incorporated as nonprofit corporations. They are located in all sections of the United States, but three-quarters are in New England or down the Atlantic Coast. They are small, remote, intimate, generally nonsectarian, and socially exclusive.

5. "Forms" refer to the benches where English boys sat in the school room for lessons. As they progressed in their studies, they moved up, from the first "form" to the sixth "form."

THE WORLD OF BOARDING SCHOOLS

CATHOLIC SCHOOLS

Although the oldest Catholic school in the country, Georgetown Preparatory School, was founded in 1789 by the Jesuits, most were founded in the early twentieth century. Catholic schools are less concentrated in New England and the Middle Atlantic states than other types of boarding schools; less than half are located in those two regions. Catholic schools are more likely to be single-sex schools—four out of five leading Catholic boarding schools are single sex. Some have become coeducational for day students, but not for boarding students.

Most of the schools have a formal connection with some branch of the Catholic church, although at least one, the Canterbury School in New Milford, Connecticut, is under lay control. Some of the girls schools were founded by the Convent of the Sacred Heart, while the boys schools have various historical ties such as the Jesuits, Benedictine monks, Franciscan priests and brothers, Marian Fathers, Brothers of the Holy Cross, or Augustinian Fathers. This variety in their historical origins leads to considerable diversity in Catholic schools, ranging from the intense scholarly emphasis of the Jesuits to the missionary approach of the Franciscans. The diversity among Catholic boarding schools suggests that many do not socialize their students for power, although some Catholic schools, like the Portsmouth Abbey School, are within the elite tradition.

WESTERN SCHOOLS

With a few exceptions, such as the Thacher School founded in 1889, most of the western schools were founded in the twentieth century, some as recently as the 1950s. The weight of tradition weighs less heavily on them because of their shorter history. They tend to be nonsectarian, and nearly two-thirds are coeducational. Usually they are less endowed than eastern schools. Often but not always, western schools have more modest physical facilities, and since they are relatively new, fewer alumni.

There are two types of western schools. Some, such as the Webb School and the Cate School in California, and Fountain Valley School in Colorado, are modeled after eastern prep schools, and others, such as Thacher and the Orme School, are designed to give city students a taste of western life, including riding, camping, and ranching. As western schools tend to emphasize individualism, they are less likely to forge a collective identity among their students.

PROGRESSIVE SCHOOLS

Progressive schools are among the most recently founded schools and the hardest to identify, because they usually do not label themselves as such. Progressivism is a difficult concept to define, as it can apply to a widely diverse range of educational philosophies. The Putney School in Vermont is a good example of the progressive tradition. In many cases the definition of progressive education depended upon the personality of the founder and/or the head of the school. Progressive schools tend to draw children of affluent, liberal, professional families, including those who are successful in the arts. Progressive schools have not traditionally sought to prepare students for exercising power, but rather encourage them to develop their individual intellectual and creative potentials.

The founders of progressive schools believed in integrating mental, manual, musical, and artistic work. They created small, always coeducational, and more authentically nonsectarian schools. Some have farms or ranches as part of the school, and require farm, household, and/or construction work from students. In some cases, students have helped construct major buildings on the campus. These shared projects tend to build very close and informal student-faculty relations.

QUAKER SCHOOLS

The first Quaker school was Oakwood, founded in 1796 in Poughkeepsie, New York. Quaker schools are all coeducational and range from the very small (one has a graduating class of fewer than 10 students) to schools with senior classes of 100 or 150.

The schools were founded to educate the children of Quakers and people in sympathy with Quaker ideals. They tend to stress, in the words of one school's self-description in *The Handbook of Private Schools* (1981, 587), "simplicity and freedom from unnecessary distractions." Quaker schools bring the members of the community together regularly for Quaker meeting, which begins with a few moments of silence, usually followed by a program. In general, they have not tried to socialize their students for power and thus they appear in this study in a cameo role.

MILITARY ACADEMIES

Military academies are like girls schools in that many were founded around the turn of the century as proprietary schools. Sometime in the twentieth century most military academies became incorporated as nonprofit organizations. A striking fact is that none are located in New England. About half are in the South Atlantic or south central states. Most military schools are for boys, and a fair number have only boarding students. Several have either become coeducational, such as New York Military Academy, or added a Girls Academy, as Culver has done; some begin as early as fifth grade.

Four military academies are affiliated with the Episcopal Church and two with the Catholic Church, but most are nonsectarian. In general, the curricula of military academies will include remedial courses, although the best-known schools stress a vigorous college preparatory curricula. While all provide military discipline and drill, they vary in terms of how much military coursework they provide, with some offering programs approved by the U.S. Department of the Army or Navy. Because military schools either educate "problem" children or prepare their students for a military career, and because military careers are not the normal pattern for America's most powerful families, most military schools are not considered part of the elite tradition.

At least some of the schools in each of these nine types could be considered among America's elite boarding schools. But not all of them are in its central core, which is defined on the basis of both clientele served and cultural and philosophical orientation. Most Catholic, military, and western schools have not drawn the children of the most powerful families in America. Progressive, Quaker, and girls schools have not tried to prepare their students for the exercise of power. Some of the schools in the Episcopal, academy, and entrepreneurial traditions have a philosophy of leadership training and have attracted the children of the upper classes. Since the exercise of power was considered a male prerogative, it is not surprising that all of those schools were boys schools at their founding, although only a few remain so today.

The Select 16

E. Digby Baltzell identified sixteen boarding schools that "serve the sociological function of differentiating the upper classes from the rest of the population . . . and set the pace and bore the brunt of criticism received by private schools" (1958, 293, 305). Indeed, the sixteen schools in table 2–1 strike one as predominantly "old, eastern, patrician, aristocratic and

English" (McLachlan 1970, 6–8). These are core schools of the elite tradition, and they play an important role in socializing their students for power. We refer to these schools as the select 16.

Others besides Baltzell have developed lists of the most socially prestigious American boarding schools and although they differ on one or two schools, there is a consensus as to which schools are the most elite (see Cookson and Persell 1978 for discussion).

The snob appeal of the most socially elite schools has its lighter side. Some preps, in fact, consider Groton to be the only boarding school worth counting. Nelson W. Aldrich, Jr., poked fun at this sense of social competition when he wrote:

> There are fifteen prep schools in the country: Andover, Middlesex, St. Paul's, Lawrenceville, Groton, Kent, Exeter, St. Mark's, St. George's, Taft, Brooks, Choate, Deerfield, Milton, Hotchkiss. It's a complete list, though mine. (In maintaining that there are no prep schools beyond these fifteen, I claim the right, as theater people do, to say that anything beyond Broadway is Bridgeport.) A Preppie from any other school springs like Gatsby "from some Platonic conception of himself." (1979, 59)

TABLE 2–1

The Select 16: Baltzell's List of the Most Socially Prestigious American Boarding Schools

School	Location	Date of Founding
1. Phillips Academy	Andover, Mass.	1778
2. Phillips Exeter Academy	Exeter, New Hampshire	1783
3. Episcopal High School	Alexandria, Virginia	1839
4. Hill School	Pottstown, Pennsylvania	1851
5. St. Paul's School	Concord, New Hampshire	1856
6. St. Mark's School	Southborough, Mass.	1865
7. Lawrenceville School	Lawrenceville, New Jersey	1883
8. Groton School	Groton, Mass.	1884
9. Woodbury Forest Sch.	Woodberry Forest, Va.	1889
10. Taft School	Watertown, Conn.	1890
11. Hotchkiss School	Lakeville, Conn.	1892
12. Choate School	Wallingford, Conn.	1896
13. St. George's School	Newport, Rhode Island	1896
14. Middlesex School	Concord, Mass.	1901
15. Deerfield Academy	Deerfield, Mass.	1903
16. Kent School	Kent, Conn.	1906

NOTE: E. Digby Baltzell, *Philadelphia Gentlemen—The Making of a National Upper Class* (Chicago: Quadrangle Books, 1958), 306. Reprinted by permission.

Aldrich's list excludes three schools with a heavy southern constituency (The Episcopal High School, The Hill School, and Woodberry Forest School) and includes two New England schools that Baltzell does not (Milton Academy and Brooks School). As Baltzell is interested in those schools that serve a national elite his list has the virtue of including more schools outside of New England.

Compared to other leading schools, the select 16 schools tend to have been founded earlier, are larger, have many more alumni—and consequently are more heavily endowed, have more buildings and playing fields, and are more likely to be located in New England or the Middle or South Atlantic states than other boarding schools.

Architecture and Aesthetics

Knowing the organizational features of boarding schools, however, does not adequately convey a sense of the quality of life at the schools, especially at the most elite schools. The transmission of status requires more than resources alone; it also requires the development of style and the acquisition of taste. "Tone" is a favorite prep word, because it captures, without defining, that elusive quality of status without gauche fanfare that the schools strive to create. Knowing the organizational features of the school alone fails to communicate the tone, which is shaped in part by the school's architectural and aesthetic beauty.

The importance of prep architecture has deep roots in England, where the building and grounds of the great public schools resemble small medieval cities captured in time and preserved by generations of caretakers. When Henry VI founded Eton College in 1440, it was his intention that it should not only supply him with scholars but become a place of pilgrimage. He lavished on the college a large collection of holy relics, including fragments of what were supposed to be the True Cross and the Crown of Thorns. College Chapel, which Henry helped to design, contains the largest church window in England.

Whether one is in the school yard, cloisters, provost's garden, or simply walking up the "Long Walk," history and the power of the British class system can be seen and felt firsthand. On any given afternoon, Eton boys hurry down to the Thames where the Eton College Boat Club stretches along the river's edge, while an apprentice sits by the window of the local tailor's shop, sewing the morning coats which young Etonians wear to class.

The buildings of Harrow are almost as venerable as Eton's. In the Fourth Form Room, Harrovians have been carving their names in the oak-paneled walls since 1660—among them Sir Robert Peel, the prime minister; Lord Byron, the poet; and in small letters to the left of the door as one exits, W.L.S. Churchill (later Sir Winston).

By English standards, American prep schools have few architectural traditions, but by American standards many prep schools seem to be steeped in tradition. Deerfield Academy is in a historic landmark area, some of its buildings having survived the period when Indians still raided up and down the Connecticut Valley. The campus of Phillips Andover Academy, which opened for classes shortly before the Continental Army struggled out of Valley Forge in 1778, is very similar to a New England colonial village, its centerpiece the chapel, its spire rising well above the abundant trees. Andover students can read in the wood-paneled Oliver Wendell Holmes Library, look at works by American artists such as Eakins, Homer, and Whistler in the Addison Gallery of American Art or just relax in the Moncrief Cochran Sanctuary, sixty-five acres of landscaped beauty which includes a brook, two ponds, and natural wild areas as well as manicured lawns and flower beds of rhododendron and laurel.

Eastern Episcopal schools reflect their founders' intention that a school should be like a family, or more specifically, a somewhat idealized Anglo-Saxon family. Usually built around a quad, or "The Circle" as it is called at Groton, Episcopal chapels, libraries, and meeting halls are often Gothic in design. The chapel at an Episcopal school is the heart of the campus: "Henry Vaughn's magnificent Gothic Revival chapel stands close to the gate of the school, symbolic of the founder's intent that religion not only be an important part of the official life of Groton School, but also make a claim on the entirety of life" (Groton School Catalogue 1981–82, 3).

As one sits in the chapel at Groton, balancing precariously on a small, rickety wooden chair that may have been used by Franklin Delano Roosevelt, the Protestant world view, so powerfully expressed in the hymn "A Mighty Fortress is Our God," seems less of an abstraction and more a reality. At St. George's School in Rhode Island, another Episcopal school, the coats of arms, armor, banners, and flags that fill the hallways give the impression that the Dragon Slayer himself would find nothing out of place in the twentieth century if he returned as a Third Form student.

Aesthetics is not limited to the well-known schools. The Darrow School in New Lebanon, New York, was once a Shaker village. A student at the Robert Louis Stevenson School in Pebble Beach, California, can daydream in the Erdman Memorial Chapel with its vista of redwood trees and the Pacific Ocean. Not far down the coast at the Ojai Valley School, students attend an open air chapel that looks out over the Ojai Valley and the Los Padres National Forest. The girls who attend the Hockaday School in Dallas, Texas, are surrounded by a $14,500,000 educational complex that includes glass covered walkways, exterior gardens, and landscaped terraces. Even the smallest boarding school devotes attention to the aesthetics of its campus, although definitions of what is aesthetically appropriate vary by geography, philosophy, and social eliteness.

The select 16 had a total plant value of $382 million in 1983, which was almost equal to their endowments of $381 million. Many schools continue to build new gyms, dorms, libraries, theatres, and science buildings with gifts from alumni and donations of other patrons. Often the architects who are called on to plan these buildings have international reputations, like I. M. Pei, who designed the Paul Mellon Arts Center at the Choate-Rosemary Hall School in Connecticut. Many schools are now in the process of building computer rooms, wings, or buildings to meet new expectations. Schools may have ten or more terminals connecting to a mainframe computer and numerous microcomputers. Phillips Exeter has several dozen computers in several locations on campus.

Careful attention is given to new designs to ensure that they are aesthetically compatible with older buildings. Many schools still use buildings that were there the year of founding. Like English boarders, American prep school students are taught the value of architectural tradition and preservation. Part of their legitimacy rests on their connection with an important historic past.

The affluence that serves as a backdrop to a boarding school education includes the fields, mountains, streams, lakes, deserts, swamps, and valleys owned by the schools. "Conspicuous consumption," in Thorstein Veblen's sense, was a mark of social honor. The lawn that has no agricultural use is as much a mark of the gentleman as the right address or club membership. Two schools alone possess land equal to 5 percent of the state of Rhode Island. If all the (often choice) real estate holdings of American boarding schools were added together, total acreage would measure in the hundreds of thousands from coast to coast. At the same time that students at St. George's school can watch Atlantic whitecaps from atop their bluff outside of Newport, Rhode Island, students at the Cate School can scan the Pacific horizon atop their bluff just above Santa Barbara, California.

In effect, the combined real estate holdings of American boarding schools represent a "Prep National Park," a preserve free from state and local taxes, where boarding school students are allowed to explore, backpack, horseback ride, rock climb, play, and temporarily escape from the pressures of adolescence and the total institution. More than a few students have had their first drink, first drugs, and first sexual encounter in the woods and ravines that surround their schools. George Shattuck, St. Paul's founder, once dreamed that his students would learn from nature "of the things . . . seen and . . . of the things unseen" (Heckscher 1980, 8). Today this dream has come true, although not in exactly the way the founder imagined.

The subliminal message carried by the aesthetics and affluence of most prep school campuses is complemented by the actual educational resources and classroom facilities the schools provide. The Cranbrook Educational Community, which encompasses the Kingswood and Cranbrook Schools, for example, has a total of nine libraries with 100,000 volumes. At the libraries the students and teachers can find not only books but "phono-discs, films, filmstrips, filmloops, multi-media kits, cassettes, slides, transparencies, maps, microfiche, games and prints" (*Cranbrook Schools Catalogue* 1982–1983, 21). The Academy Library at Phillips Exeter has a 250,000 volume capacity, and the two libraries at Northfield-Mount Hermon have over 93,000 volumes—350 current periodicals and the *New York Times* on microfiche, dating back to its first issue in 1851. Even a small school, like the Fountain Valley School in Colorado with 225 students, has a library of 20,000 volumes. At the Portsmouth Abbey School, the first two floors of the Manor House are used as a library, containing nearly 24,000 volumes.

Music, art, and theater facilities are abundant at boarding schools. Phillips Exeter's Frederick R. Mayer Art Center contains the art department's studios and classrooms, the Lamont Gallery, and student grill. Exeter musicians can practice in the Lewis Perry Music Building, which contains group and individual practice rooms for instruction and rehearsal.

Virtually every prep school has a performance program that includes theater, music, and dance. At the small Wooster School in Connecticut, for instance, there is a performance center where students produce modern dance events, often with original music, as well as perform plays. The Paul Mellon Arts Center at Choate-Rosemary Hall is, to quote a school publication, "itself a work of art, a living sculpture which demands artistic reaction to line and form and spatial relations" (*Choate Rosemary Magazine* Fall 1981, 7). The structure houses an 800-seat theater designed by George Izenour, a leading theater architect.

Historically, the classical, humanist tradition of scholarship has been the core of the boarding school curricula. Today, however, science and mathematics are part of the core curricula. Most prep schools can offer facilities and equipment that rival many small colleges. The Jansen Noyes Science Building at the Lawrenceville School, for example, has modern facilities for physics, biology, and chemistry. The first floor of the building contains "five large classrooms, two combined classroom-laboratories, physics and biology laboratories, biology preparation room, and lecture room. On the second floor are five laboratories for physics and chemistry, stock rooms, three classrooms, faculty workshop and laboratory, science library, and planetarium" (*Lawrenceville Experience* 1982–83, 18). The Helen C. Boyden Science Center at Deerfield Academy houses New England's second largest planetarium and 12,000 square feet of open laboratory space.

The Best of All Possible Worlds

In preserving the past while adapting to the future, many boarding schools seem idyllic, almost magical, communities which can easily seduce outsiders as being the best of all possible worlds. No one knows exactly how aesthetics affects consciousness, but it is reasonable to suppose that the shared experiences of coming of age within the walls of a cloistered elite school must have some impact on its students.

In one sense the beauty of prep school campuses is an exterior validation of the student's sense that "Yes, I am special," or perhaps even, "Yes, I am beautiful." A girl wrote that what she liked best about boarding school was "the design of the school; it's a beautiful place to work. I don't think I would have the same attitude if it was built and designed differently." A headmaster articulated his belief that architecture affects a student's psyche when he reported that a student said, "This school requires quality in what I do, because I have leaded glass windows in my bedroom."

The facilities of the elite schools also make learning easier than in many public schools, where facilities can be limited, or inadequate. Surrounded by so much educational opportunity, the prep school scholar has the opportunity to create an individualized educational experience, although opportunities are often left unexplored. As total institutions in aesthetic surroundings, many boarding schools seem almost like island paradises within the larger educational system.

3

The Chosen Ones

FOR the vast majority of public high-school students, admission to school is a straightforward process. Students either attend the school in their community or, if they have special talents or needs, they may be admitted to a specialized public school where admission is based on openly stated criteria. Private schools, including boarding schools, are rarely democratic from the standpoint of admission. Like private corporations, country clubs, and cooperative real estate holdings, private schools have the right to choose whom they will or will not admit. And while it is their stated policy not to discriminate on the basis of race or religion, the social traditions of the schools have meant that their student bodies have tended to be homogeneous in terms of family background, religion, and race.

Acceptance into an elite boarding school is in itself a form of ritual, the first step in the prep rite of passage. There was a time when a parent simply rang up the head or dropped by the school and a deal was struck, but by and large those days are gone. Today, applicants and their families must find their way through a maze of forms, letters of recommendation, transcripts, school visits, and interviews. Tenacity is essential to mastering the ritual of acceptance because for the majority of students entrance into the status seminary is not easy, nor is it meant to be. The schools have certain standards to uphold, and often those standards have less to do with ability or willingness than background and style. Tradition weighs heavily in the admissions process and parvenus are at somewhat of a disadvantage in the scramble for acceptance, as they may have yet to learn the subtlety of the prep code, or worse, may not know that such a code exists.

The schools must strike a balance between their ideal class and the class that can be formed from the applicant pool; generally the more elite the school the more carefully the class can be crafted. Tuition at the elite schools is very high and many heads feel obligated to "sell" their schools as good economic and social investments for families. A headmaster at a select 16 school calculated that it cost a family approximately $45 a day to send their child to his school. Where else, he maintained, could you get three meals a day, outstanding facilities, and the best possible education for such a small amount?

Part of the appeal of boarding schools for many parents and students is that they have a choice among a number of different types of schools. The power of choice may indeed be one of the hallmarks of upper-class and high-status life-styles. To hand tailor a child's education by selecting an appropriate school may be worth considerably more than $45 a day for many parents—it may be considered essential for the proper transmission of status.

Boarding Schools and the Educational Marketplace

Students have been enrolling in boarding schools since before the American Revolution. As early as 1742, when the Countess Benigna von Zinzendorf founded the Moravian Seminary for Girls and the Moravian Preparatory School for Boys in Pennsylvania, a small fraction of American families saw the value of sending their children away to school. The New England academies, such as Andover (1778), Exeter (1781), Deerfield (1797), and Milton (1798) educated the sons of some of the new nation's most illustrious families. Andover enrolled Washingtons, Lees, Quincys, and Lowells; Paul Revere designed the school seal and John Hancock signed the school's Act of Incorporation. The connection between the academies and elite colleges was established early; between 1768 and 1790, one-quarter of Harvard's students were alumni of the Governor Dummer Academy in Massachusetts, which was founded in 1763 (*Handbook of Private Schools*, 1980).

Until the latter part of the nineteenth century, the boys boarded with local families rather than at the schools themselves. The academy tradition spread south and westward and by 1850 there were more than 6,000 incorporated and unincorporated academies (McLachlan 1970, 35). Early in the nineteenth century, a number of academies for girls were established, usually called female seminaries. They were less academically demanding than the boys' academies, as girls were expected to be little more than decorous appendages to men, and did not go on to higher education. Emma Willard pioneered the idea that women should have equivalent educations when she opened the doors of the Troy Female Seminary in 1821 (now the Emma Willard School). Most other female seminaries opened during this period did not advocate women's intellectual equality as strongly as Emma Willard. When Miss Porter's was founded in 1843, the curriculum emphasized the traditional nineteenth century female virtues of good breeding and gentleness.

The first true New England boarding school was the Roundhill School, founded in 1823 by Joseph Green Cogswell and George Bancroft. Harvard provided two-thirds of the mortgage money necessary to buy the school's site. Cogswell and Bancroft embraced aspects of the Enlightment such as the belief in education and reason, but still clung to many traditional Puritan beliefs. They tried to keep their school operating, but for financial reasons it closed in 1834. And while a handful of boarding schools opened and closed in the period after Roundhill, it was not until 1856 that the idea of founding a great boarding school in New England was rekindled with the establishment of St. Paul's in New Hampshire.

From the founding of St. Paul's until the end of the century, sixty-one elite boarding schools were established in the United States, and by 1879, 73 percent of all secondary school students were enrolled in private schools, including boarding schools (Kraushaar 1972, 13). However, in the decade following this private school boom, expansion of the public high-school system reduced the number of students in private schools to 30 percent, and by the beginning of the twentieth century only 10 percent of the high-school age population was enrolled in private schools, of which less than one percent were in the elite boarding schools.

The prep schools operated as exclusive clubs—Catholics, blacks, and Jews need not apply. From the 1880s onward the schools developed their reputation for snobbishness, and that they were is undeniable. Immigration had created among the WASPs a fear of ethnic "contamination." Thus, it was during the decades of massive immigration—from 1880 to 1909, in the 1920s, and again in the 1960s—that most of these schools were established (see figure 3–1), although other issues undoubtedly were operating during the 1960s. Commenting on the earlier eras, James McLachlan has written:

THE WORLD OF BOARDING SCHOOLS

It would hardly be surprising that a 1903 survey of family boarding schools would state quite bluntly that they were being founded in part because of parents' feelings that "in certain localities the companions of the boy in all but the higher grades of day school are, from their nationality, objectionable personal habits, or what not, undesirable." (McLachlan 1970, 214)

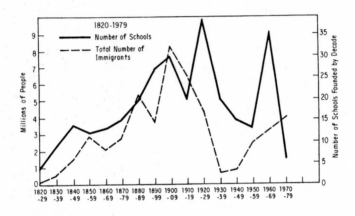

FIGURE 3–1

Immigration to the United States by Decade. Paralleled to Number of Elite Schools Founded, by Decade, 1820–1979

SOURCE: Adapted from a chart prepared by the U. S. Bureau of Census and from data in *The Handbook of Private Schools* (Boston: Mass, Porter Sargent, 1981).

After World War I, there was a little more geographic and religious expansion. Midwestern schools, such as Cranbrook in 1926, were established and Catholics started a prestigious school in 1926 with the founding of Portsmouth Priory in Rhode Island. Yet prep schools remained extraordinarily conservative in their social outlook and non-establishment families rarely sent their children away to school.

This changed with the founding of the Putney School in 1935. Progressive and Rousseauian, Putney paved the way for many of the alternative schools that sprang up in the 1960s. Nonreligious and distinctly liberal, Putney made a point of not being socially exclusive. It was during the period of Putney's founding that non-elite educators began to advocate closer relations between faculty and students, and because education was a preparation for life, self-reliance was seen as a virtue. The tiny Midland school in California, founded in 1932, is an example of how non-establishment parents and educators were already beginning to rebel against the size and bureaucracy of the U.S. public school system.

After World War II, enrollment patterns remained fairly steady in boarding schools as the number of schools expanded slowly, but in the 1960s the storm broke. Students simply refused to accept the discipline that many schools tried to impose and either left or did not enroll in the first place. This was partly possible because in the post-*Sputnik* period public education was undergoing a rapid and positive transformation.

Prodded in part by practicalities, boys schools discovered the virtues of coeducation in the late 1960s. By admitting girls, boys schools could accomplish a number of organizational goals simultaneously. The schools became more attractive to boys, as well as girls, and acquired a much larger pool from which to draw qualified students. It followed that with the spread of coeducation, girls school applications declined.

While there have been changes in the boarding school marketplace, the motivations of upper-class families have remained relatively constant. For them an elite school is part of their children's preparation for life. Susan Ostrander, who studied upper-class women, was told by one woman, "My husband wanted to repeat his educational history . . . and that of his own father." Another noted, "It's helpful when you move to a new city and want to get invited into the local social club." An upper-class mother commented on the social as well as educational advantages of exclusive schools: "You don't go to private school just for your education. You go there to be separated from ordinary people." Another said, "I don't want my children to be exposed to the things that go on in public schools, drugs and vandalism" (Ostrander 1984, 84–85).

Part of the elite tradition is the continuity a family establishes by sending several generations to a single school. Fifty-four percent of our sample of 2,475 students have at least one relative who attended a boarding school (the figure for Episcopal schools is as high as 73 percent). Among the 54 percent, 53 percent have one or more relatives who attended the same school.

But to fill their beds, even the most selective prep schools have had to compete for the children of parvenu families by adopting a number of public relations strategies. Virtually every school, for instance, has an extensive kit of materials, including lavishly printed brochures generously illustrated with photographs of the students already enrolled, and listing school activities, faculty, and curriculum. These brochures are considerably more expensive and extensive than those of boarding schools in England. In England some schools have begun to hire public relations firms to do brochures "like the American schools do," according to one English head, though many still have a simple descriptive page or two.

In the parlance of the marketplace, certain schools may become "hot" or "cold." A hot school is usually one that was once socially prestigious, fell on hard times, and is now on the rebound. Schools often become hot after the arrival of a new head. The boarding school world is small, and gossip, for good or for ill, travels fast and reputations can ride on the most casual of parents' cocktail chatter. As the rumor mill tends to be slightly behind reality, schools on their way down have a short grace period before their reputations tumble and schools on their way up must wait a few years for their reputations to spread. The select 16 and other very elite schools, of course, can weather these highs and lows without much effort, but for schools whose market position is less predictable, the grapevine of parental opinion can be critical.

Getting In: Raw Material and Prep Poise

When heads appoint teachers to various positions within a school, there is room for a certain margin of error. If a young English teacher turns out to be a magnificent educator, but a mediocre third-string soccer coach, the foundations of the school are not rocked. But when a head appoints an admissions director, he or she is entrusting the future of the school to that individual, because the admissions director is the school's most important gatekeeper. Aside from those students that are admitted on the basis of what the British call "headmaster's choice," all incoming students must, ultimately, measure up to the standards set by the admissions office. Loyalty, discretion, and judgment are the essential qualities of an admissions officer, and a certain amount of sophistication, good looks, and humor do not hurt. The admissions director must have an acute awareness of the school's needs, as well as the expectations of parents.

Parents expect the elite schools to look elite. Most schools have spacious admissions offices where the emphasis is on understatement and traditional tastes. The antique clock and furniture, along with the original oil paintings and Persian rugs, create an aura of exclusiveness. Some schools wear their status openly by displaying the portraits or busts of their more illustrious alumni. In general, one would hesitate to raise one's voice in the admissions offices of the most elite schools.

Admissions officers and admissions committees are adept at creating student bodies that are tailored specifically for their schools. Certain basic qualities are required of each class admitted; they must be demographically distributed according to the school's admissions goals, ambitious, and reasonably athletic. Schools vary widely on the number of scholarship students they will accept and on the emphasis placed on prior academic ability. Every class must have musicians, artists, athletes, and thinkers if they are to be successful.

A school filled with "brains" stands the risk of driving away the less brainy but wealthier families. A school that is entirely "prepped out" may find its reputation among college admissions officers slipping. Too many "jocks" make teachers unhappy, too few jocks make students and alumni unhappy. Moreover, the picture is complicated by the search for diversity. Girls at coed schools must be as strong academically and socially as boys, otherwise they cannot hold their own.

It is generally believed that prep school students are highly qualified. At the more selective schools, students must take the Secondary School Aptitude Test (SSAT). Unlike colleges, however, the prep schools do not uniformly publish the range and average scores of entering students on these tests. Although entering freshmen in some select 16 schools, such as Groton and Exeter, have high median SSAT scores, other elite schools admit a number of students whose scores fall below the average.[1] Student grades and recommendations are also required for admission, although how the schools evaluate these measures is not known, underscoring the private nature of these institutions.

It is not by chance that most prep school students have shiny, well-combed hair, are trim, healthy, and at least reasonably attractive. The social psychiatrist Robert Coles contrasts the attention to appearance and self of privileged children with that of other children:

> With none of the other American children I have worked with have I heard such a continuous and strong emphasis put on the "self." In fact, other children rarely if ever think about themselves in the way children of well-to-do and rich parents do—with insistence, regularity, and, not least, out of a learned sense of obligation. These privileged ones are children who live in homes with many mirrors. They have mirrors in their rooms, large mirrors in adjoining bathrooms. When they were three or four they were taught to use them; taught to wash their faces, brush their teeth, comb their hair. Personal appearance matters and becomes a central objective for such children. (Coles 1977, 380)

Part of the screening process is to weed out those who will not fit in. Discovering what "fitting in" actually meant to admissions officers was difficult, however, because they were guarded in how much information

1. The median score nationally on the SSAT is 309 and a score of 348 places a student in the 99th percentile. The median score for Groton and Exeter is 325.5 (*Independent Schools: A Handbook* 1982).

they would reveal. After all, merit is only part of the criteria for admission; other intangibles, such as family wealth and social standing, also count for a great deal.

Thus the admissions process remains relatively secretive, although even the most casual observation of the students who go to the most elite schools leads one to believe that the presentation of the self plays an important role in how students are selected for admission. Part of the prep presentation of self is the public display of confidence and control—poise. The first step on the road to "being somebody" is to "act like somebody," even if you are not quite sure who that somebody is.

Schools vary in how they actually go about deciding who will be offered a place, who will be put on the waiting list, and who will "not be invited to attend"—reject is not a boarding school word. Most schools claim to need all the information on applicants by the end of January, although many will entertain applications after that date. Some schools have rolling admissions, evaluating applications more or less continually. Generally, a set of complete folders is read by a committee composed of faculty members from different departments, some coaching staff and, very probably, the admissions director and one or two assistants. Each member of a committee will read a great number of applications, ensuring that the biases of any single reader do not unduly influence the decision-making process. Naturally, these group readings entail a certain amount of horse trading and informal information sharing: children of alumni will have certain advantages, as will outstanding students and athletes.

An important element in the decision-making process is trying to estimate which families will send their children to a particular school if they are admitted. No school wants to admit a large number of students who then choose to go to other schools. Not only is a school's prestige on the line, but, practically speaking, there is a problem of determining the ratio of acceptances to enrollments. If too many students enroll, there is overcrowding; if too few enroll, the consequences are obvious. So the question of determining which parents are serious about sending their children to a prospective school is an important consideration. A waiting list, therefore, becomes a school's insurance policy against finding itself, come fall, underenrolled.

Rejection from an applicant's school of choice can be traumatic to both students and their families. The families have invested themselves in the admissions process and rejection implies not only a lack of academic attainment, but a lack of social standing as well. Often rejection notices are couched in terms not of the student's failure, but of the school simply not having enough places. Some schools will counsel parents on alternative boarding schools that might be appropriate for their child. A student who fails to gain admission to a top boarding school may have to be content with a school with a somewhat less prestigious reputation. Competition among schools of similar prestige is intense, but it is minimal among schools of differing prestige.

Like the minuet of the seventeenth century, the admissions dance is highly stylized and a bit baroque. The complexity of the admissions process, of course, is not accidental. Boarding schools must retain a firm grip on who they admit, because, if the "wrong" students are admitted, then the historical mission of the schools to mold patrician and parvenu into an elite cadre will be jeopardized. The raw material must be suitable to the "treatment."

An examination, then, of who actually goes to boarding schools reveals a great deal about the schools and their perception of their place within the larger educational and social system. If people can be known by the company they keep, cannot schools be known by the students they admit?

Prep School Families

INCOME

F. Scott Fitzgerald is reputed to have once said to Ernest Hemingway, "The rich are different from you and I." To which Hemingway replied, "Yes, they have more money." If Fitzgerald had said, "Preps are different than you and I," Hemingway's response would have been the same: One only has to glance at the endowments of most of the major schools to see that their alumni are affluent. It is not uncommon for an elite school to net more than a million dollars a year in their annual fund drive. Happen by an elite school during a parents' weekend, and the collective value of the automobiles in the parking lot would be enough to build a reasonably well-equipped public school in a low-income neighborhood.

An accurate estimate of income for any group, especially the well-to-do, is difficult to obtain. Even the IRS is baffled at times by how people with low taxable incomes can live so well. To complicate matters further, income can be either earned or unearned (that is, based on the ownership of productive resources), and wealth is a whole other story. We had no measure of parental wealth, but we did include an income question on our questionnaire. To some, this methodology might appear problematic, as students' knowledge of their parents' income may be questionable. Yet, there is a considerable amount of research evidence that adolescents and parents come close in their independent reports of various aspects of family life (for example, see Jessop 1982). Girls tended to answer, "Don't know," more than boys did, but other than that, there was no particular pattern to how students responded. Thus, our information is drawn equally from each of the twenty schools in the questionnaire sample.

Because we did not want to exclude from our analysis the 39 percent of students who did not know the answer to the income question, we developed a statistical method of estimating incomes based on other items from the questionnaire. We used a prediction equation of ten family background items that were highly associated with income. The effect of including the estimated income with the reported incomes was to raise somewhat the level of incomes for the whole sample, especially in the $75,000 to $100,-000 category. To guard against unduly inflating our measure, we excluded scores that were above any actually reported incomes. We also compared the predictive effect of our estimated income with the predictive effect of actually reported income in relation to a student's SAT scores. Because we found that the estimated incomes and the reported incomes were virtually identical in their predictive power, we concluded that the estimated measure was an adequate substitute in those cases which did not report income.

Forty-six percent of the boarding school families in our sample of twenty schools have annual incomes of more than $100,000 a year. An additional 20 percent of boarding school families have incomes between $75,000 and $100,000 per year. Only 3 percent have incomes of less than $15,000, 7 percent fall into the $15,000 to $25,000 a year range, and 24 percent fall between $25,001 and $75,000 a year. By contrast, in 1981, 9.7 percent of all American families earned more than $50,000 a year, and the median family income was slightly less than $24,000 a year. Forty-one percent of American families made less than $20,000 a year which, after taxes, equals about what it costs to send one child to boarding school for one year.

Students who board at school are only slightly more affluent than day students, but the families that send their daughters to girls schools are very well off indeed, even compared to other boarding school families; 58 percent have incomes in excess of $100,000 a year. Students at all-boys schools also come from affluent families; 53 percent have incomes in excess of $100,000 a year.

Foreign students are as affluent as the Americans, as are the Asian-American students in our sample. Among black students, there are also affluent families; 15 percent come from $100,000 or more a year homes.

There were no major differences between freshmen and seniors in our sample, although freshmen appeared to come from slightly wealthier families (perhaps because they can afford four years of boarding school, whereas seniors, due to finances, may not have attended for all four years). A wealthy group of students come from Jewish homes, 41 percent having incomes of $100,000 a year or more. Presbyterians, Episcopalians, and Catholics are the next most wealthy groups, although Catholics are a weak fourth in affluence.

Parents who are prep school graduates have higher incomes than those who are not prep school graduates, and students who reported three or more relatives as boarding school alumni are proportionately more wealthy; 54 percent of these families have incomes exceeding $100,000 a year.

PARENTAL EDUCATION AND OCCUPATIONS

Income alone, however, is inadequate as a single descriptor of American boarding school families. This is a world where money matters, but other things matter as well. Boarding school families in our sample are well educated; 85 percent of the fathers have B.A.'s, as do 75 percent of the mothers. Nearly two-thirds of the fathers have attended graduate or professional school, compared to less than one-tenth of the fathers of high-school seniors nationally. One-third of boarding school mothers have attended graduate or professional schools, while nationally less than one in twenty mothers of high-school students have attended graduate school.

Given the high educational level of these families, it is not surprising that 50 percent of the fathers are professionals and 40 percent are managers. Specifically, 12 percent of our sample's fathers are doctors, 10 percent are attorneys, and 9 percent are bankers, with other professions following far behind. The academies attract some children of teachers, writers, and editors, but, proportionately, their number is small compared to the children of doctors, lawyers, and bankers. Progressive schools attract the children of doctors, girls schools attract bankers' and lawyers' daughters, with lawyers also preferring Episcopal schools for their children. College teachers seem to choose progressive schools, with academies running second.

Sixty-three percent of the mothers of boarding school students work, slightly less than the national average for mothers of high-school students, 71 percent of whom work. Of those who are not working, most are housewives. Boarding school mothers are less likely than the fathers, but more likely than either men or women in the national population, to occupy professional and managerial jobs. Slightly more than one-third of these mothers are professionals, and one in eight are managers or administrators.

One out of thirteen are clerical workers. The rest are scattered across various other occupations.

MARITAL STATUS

Boarding school families in this sample are stable in terms of the percentage who remain married. Seventy-five percent of the parents in this sample are married. This is virtually the same figure reported by the recent National Association of Independent Schools (NAIS)[2] survey (Talbot 1983). Thirteen percent of the parents in our sample are divorced, 2 percent separated and 4 percent widowed. The remaining 6 percent of the students are living with step-parents or other relatives. Foreign families are also stable: 82 percent of the parents are married. Families that send their children to Episcopal, Catholic, or academy schools are the most stable, with the marriage rate above 80 percent. Western schools tend to attract a higher percentage of students whose parents are divorced, while less than one-half of progressive school parents are married.

GEOGRAPHICAL ORIGINS

In a survey of the catalogues of the 55 schools we visited, we found that it is not uncommon for a school with between 500 and 600 students to have representatives from thirty or more states and students from at least two dozen foreign countries. Even smaller schools, with between 200 and 300 students, will have students from twenty or more states and ten or more foreign countries. Some schools, however, count students as coming from foreign countries when, in fact, they are children of United States citizens serving overseas, often in the State Department or with multinational corporations. Based on our questionnaires at 20 schools, we found that foreign students, that is, non-U.S. citizens, make up between 3 percent and 11 percent of the schools' student bodies. On average, 7 percent of American boarding school students are non-citizens. Catholic schools have the most foreign students, while Episcopal schools have the fewest. Many foreign students come from high-income families in the Middle East, South America, and Asia.

While most boarding schools do have cosmopolitan student bodies, they also support local constituencies. A Massachusetts school will have a good number of students from that state and nearby states, and there are generally a large number of Californians in California schools. Despite the conscious attempts by several large schools to draw "national student

2. The NAIS is a national organization that many private schools join. In the 1981 *Handbook of Private Schools'* population of 289 leading secondary boarding schools, 78 percent belong to NAIS.

bodies," the majority of students even at those schools live within a five-hour drive. Smaller schools draw even more heavily from their immediate state or region.

GLOBAL TRAVEL

Boarding school families travel a great deal and they take their children with them. Sixty-nine percent of the students in the questionnaire sample of 20 schools have traveled outside of the United States, half of them have been to Europe, 15 percent to Asia, 13 percent to South America, 8 percent to Africa, and 4 percent to Australia. Progressive, entrepreneurial, academy, and western school families must be hopping on and off planes regularly, as less than 13 percent of these students have never been outside of the United States. Jewish families are the top travelers—only 12 percent have not been outside the United States. Among black students, 44 percent have never been outside of the United States.

It is by no means unusual that boarding school students, no matter what their grade level, are better traveled than their teachers, creating an interesting paradox. In the teaching of geography, for instance, one may wonder who is the expert and who is the learner? And many of these students are not just tourists. Quite often they visit foreign families and stay for extended periods. This sense of internationalism is an important part of boarding school culture, and undoubtedly some students feel that the world is their oyster.

BOOKS AND COMPUTERS

Boarding school families in the questionnaire sample own a great many books: 51 percent have 500 books or more in their home, and less than one percent have fewer than 25 books. Progressive school parents must be inveterate readers, as 70 percent have libraries of more than 500 books, as do 60 percent of Episcopalian families. Western school families tend to read less than other boarding school families, or, at least, collect fewer books, since only 40 percent of them have more than 500 books. Academy school families have only slightly larger than average libraries, as do entrepreneurial school families. Catholics own fewer books than the average boarding school family, and minorities do not appear to make heavy investments in books.

Despite the linear orientation of boarding school families, they are entering the computer age, with 21 percent owning computers. Western school families are most likely to own a computer, nearly one-third do, while Catholic school families have the fewest home computers. Thirty-six percent of Asian boarding school families have computers, as do 28 percent of Jewish families. Nationally only 8 percent of households have home computers, and even in Silicon Valley only an estimated 25 percent of households have them (Rogers and Larsen 1984, 171).

LEGACIES

Elite schools vary in the number of alumni they admit or attract and in the last decades former public school families have been attracted to them. A 1983 National Association of Independent Schools study of boarding schools found that 57 percent of their students had come from public school and that 41 percent of their respondent's parents had never attended an independent school. For 53 percent of the students in the NAIS study at least one member of their extended family had attended boarding school. In our study, we found a similar percentage—54—of those attending boarding school have at least one relative who attended boarding school. These "legacy" students create a critical mass at many boarding schools, especially at the Episcopal, girls and academy schools whose student bodies are between 55 and 75 percent legacy students.

Legacy students differ from their non-legacy peers in terms of their backgrounds. They are more likely to be white and Episcopalian, their fathers are more educated and their mothers slightly more educated than non-legacy parents. No matter what legacy students' religious backgrounds, their parents are far more likely to hold prestigious occupational positions, and earn more than non-legacy families. Sixty percent of the students in our questionnaire sample who came from families earning more than $100,000 a year are legacies; only 2 percent have incomes of less than $15,000 a year.

For our study, we created a measure we called deep-prep. Deep-prep students are those who have had three or more relatives who attended boarding school. Over 26 percent of our questionnaire sample were deep-prep students, and they were predominantly Episcopalian, Presbyterian, and other Protestant denominations. Episcopalian schools have as many as 42 percent of their students come from deep-prep families. Girls schools also have many deep-prep families, and apparently the progressive tradition has become intergenerational, because the progressive schools attract a number of deep-preps. Academies have relatively few—16 percent— deep-preps. Girls are slightly more likely to come from deep-prep families than boys. Sixty-six percent of deep-prep fathers have graduate or professional degrees, and their wives are nearly all college graduates.

Because boarding schools have historically educated the sons and daughters of America's Protestant Establishment, we created a measure that identified those Episcopalian and Presbyterian students who have at least one relative who was a boarding school alumnus, are white, and who have an estimated family income of more than $100,000 a year. Eight percent of the sample fell into this category. These families tend to send their children to the entrepreneurial, girls, academy, and Episcopal schools. One-sixth of all girls schools' families are Protestant Establishment, as are 40 percent of the students at Episcopal schools—to no one's surprise.

Self-Perceptions and Life Goals

Both freshmen and seniors in our survey of 2,475 students were asked a series of questions about their self-esteem, sense of efficacy, and major life goals. Respondents had the opportunity to "Strongly agree," "Agree," "Disagree," or "Disagree strongly" to such questions as, "I feel I am a person of worth on an equal plane with others." The more strongly students agreed with statements such as these, the higher their self-esteem. Questions such as "When I make plans, I am almost certain I can make them work," were answered in the same way as the self-esteem questions and were used to measure efficacy.

Not surprisingly, boarding school students have a high degree of both self-esteem and efficacy. Most students strongly agree or agree with such questions as "I am a person of worth," and most students believe "I can make things work." Religious differences accounted for little of the variations in their responses. Students from legacy families have higher self-esteem and sense of efficacy than other students, and Asian students have the highest self-esteem and the lowest sense of efficacy. Black students are lowest in self-esteem and second to whites on the efficacy measure.

Perhaps most interesting from a socialization point of view is that the earlier students enter boarding school, the higher their self-esteem, while students entering at eleventh grade have the highest sense of efficacy. Thus, a girl who enters boarding school in the ninth grade from a legacy family is likely to have the highest self-esteem, while a nonlegacy black male who enters after the tenth grade is likely to have the lowest self-esteem. Students from white, high-income legacy families are likely to have a greater sense of efficacy than other types of students. On balance, however, the differences between students on these measures were small compared to their general similarity.

Students were also asked to indicate how important certain life goals were to them. They could rank each life goal as "Not important," "Somewhat important," and "Very important" (see table 3–1). Ranking these life goals according to how many students thought they were "Very important," an interesting pattern develops.

Boarding school students place a great deal of importance on friendship, work, marriage, and leisure and considerably less importance on money per se, correcting social inequalities, or being community leaders. Keeping in mind that the respondents are adolescents, it is not surprising that they attach such high importance to friendship. But there is not a great deal of social concern in their responses; students are three times more likely to indicate that their leisure time is more important than correcting social inequalities.

When the overall sample is broken down into sub-groups some interesting differences between groups emerge. For instance, there is a strong inverse relationship between family income and wanting to correct inequalities; the higher the income, the less interest in correcting them; the lower the income, the greater the interest. Few deep-prep students thought that having money was very important, but students with fewer legacies or no legacy at all whose families had incomes in excess of $100,000 a year were more likely than other students to say that having money was a "very important" life goal.

TABLE 3–1

Life Goals Among Boarding School Students

Rank of Goal	Goal	Students Who Ranked Goal "Very Important"
1	Having strong friendships	2,250
2	Being successful in my line of work	1,952
3	Finding the right person to marry and having a happy family life	1,894
4	Having leisure time to enjoy my own interests	1,893
5	Being able to find steady work	1,702
6	Being able to give my children better opportunities than I've had	1,370
7	Having children	1,074
8	Having lots of money	694
9	Working to correct social and economic inequalities	591
10	Being a leader in my community	428
11	Living close to my parents and relatives	413
12	Getting away from this area of the country	292

NOTE: Goals were ranked "Very Important," "Somewhat Important," and "Not Important" by 2,475 students at 20 schools.

Black students are much more success-oriented than white or Asian students. Black students are more likely to indicate that instrumental life goals such as being successful in work are very important, but they are also more likely to want to work to correct social inequalities. Over one-third of the blacks indicated that correcting social inequalities is important to them, while less than one-fourth of the whites indicated that the issue is very important in their lives.

Day and boarding students are similar in their responses, as are the legacy and nonlegacy students. Students from married-parent homes are more likely to value marriage than students from divorced or separated homes. Boarding school students tend to have higher occupational aspirations than their parents, and considering that most of their parents are successful, we get a sense of the climate of ambition at most boarding schools.

Boarding School Student Bodies

FRESHMEN AND SENIOR COMPARISONS

Boarding school student bodies tend to be stable through time. To cite a few examples, 86 percent of freshmen were white, and 88 percent of the seniors were white. Sixty-two percent of freshmen fathers had a graduate or professional degree, while 60 percent of the twelfth-graders' fathers had achieved the same educational level. Forty-one percent of both freshmen and senior fathers owned their own business. Sixteen percent of both groups' mothers owned their own business. Freshmen and senior families had similar incomes. Fifty percent of the freshmen fathers were professionals, while 49 percent of the seniors' fathers were professionals.

Freshmen and senior families were similarly distributed according to the number of their family members who had attended boarding school; 14 percent of both groups had three or more relatives who were boarding school alumni. Seventy-five percent of freshmen families were married, while 74 percent of the parents of seniors were still married.

While differences between students who enter boarding school at different grade levels are relatively small, there are some patterns that warrant mention. Sixty-one percent of seniors who entered in the ninth grade, for instance, tend to come from boarding school families. And 64 percent are attending the same school that one or more of their relatives attended.

Religious differences between students who enter at different grade levels are small. Episcopalians comprise 22 percent of the students entering at all levels, except for the post-graduate (PG) year.[3] Catholics send their children away somewhat later, as they comprise 34 percent of the twelfth-grade entrants and 44 percent of the post-graduates are Catholic. Of the seniors who entered in the tenth and eleventh grades, there are a few important differences. Girls, however, comprise a 55 percent majority of the eleventh-grade entrants. More minorities and non-U.S. students enter the schools in the tenth grade in particular; 50 percent of the black students enter in the tenth grade, while 44 percent of the Asians enter at that level. By the eleventh grade, less than half of the students entering boarding school have had a family member with previous boarding school experience.

Families of post-graduates appear to be extremely stable (85 percent have married parents), but somewhat less affluent than other boarding school families. Few of these families have traveled extensively, and, as a group, they have fewer books in their homes than other families.

DAY STUDENTS

Overall, 24 percent of the respondents in our sample were day students. The lowest percent of day students at any school was 2 percent and the highest proportion was 62 percent. The entrepreneurial, girls, and Catholic schools are likely to be one-third day students, the academies, Episcopal, and progressive schools have less than 20 percent, and the western schools less than 10 percent. Select 16 schools have more boarding students (85 percent) than other schools (68 percent).

Day students, as a group, are quite similar to boarding students in terms of their family backgrounds. Much like freshmen-senior comparisons, one is struck by the homogeneity between day and boarding students. If anything, day students are from more stable homes (81 percent of their parents are married), are better traveled, and have slightly larger libraries than boarding students. Day families have as high incomes as boarding families, and many day-school fathers are doctors. In general, day-school fathers have slightly higher occupational prestige scores than boarding-school fathers. Less than 2 percent of day students are black. The day-school population appears to be composed primarily of the children of local professionals. The number of day girls and day boys is nearly equal and there are more freshmen day students than senior day students.

3. The PG year is a repeat of the senior year of secondary school by a student who comes in after graduating from another high school.

THE ISSUE OF DIVERSITY

"Diversity" is a prep school watchword. In the last twenty years, boarding schools have been proud of the increasing diversity of their student bodies. But how truly diverse is the boarding school world?

It is no surprise that the boarding school world is basically white. Ninety percent of boarding school students are Caucasian,[4] compared to 83 percent for the population at large. Episcopal, girls, and Catholic schools are more than 90 percent white.

Through private programs such as *A Better Chance,* black students from disadvantaged backgrounds are given opportunities to attend boarding schools, yet their representation in boarding schools is below their representation in society; 12 percent of the American population and 19 percent of the public high-school population was black in 1982. No private boarding school comes close to this number of black students. Some boarding schools have as few as one percent black students and, on average, 4 percent of boarding-school students are black. While a number of these students have low-income backgrounds, and receive scholarships, boarding schools also attract a great number of the black middle class; 29 percent of the black students in the sample had a relative who had attended boarding school, and 36 percent of the black fathers in the sample had obtained a graduate or professional degree. Thirty-two percent of the mothers had obtained a graduate or professional degree and 22 percent of the fathers owned their own business. Compared to the statistics for the black population in general, the divorce rate among black boarding school families is low, and their income is high. Eighty percent of black mothers work, and one-third of the black students are Baptists.

Surprisingly, there are more Asian students in this sample than blacks. Five percent is Asian. The academies, entrepreneurial, and western schools enroll a high number of Asian students. At least one-third of them are non-U.S. citizens, although 53 percent of these students indicated that one or more of their relatives attended boarding school. Seventy-four percent of the fathers have obtained a professional or graduate degree and 42 percent own their own business. Asian families have the lowest divorce rate of any group (93 percent have married parents) and have traveled a great deal, especially in North America and Asia. One-quarter of the Asian fathers earn $100,000 or more a year.

---

4. The exact percentage of whites in the questionnaire sample of twenty schools is 90.3, of blacks, 4.3, and of Asians, 5.3. Due to rounding, the total percent equals 99 rather than 100.

THE WORLD OF BOARDING SCHOOLS

RELIGION

There was a time when elite schools simply did not accept non-Protestants, but today one-quarter of all boarding-school students are now Catholic, close to the 27 percent of Catholic-Americans. Naturally, the Catholic schools attract Catholics in large numbers, but academies, entrepreneurial, girls, and to a lesser extent, the western schools also attract them. Episcopal and progressive schools have the fewest Catholics.

The accusation of anti-Semitism has been laid at the doorstep of boarding schools since the late nineteenth century. But today 11 percent of the students in our sample of 2,475 are Jewish, compared to less than 3 percent in the general population. Entrepreneurial schools enroll a particularly high number of Jewish students (16 percent), followed by progressive schools, western schools, and the academies. In our sample there were no Jewish respondents at either the Episcopal schools or the Catholic schools. Jewish families have fewer legacies than any other group except blacks. They are the most highly educated group: 71 percent of Jewish fathers have professional or graduate degrees, and 45 percent of Jewish mothers have the same level of education. Sixty-five percent of Jewish fathers own their own business, and 22 percent of Jewish mothers own their own business. The divorce rate among Jewish families is relatively high in our sample, compared to other religious groups.

SEX

Another major admissions decision within the last two decades has been to admit girls to what were formerly all-boys schools. Overall, 39 percent of our sample were female. Progressive schools, western schools, and public schools come close to having equal numbers of girls and boys, partly, of course, because many of them have always been coeducational. The girls at boarding schools have similar family backgrounds to the boys'. Proportionately, there are a few more girls who come from Episcopalian homes. Girls who attend coed schools come from families with slightly lower incomes than do the boys at coed schools. Girls' mothers tend to work outside of the home a little more often than boys' mothers and, interestingly, they tend to come from families with a strong boarding-school tradition. Girls' mothers are slightly more educated than boys' mothers and slightly more likely to be divorced.

Stability and Continuity in the Prep School World

In sum, boarding school students are overwhelmingly from high-income professional and managerial families. Three-quarters of their parents are married, only 7 percent are non-citizens, 5 percent are Asians, and 4 percent are black. More than half (54 percent) of the students have one or more relatives who also attended boarding school. The students and their families travel widely; nearly three-quarters have traveled outside of the United States.

The students have a high degree of self-esteem and efficacy and value having strong friendships more than anything else as their life goal, although they seek even higher status occupations than the already high ones held by their parents.

The schools exhibit a rather remarkable capacity to maintain stability in the students they admit. Whether it is comparisons between day and boarding students, freshmen and seniors, or boys and girls, the relatively new arrivals closely resemble their traditional counterparts. Yet, there does appear to be some increase in the racial and religious diversity of current student bodies compared to traditional ones.

Boarding school students, by any reasonable standard, are elite—whether they come from the old monied patrician families or upwardly mobile parvenu families. Boarding schools not only choose their students, they can create their student bodies with precision. With the exception of coeducation, change has been slow in the boarding school world, and decisions are made carefully with a view to their long term effect. Public schools and even many private day schools simply do not have this option. The select 16 boarding schools can be particularly selective in who they admit. Having gained admission to a boarding school, the chosen ones are ready to embark on the "the prep rite of passage," which we discuss in the next section.

PART

II

THE PREP RITE
OF PASSAGE

4

Cultural Capital: Curricula and Teachers

BORROWING from the British, early American headmasters and teachers advocated a boarding school curriculum that was classical, conservative, and disciplined. It wasn't until the latter part of the nineteenth century that such "soft" subjects as English, history, and mathematics were given a place beside Latin, Greek, rhetoric, and logic in the syllabus. It was the early schoolmasters' belief that young minds, especially boys' minds, if left to their own devices, were undisciplined, even anarchic. The only reliable antidote to mental flabbiness was a rigorous, regular regime of mental calisthenics. A boy who could not flawlessly recite long Latin passages was required to increase his mental workouts. Classical languages were to the mind what cold showers were to the body: tonics against waywardness.

Girls, with some exceptions, were not thought of as needing much mental preparation for their future roles as wives and mothers. Their heads were best left uncluttered by thought; too much book learning could give a girl ideas about independence. Besides, the great majority of them were not going on to college, where even more classical languages were required.

As an intellectual status symbol, the classical curriculum helped distinguish gentlemen from virtually everyone else and thus defined the difference between an "educated" man and an untutored one, as well as the difference between high culture and popular culture. Such a division is critical to exclude nonmembers from groups seeking status. For a long time a classical curriculum was the only path to admission to a university, as Harvard and many others required candidates to demonstrate proficiency in Latin and Greek (Levine 1980). Thus, the curriculum of boarding schools has long served both social and practical functions.

Culture, much like real estate or stocks, can be considered a form of capital. As the French scholars Pierre Bourdieu and Jean-Claude Passeron (1977) have indicated, the accumulation of cultural capital can be used to reinforce class differences. Cultural capital is socially created: what constitutes the "best in western civilization" is not arrived at by happenstance, nor was it decided upon by public election. The more deeply embedded the values, the more likely they will be perceived as value free and universal.

Thus curriculum is the nursery of culture and the classical curriculum is the cradle of high culture. The definition of what is a classical course of study has evolved, of course, since the nineteenth century. Greek and Latin are no longer required subjects in most schools—electives abound. But the disciplined and trained mind is still the major objective of the boarding school curriculum.

> The Groton curriculum is predicated on the belief that certain qualities of mind are of major importance: precise and articulate communication; the ability to compute accurately and to reason quantitatively; a grasp of scientific approaches to problem-solving; an understanding of the cultural, social, scientific, and political background of Western civilization; and the ability to reason carefully and logically and to think imaginatively and sensitively. Consequently the School puts considerable emphasis on language, mathematics, science, history, and the arts. (*Groton School* 1981–82, 15)

The contrast between the relatively lean curricula of many public schools and the abundant courses offered by boarding schools is apparent. In catalogues of the boarding school's academic requirements, courses are usually grouped by subject matter, and at the larger schools course listings and descriptions can go on for several dozen pages. Far from sounding dreary, the courses described in most catalogues are designed to whet the intellectual appetite. Elective subjects in particular have intriguing titles such as "Hemingway: The Man and His Work," "Varieties of the Poetic Experience," "Effecting Political Change," "Rendezvous with Armageddon," and for those with a scientific bent, "Vertebrate Zoology" and "Mammalian Anatomy and Physiology."

Boarding school students are urged to read deeply and widely. A term course on modern American literature may include works from as many as ten authors, ranging from William Faulkner to Jack Kerouac. Almost all schools offer a course in Shakespeare in which six or seven plays will be read.

In history, original works are far more likely to be assigned than excerpts from a textbook. A course on the Presidency at one school included the following required readings: Rossiter, *The American Presidency;* Hofstadter, *The American Political Tradition;* Hargrove, *Presidential Leadership;* Schlesinger, *A Thousand Days;* Kearns, *Lyndon Johnson and the American Dream;* and White, *Breach of Faith.* Courses often use a college-level text, such as Garraty's *The American Nation* or Palmer's *A History of the Modern World.* Economic history is taught as well—in one school we observed a discussion of the interplay between politics and the depression of 1837—and the idea that there are multiple viewpoints in history is stressed. It is little wonder that many prep school graduates find their first year of college relatively easy.

An advanced-placement English class uses a collection of *The Canterbury Tales* by Geoffrey Chaucer that includes the original middle English on the left page and a modern English translation on the right. An advanced third-year French course includes three or four novels as well as two books of grammar and readings. Even social science courses require a great deal of reading. In a course called "An Introduction to Human Behavior" students are assigned eleven texts including works from B. F. Skinner, Sigmund Freud, Erich Fromm, Jean Piaget, and Rollo May.

Diploma requirements usually include: 4 years of English, 3 years of math, 3 years in one foreign language, 2 years of history or social science, 2 years of laboratory science, and 1 year of art. Many schools require a year of philosophy or religion and also may have such noncredit diploma requirements as: 4 years of physical education, a library skills course, introduction to computers, and a seminar on human sexuality. On average, American public high-school seniors take one year less English and math, and more than a year less foreign language than boarding school students (Coleman, Hoffer, and Kilgore 1982, 90). Moreover, in the past two decades there has been a historical decline in the number of academic subjects taken by students in the public schools (Adelman 1983).

Because success on the Scholastic Aptitude Test is so critical for admission to a selective college, it is not uncommon for schools to offer English review classes that are specifically designed to help students prepare for the tests. Most schools also offer tutorials and remedial opportunities for students who are weak in a particular subject. For foreign students there is often a course in English as a second language.

As the arts will be part of the future roles of boarding school students, the music, art, and theater programs at many schools are enriching, with special courses such as "The Sound and Sense of Music," "Advanced Drawing," and "The Creative Eye in Film." Student art work is usually on display, and almost every school will produce several full-length plays each year, for example, *Arsenic and Old Lace, A Thurber Carnival, Dracula,* and *The Mousetrap.*

Music is a cherished tradition in many boarding schools, in keeping with their British ancestry. The long-standing "Songs" at Harrow, made famous because Winston Churchill liked to return to them for solace during World War II, are a remarkable display of school solidarity. All 750 boys participate, wearing identical morning coats with tails. Every seat is filled in the circular, sharply tiered replica of Shakespeare's Globe Theater as the boys rise in unison, their voices resonating in the rotunda.

The belief that a well-rounded education includes some "hands-on" experience and travel runs deep in the prep view of learning. Virtually every boarding school provides opportunities for their students to study and work off campus. As volunteers, Taft students, for instance, can "tutor on a one-to-one basis in inner-city schools in Waterbury, act as teachers' helpers in Waterbury Public Schools and work with retarded children at Southbury Training School." They can also work in convalescent homes, hospitals, and day-care centers, and act as "apprentices to veterinarians and help with Girl Scout troops" (*Taft* 1981–82, 21). At the Ethel Walker School in Connecticut, girls can go on whale watches, trips to the theater, or work in the office of a local politician. The Madeira School in Virginia has a co-curriculum program requiring students to spend every Wednesday participating in volunteer or internship situations.

Generally speaking, the schools that take the position that manual labor and firsthand experience are good for the soul as well as the mind and body, are more progressive in orientation than other schools. At the Putney School every student has to take a tour of duty at the cow barn, starting at 5:30 A.M. In their own words, "Putney's work program is ambitious. We grow much of our own food, mill our own lumber, pick up our own trash, and have a large part in building our buildings. . . . Stoves won't heat until wood is cut and split" (*The Putney School* 1982, 3).

Various styles of student-built structures dot the campus of the Colorado Rocky Mountain School, and at the tiny Midland School in California, there is no service staff, except for one cook. When the water pump breaks, faculty and students fix it, and when buildings are to be built, faculty and students pitch in. "We choose to live simply, to distinguish between our needs and our wants, to do without many of the comforts which often obscure the significant things in life" (*Midland School* 1983, 1). The creed of self-reliance is reenacted every day at Midland. When a trustee offered to buy the school a swimming pool, he was turned down. Lounging around a pool is not part of the Midland philosophy.

Travel is very much part of the prep way of life and is continued right through the school year. Not only are semesters or a year abroad (usually in France or Spain) offered, but at some of the smaller schools, everyone goes on an extensive field trip. Every March at the Verde Valley School in Arizona the students travel to "Hopi, Navajo and Zuni reservations, to small villages in northern Mexico, to isolated Spanish-American communities in northern New Mexico and to ethnic neighborhoods of Southwestern cities. They live with native families, attend and teach in schools, work on ranches, and participate in the lives of the host families and their communities" (*Verde Valley School* 1982–83, 9). Not all boarding schools, of course, place such a high value on rubbing shoulders with the outside world. At most of the academies, entrepreneurial, and girls schools the emphasis is on service rather than sharing.

While boarding schools may vary in their general philosophy, the actual curricula do not widely differ. The pressures exerted on prep schools to get their students into good colleges means that virtually all students must study the same core subjects. Although not quick to embrace educational innovation, many boarding schools have added computers to their curricula. This has no doubt been encouraged by announcements by a number of Ivy League and other elite colleges that they want their future applicants to be "computer literate." While people at most boarding schools, or anywhere else for that matter, are not quite sure what is meant by computer literate, they are trying to provide well-equipped computer rooms and teachers who can move their students toward computer proficiency.

For students who have particular interests that cannot be met by the formal curriculum, almost all schools offer independent study, which gives students and teachers at boarding schools a great deal of intellectual flexibility. At Groton, for example, independent study can cover a diverse set of topics including listening to the works of Wagner, conducting a scientific experiment, or studying a special aspect of history.

The boarding school curriculum offers students an abundant buffet of regular course work, electives, volunteer opportunities, travel, and independent study, from which to choose a course of study. By encouraging students to treat academic work as an exciting challenge rather than just a job to be done, the prep schools not only pass on culture but increase their students' competitive edge in the scramble for admission to selective colleges.

The Importance of Sports

Even the most diligent student cannot sit in classrooms all day, and because the prep philosophy emphasizes the whole person, boarding schools offer an impressive array of extracurricular activities, the most important of which is athletics. At progressive schools, the competitive nature of sport is deemphasized. The "afternoon out-of-door program" at Putney, for example, allows for a wide variety of outdoor activities that are noncompetitive; in fact, "skiing is the ideal sport for Putney as one may ski chiefly to enjoy himself, the air, the snow" (*The Putney School* 1982, 15).

Putney's sense that sport should be part of a communion with nature is not shared by most other schools, however. At most prep schools sport is about competition, and even more important, about winning. An athletically powerful prep school will field varsity, junior varsity, and third-string teams in most major sports. A typical coed or boys school will offer football, soccer, cross-country, water polo, ice hockey, swimming, squash, basketball, wrestling, winter track, gymnastics, tennis, golf, baseball, track, and lacrosse. For the faint-hearted there are alternative activities such as modern dance, cycling, tai chi, yoga, ballet, and for the hopelessly unathletic, a "fitness" class. A truly traditional prep school will also have crew like their English forbears at Eton and Harrow. Certain schools have retained such British games as "Fives," but most stop short of the mayhem masquerading as a game called rugby.

Prep teams compete with college freshmen teams, other prep teams, and occasionally with public schools, although public school competitors are picked with care. Not only is there the possible problem of humiliation on the field, there is the even more explosive problem of fraternization in the stands when prep meets townie. Some schools, known as "jock" schools, act essentially as farm teams for Ivy League colleges, consistently providing them with athletes who have been polished by the prep experience. Many prep schools take public high-school graduates for a post-graduate year, as a way of adding some size and weight to their football teams.

Prep girls also love sports; they participate as much as the boys, often in the same sports, and with as much vigor. A girls' field hockey game between Exeter and Andover is as intense as when the varsity football teams clash. Horseback riding at girls schools is still popular; a number of the girls go on to ride in the show or hunt circuit. Unlike many of the girls in public schools, the boarding-school girl is discouraged from being a spectator. Loafing is considered to be almost as bad for girls as it is for boys.

During the school year the halls of nearly all prep schools are decorated with either bulletins of sporting outcomes or posters urging victory in some upcoming game. Pep rallies are common, as are assemblies when awards are given and the competitive spirit is eulogized. Often the whole school will be bussed to an opponent's campus if the game is considered to be crucial or if the rivalry is long-standing.

Alumni return to see games, and there are frequent contests between alumni and varsity teams. Because preps retain the love of fitness and sports, it is not uncommon for the old warriors to give the young warriors a thrashing. Similarly, the prep life also invariably includes ritual competitions between, say, the girls field hockey team and a pick-up faculty team.

Nowhere is the spirit of victory more pronounced than on the ice of the hockey rink. Few public schools can afford a hockey rink so prep schools can attract the best players without much competition. Some prep schools import a few Canadians each year to fill out the roster. Speed, strength, endurance, and fearlessness are the qualities that produce winning hockey and more than one freshman team from an Ivy League college has found itself out-skated by a prep team. Whatever else may be, in Holden Caulfield's term, "phony" about prep schools, sports are for real. This emphasis on sport is not without its critics. At the Harrow School in London, the new headmaster, who was an all-England rugby player, has begun a program to reward artistic and musical prowess as well as athletic and academic skills.

The athletic facilities at prep schools are impressive, and at the larger schools, lavish. Acres and acres of playing fields, scores of tennis courts, one or more gyms, a hockey rink, a golf course, swimming pools, squash courts, workout rooms—all can be found on many prep school campuses. Generally, the facilities are extremely well maintained. The equipment most preps use is the best, as are the uniforms. One boy described how "when your gym clothes get dirty, you simply turn them in at the locker room for a fresh set." The cost of all this, of course, is extraordinary, but considered necessary, because excellence in sport is part of the definition of a gentleman or a gentlewoman.

The pressure for athletic success is intense on many campuses, and a student's, as well as a school's, social standing can ride on the narrow margin between victory and defeat. Perhaps because of this, schools generally take great pains to play schools of their own size and social eliteness. A study of who plays whom among prep schools reveals that schools will travel great distances, at considerable expense, to play other prep schools whose students and traditions are similar to their own.

Extracurriculars and Preparation for Life

Not all prep school extracurricular activities require sweating, however. Like public school students, preps can work on the school newspaper, yearbook, help to organize a dance, or be part of a blood donor drive, and are much more likely than their public school counterparts to be involved in such activities. For example, one in three boarding school students are involved in student government compared to one in five public school students, and two in five are involved in the school newspaper or yearbook compared to one in five. This evidence is consistent with other research. Coleman, Hoffer, and Kilgore (1982) found that private school students participate more in extracurricular activities than do public school students. The fact that more boarding school students than public school students are involved in activities provides additional opportunities for them to practice their verbal, interpersonal, and leadership skills.

The catalogue of clubs at prep schools is nearly endless. The opportunity for students to develop special nonacademic interests is one of the qualities of life at prep schools that distinguishes them from many public schools. Special interest clubs for chess, sailing, bowling, or gun clubs are popular at boys schools. One elite boys school has a "war games" club. As the boys at this school are feverishly calculating their country's next strategic arms move, the girls in a Connecticut school are attending a meeting of Amnesty International. Girls, in general, tend to spend their off hours studying the gentler arts such as gourmet cooking and art history. One girls school has a club with a permanent service mission to the governor's office.

At some schools students can learn printing, metalwork, or woodworking. The shop for the latter at Groton is amply equipped and much of the work turned out by the students is of professional quality. The less traditional schools offer clubs for vegetarian cooking, weaving, quilting, folk music, and—in subtle juxtaposition to the Connecticut girls school—international cooking. At western schools, the horse still reigns supreme and many students spend endless hours riding, training, cleaning, and loving their own horse, or a horse they have leased from the school.

With the prep emphasis on music, choirs, glee clubs, madrigals, chamber music groups, as well as informal ensembles are all given places to practice. Most schools also have individual practice rooms, and like athletic teams, many prep musicians travel to other schools for concerts and performances.

Some schools offer a five week "Winterim," during which students and faculty propose and organize a variety of off- and on-campus activities and studies. Such a program breaks the monotony of the usual class routine in the middle of winter, a season teachers repeatedly told us was the worst time at boarding school. It also enables students and faculty to explore new areas or interests in a safe way, that is, without grades.

In prep schools there is a perceived need for students to exercise authority as apprentice leaders early in their educational careers. The tradition of delegating real authority to students has British roots, where head boys and prefects have real power within the public schools. Head boys can discipline other boys by setting punishments and are treated by headmaster and housemasters alike as a part of the administration. In the United States, student power is generally more limited, although at the progressive schools students can be quite involved in the administrative decision-making process.

Virtually all prep schools have a student government. The formal structure of government usually includes a student body president, vice president, treasurer, secretary, class presidents, and dorm prefects, representatives, or "whips," as they are called at one school. Clubs also have presidents and there are always committees to be headed. Some schools have student-faculty senates and in schools like Wooster, in Connecticut, students are expected to play a major part in the disciplinary system. An ambitious student can obtain a great deal of experience in committee work, developing transferable skills for later leadership positions in finance, law, management, or politics.

The office of student body president or head prefect is used by the administration primarily as an extension of the official school culture, and most of the students who fill these offices are quite good at advancing the school's best public relations face. A successful student body president, like a good head, is artful in developing an easy leadership style, which is useful because he or she is in a structural political dilemma. Elected by the students but responsible to the school administration, the student politician is a classic go-between, always running the danger of being seen as "selling out" by students and as "uncooperative" by the administration. Occasionally students rebel against too much pandering to the administration and elect a rebel leader, who makes it his or her business to be a thorn in the side of the administration. A number of heads and deans of students watch elections closely, because if elections go "badly" it could mean a difficult year for them.

The actual content of real power varies by school. At some, authority is more apparent than real; at others, student power can affect important school decisions. At Putney, the "Big Committee" is composed of the school director, student leaders, and teachers. The powers of the Big Committee are laid out in the school's constitution, and students at Putney have real input into the decision-making process. At the Thacher School in California, the Student Leadership Council, which is composed of the school chairman, presidents of the three lower classes, and head prefects, is not only responsible for student activities and events, but also grants funds to groups who petition for special allocations. The power of the purse is learned early in the life of a prep school student. At the Westtown School in Pennsylvania, the student council arrives at decisions not by voting yea or nay, "but by following the Quaker custom of arriving at a 'sense of the meeting'" (*Westtown School* 1982–83, 25).

Not all students, of course, participate in school politics; it may well be that many of the students most admired by their peers never run, or never would run, for a political position. The guerrilla leaders who emerge and flourish in the student underlife—or counterculture—may have far greater real power than the "superschoolies" that tend to get elected to public office.

In most coeducational schools boys tend to monopolize positions of power. The highest offices are generally held by boys; girls are found in the vice presidential and secretarial positions. Politics can be important to prep families and we suspect that a number of prep boys arrive at boarding school with a good supply of political ambition. One of the reasons advanced in support of all-girls schools is that girls can gain important leadership experience there.

Some schools try to capture what they see as the best aspects of single-sex and coed schools. They do this by having boys and girls elect distinct school leaders, by having certain customs, places, and events that they share only with members of their own sex, and by having classes, certain other activities, and social events be coeducational. These schools, often called coordinate schools, see themselves as offering the chance to form strong single-sex bonds, to build self-confidence in adolescents, and to provide experience in working and relating to members of both sexes. Girls at coed schools more generally are likely to say they think in ten years they will find the social skills they learned to be the most valuable part of their boarding-school experience.

Learning by Example

Part of the social learning students obtain is exposure to significant public personalities. Virtually all the schools have guest speaker programs in which well-known people can be seen and heard. Some of the speakers that have appeared at Miss Porter's School in the last several years include Alex Haley, author; Russell Baker, humorist; Arthur Miller, playwright; and Dick Gregory, comedian. At the boys schools there is a tendency to invite men who are successful in politics and journalism. Recent speakers at the Hill School include: James A. Baker III, Secretary of the Treasury (Hill class of 1948); James Reston, columnist; Frank Borman, astronaut and president of Eastern Airlines; and William Proxmire, United States senator (Hill class of 1934).

Inviting successful alumni to return for talks is one of the ways boarding schools can pass on a sense of the school's efficacy. Throughout the year panels, assemblies, and forums are organized for these occasions. Often the alumni speakers will also have informal sessions with students, visit classrooms, and stay for lunch, tea, or supper.

In keeping with cultural environments of prep schools, especially the select 16 schools, professional musicians, actors, and dancers are regularly invited to perform. Art and sculpture exhibits are common and some schools, such as Andover and Exeter, have permanent art galleries. The art at prep schools is generally either original works by artists such as Toulouse-Lautrec, Matisse, or Daumier, or the work of established contemporary artists such as Frank Stella, who graduated from Andover. At a large school there may be so much cultural activity that it is unnecessary to leave campus for any kind of high cultural event.

Those who come to elite boarding schools to talk or perform are the makers of culture. For adolescents seeking to be the best, these successful individuals give them a sense of importance and enpowerment. All around them are the symbols of their special importance—in Groton's main hallway hangs a personal letter from Ronald Reagan to the headmaster, reminding the students that Groton "boasts a former President of the United States and some of America's finest statesmen." Five or six books a year will be published by a school's alumni; Exeter in particular has many alumni authors, including James Agee, Nathaniel G. Benchley, John Knowles, Dwight Macdonald, Jr., Arthur M. Schlesinger, Jr., Sloan Wilson, and Gore Vidal. Roger L. Stevens, Alan Jay Lerner, and Edward Albee are all Choate-Rosemary Hall alumni, adding luster to a theater program that trains many professional actresses and actors. A student at an elite school is part of a world where success is expected, and celebrity and power are part of the unfolding of life. Not every school is as culturally rich as the elite eastern prep schools, but in the main, most schools work hard to develop an appreciation for high culture. At the Orme School in Arizona, a week is set aside each year in which the whole school participates in looking at art, watching art being made, and making art.

Nowhere is the drive for athletic, cultural, and academic excellence more apparent than in the awards, honors, and prizes that are given to outstanding teams or students at the end of each year. Sporting trophies are often large silver cups with the names of annual champions engraved on several sides. At some schools the triumphs have come with enough regularity to warrant building several hundred yards of glass casing to hold the dozens of medals, trophies, and other mementos that are the victors' spoils. Pictures of past winning teams, looking directly into the camera, seem frozen in time.

Academic prizes tend to be slightly less flashy but no less important. Much like British schoolmasters, American schoolmasters believe in rewarding excellence, so most schools give a number of cultural, service, and academic prizes at the end of each year. There is usually at least one prize in each academic discipline, as well as prizes for overall achievement and effort. There are service prizes for dedicated volunteers, as well as debating and creative writing prizes. Almost all schools have cum laude and other honor societies.

Sitting through a graduation ceremony at a boarding school can be an endurance test—some schools give so many prizes that one could fly from New York to Boston and back in the time it takes to go from the classics prize to the prize for the best woodworking or weaving project. But of course, the greatest prize of all is graduation, and more than a few schools chisel, paint, etch, or carve the names of the graduates into wood, stone, or metal to immortalize their passage from the total institution into the world.

The Road Not Taken: The Boarding School Teacher

Educating a child at a prep school is extremely expensive and parents can find themselves having to scramble to meet the high tuition fees required by the schools. But complaints about the high cost of an elite education have a slightly hollow ring, not only because most prep school families are wealthy, but because whether they are aware of it or not they are the beneficiaries of a unique financial partnership. Without the indirect subsidy that teachers provide to parents by working for pay that is only slightly above the minimum wage, the tuitions at most schools would probably have to double to meet the schools' running expenses. It is true that wages are not the only form of compensation that boarding school teachers receive; most are offered free housing and, if they are willing to eat with the students, three meals a day seven days a week. But on balance, the relative impoverishment of boarding school teachers is what, in the end, balances the boarding school budget.

This silent partnership is one of the most enigmatic yet potentially revealing aspects of the prep school world because the teachers are, in the words of more than one head, the "heart and soul" of any school. Students come and go, but the faculty goes on. Senior faculty in particular are the embodiment of what the school has been, is, and will be. The faculty's importance rests not only in their numbers but in their culture, which is invisible to most parents, irrelevant to most students, and mistrusted by more than a few heads. Understanding this culture is not easy for an outsider because it is a highly codified world where the keys to perception are kept carefully locked away from strangers. Teaching at a boarding school is, according to the teachers, "a way of life," much like a religious vocation where service gives life meaning.

Normally we associate devotion and sacrifice with service to the poor or disadvantaged; how do we understand that same dedication in the case of prep school teachers who, in the words of one, are "missionaries to the rich"?

Almost everyone who teaches in prep schools could be doing something else. Unlike many public school teachers who are upwardly mobile and drawn to teaching because of money and convenience (Lortie 1975, 31), the prep school teacher has chosen a career that provides little social mobility. Young teachers are often surprised to learn that despite being hired at a well-known school their status in the outside world remains low. This is ironic because by and large most prep school teachers are quite accomplished. Roughly 75 percent of the 382 teachers surveyed have attended a private college and many of them are graduates of Ivy League and other selective colleges. At one academy, 25 out of 80 teachers are Ivy League graduates, 11 coming from Harvard. Sixty percent of prep school teachers have a masters degree and 5 percent have Ph.D.'s (Cookson 1980). A high proportion of boarding school teachers are prep school graduates and some prep school teachers are scholars who hold academic chairs at the schools.

THE PREP RITE OF PASSAGE

Not only are prep school teachers well educated, but they often come from professional families, bringing varied experience to their jobs. It is not unusual to find prep school teachers who were athletic stars in college, have backpacked in the Brazilian jungle, spent time in the Peace Corps, lived in Europe, written a book, or built their own boat. Two-thirds of boarding school teachers are male, which contrasts with public schools, where men comprise only a little more than half of all secondary school teachers (U.S. Bureau of the Census 1984, 151).

It should be apparent, then, that the road not taken by the prep school teacher is the highway of affluence and social status; the road taken is the wooded trail of commitment to youth and intellectual pursuits. In a survey that included both private day school and boarding school teachers both groups rated "knowledge and ability," "dedication to children," and "kindness" as the top three attributes of a teaching professional. Education courses and previous experience were the lowest ranked items. "Tolerance and consideration" and "the ability to deal effectively with students" were the most important qualities of an "outstanding" teacher in the eyes of the respondents (Cookson 1980).

Boarding school teachers have very little job security, certainly no union to represent them, and in almost all cases no tenure. At most schools their relationship with the head borders on the feudal, and they have little recourse if they fail to receive promotions or are dismissed, even without a stated cause. But as vulnerable as they are, very few prep school teachers would want a union or tenure. When asked if they had tenure many teachers responded, "No, thank God." Trying to unionize the elite schools would no doubt prove to be a quixotic and short adventure.

This is because prep school teachers prize their independence. When asked what they liked best about teaching they responded, "working with students," "watching young minds develop," as well as being able to teach as they liked without a central administration prescribing lesson plans or insisting on a set method of teaching. The small classes at boarding schools can make teaching enjoyable. To be among curious adolescents can be exhilarating but it can also be disillusioning when students "tune-out" or resist learning. One teacher wrote on his questionnaire that the worst thing about teaching was "that group of contemporary students who are making Spengler's predictions in *The Decline of the West* a reality."

What prep school teachers like least about their jobs is paperwork, committee work, and busy work—including "administrivia." Some spoke of "colleagues that gossip," and "the confining, demanding seven days per week of boarding school; also the cliques and favoritism. . . ." Another wrote that what she least liked was "the police duties of a boarding school;

trying to determine who lies, drinks, imports dope, etc., catching them, and passing judgements."

Teacher, dorm monitor, coach, friend, policeman, and colleague: the prep school teacher wears many different occupational hats in the course of a single day. This way of life for some is a fulfillment. "Where else can you teach classes in the morning, play games in the afternoon, and read for your classes and yourself at night?" asked one contented teacher. For others, the experience of working within the total institution can be a deprivation leading to depression and a growing sense of isolation which sometimes can be the cause of burn-out, an occupational ailment affecting more and more teachers and causing heads to invest more time and resources in professional problems and development.

Triple Threats, Double Duties, and Singular Rewards

During the nineteenth century and for most of the twentieth century, prep school heads had available to them a small but relatively homogeneous pool of prospective teachers from which to draw their faculties. Like British schoolmasters, the early American schoolmasters had the tendency to stay at their school for many years; a career of fifty years at a single school was not unheard of. More than likely, the classic schoolmaster or schoolmistress was unmarried and very orthodox on matters of religion, deportment, and breeding. These were the days of the prep school boom when Anglophilia was at its height and overt starchiness and snobbery were not considered bad taste.

Each school has its legendary great teachers, and paging through old yearbooks one comes across faded photographs of other, forgotten great teachers, their faces poised between quizzicality and contentment. Alumni bulletins will very often do a sentimental story about old so-and-so, who gave so much to the school, and some of the larger schools have set up special academic chairs in honor of a great teacher.

Even today, most schools have a grand old man or woman who provides a living link between the past and present and is treated with great deference. This is not to say that all teachers have been gentle souls; on the contrary, according to our alumni interviews, the schools have harbored a substantial number of bizarre characters. Over time, boarding schools have certainly attracted their share of drinkers, lechers, and incompetents. Nearly all alumni can recount at least one teacher who frightened them either through physical force or mental torture. At one school, a particular teacher had the habit of stationing himself by the bathroom door, "disciplining" the boys as they came to and from the shower.

Sexual relations between teachers and students is a taboo subject, but more than one teacher has had to leave school before the end of the year because they misconstrued the meaning of a "close faculty-student relationship." A number of liaisons of a homosexual or heterosexual nature may go undetected and therefore unpunished. During the sixties some of the more adventurous schools became well known for their swinging life styles, but this is a luxury that parents seem less willing to finance at present.

Whether a boarding school teacher was lovably eccentric, boringly square, or unpleasantly bizarre, heads from the earliest days expected their teachers to work long hours at many tasks. At the boys schools teachers were expected to teach, coach, and supervise a dorm—the so-called "triple threat." Like their British counterparts, the ideal schoolmaster was a genuine amateur: part scholar, part athlete, part counselor. However unlike the British, the American teacher could not set up his own boarding "house" for students and charge fees as a way of supplementing his income. At the girls schools, labor was divided between the academic staff (teachers) and residential staff (housemothers), and gym teachers, an arrangement still in operation.

While at school no teacher could claim to be off duty; informal as well as formal obligations were continuous. Monitoring of students was constant—be it at meals, in the dorms, at study halls, on the field, in class, around the grounds, or in the halls. Preparing for and attending chapel, attending teas, dealing with parents, and managing one's personal life all had to be squeezed into busy days. Double duty was business as usual for the boarding school teacher.

For heads the willingness of so many to work so hard for so little was an administrative delight. As the young triple threats aged they either were elevated to the status of "great teacher" or were let go. A continuous flow of youthful energy was thus ensured. A school could hum along for years staffed by hard-working, loyal teachers who asked only that they be left free to teach how they pleased, a singular reward that most heads were only too glad to grant. Teacher evaluation was conducted by rumor, gossip, how much damage there was in the dormitories they supervised, and general impressions along the grapevine. Basically you either "fit in" (a favorite administrative phrase) or you did not.

In our interviews, many heads spoke of the changes they had witnessed among their faculties. Since the 1960s, in particular, the profile of the boarding school teacher has changed considerably. Teacher prospects are more likely to be married, have children, have some public school background, and consider themselves professionals who expect some privacy and time for a personal life. To the older heads this suggests a lack of commitment, but wealthy bachelors and spinsters are in short supply and the schools have had to adjust to the new boarding school teacher. Clever heads have followed the path of least resistance and discovered that it is "healthy" to have lots of small children on campus. They "encourage" professional growth and are "stimulated" by faculty without prep school backgrounds. Enlightened leadership provides for sabbaticals, paid summer graduate study, travel to conferences, release time for special projects, on-campus workshops, as well as good health and dental plans.

Salaries are still low by public school standards. A beginning teacher may start for something less than $10,000 a year; a senior teacher is unlikely to make much more than $30,000 at even the best endowed schools. Many teachers supplement their incomes by taking on extra administrative duties, coaching, and working during vacations and summers as chaperones and guides for school-sponsored overseas trips. Some also work in camps, Outward Bound programs, and summer sessions.

Over time the amateur ideal has become a bit tarnished by its abuse, which is apparent in the area of faculty evaluation. At many schools, the casual armchair evaluations so favored by generations of heads have been replaced by more systematic methods of evaluation. Presumably, a formal, open method of evaluation decreases paranoia and increases a sense of accountability and professionalism. It also provides administrators with reams of information about teachers, which can be a mixed blessing for those who are something less than great in front of a class. In a litigious society, heads also feel they should collect systematic records of work performance in order to prove due process in any court case arising from a contested dismissal decision. Formal evaluation increases paperwork and draws off teacher and administrator time. One head contrasted "real humanity" with "the pretense of professionalism."

It is difficult to evaluate properly in any mechanical way the many informal but critical attitudes and behaviors prep school teachers must have if they are to do their jobs. Formal evaluation can actually increase paranoia; one dean of faculty remarked with a glint in his eye that it was time for the faculty "to pull up their socks." An "or else" would have been redundant. Generally, boarding school teachers look to department heads or senior faculty for help and support in the classroom. Administrator observations and discussions are the least helpful forms of evaluation, according to teachers (Cookson 1980).

For many heads, and teachers as well, overly elaborate methods of evaluation have an aura of hypocrisy about them. One teacher wrote that most evaluation was little more than a way of providing "a rationale for the school's official conduct/attitude toward a teacher." Most heads consider the hiring process much more critical for producing a good faculty than *ex post facto* methods of evaluation, which is like closing the barn door after the horses have escaped.

Hiring new teachers at boarding schools is a time-consuming process that is taken seriously by the head, other administrators, and teachers. After all, they all have to live with this person. Therefore good paper credentials are only the first hurdle. Much more important are the candidate's personal qualities. Most schools, in fact, have stacks of résumés sent directly from job applicants or by teacher employment agencies. Because teachers must perform more than one job at boarding schools, it takes a certain skill to locate individuals with multiple talents, so knowing how to read these résumés is something of an art form. Finding a German teacher might not present too many problems, but finding a German teacher who can coach third-string soccer and is willing to live in a dorm is another matter.

Balance is the key not only to enrolling a good class but a good faculty as well. Each school's definition of balance is somewhat different, but basic elements have to do with academic skills, sports skills, artistic skills, as well as such personal characteristics as sex, age, experience, morality, and, last but by no means least, enthusiasm. "I look for someone who is excited about teaching kids and excited about their subject. Someone who will set kids on fire," said one faculty dean. The five most important qualities heads look for in new teachers are: knowledge and ability, verbal facility, independence of thought, kindness, and personal style and manners (Cookson 1980).

Because a teacher's personal qualities are so critical at a boarding school, educational background and previous experience are considered to be less important than they might be in other job situations. Schools are particularly leery of college and university teachers when they try to "trickle down" from higher to secondary education, feeling that the lonely, self-interested scholar usually lacks the flexibility required to cope with boarding school life or adolescent antics. According to the heads, deans, and teachers we spoke to, single and married men tend to adjust to boarding school life somewhat better than single women, who often feel socially stifled by living in relative isolation.

In searching for teachers, heads will rely on informal networks as well as formal channels. Personal references and recommendations from other boarding school heads or teachers are taken seriously. Many heads feel that mentoring good young teachers is an important part of their job. "We have an obligation to bring good people into teaching," one head remarked.

Without commitment on the part of the teachers, boarding schools would not only lose their tone, they would also lose their students. In an interview with us, one head wondered, "Can we bring into this business people with energy, time, and conviction, to be surrogate parents as well as good teachers? If not, all hell will break loose. Some parents have done a lousy job. You need teachers who will do what their heart tells them to do rather than what their contract says." According to another head, "It's harder to get this kind of total commitment from faculty today. There are fewer cultural supports for them and what they are doing. 'Why are you taking that seriously?' parents ask. Parents are sending out conflicting signals, the authorities are giving off such mixed signals."

It is this devotion that department chairmen, deans of faculties, and heads look for among prospective candidates. When applicants are invited to visit a school they should expect a long, exhausting day. They will have to meet and impress a small regiment, including in most cases the department head, dean of faculty, and the head. If after the ordeal the applicant is still able to smile, this may be treated as *prima facie* evidence that he or she has the stamina to survive the fishbowl life of the boarding school.

Faculty Culture, Pride, and Poignancy

If the shape of boarding school faculties were drawn in terms of the age differences of the teachers, it would resemble an hour glass. At the bottom are the young "short-timers" who come to work at the schools generally right out of college, spend a year or two, then move on to other occupations or go back to graduate school. Those that do remain join forces with the older faculty already in place, causing the upper bowl of the hour glass to swell out. The senior faculty are the role models not so much for the students but for the other teachers. Senior faculty are the arbiters of style, tone, and the parameters that define each school's adult community. At some schools, where the faculty have a great deal of organizational power, their influence is publicly recognized and utilized. At the smaller schools, where the head shares almost no official authority with teachers, the power of the faculty is covert, well hidden, but no less important. Friendship networks spread out from a nucleus of senior faculty to some younger faculty, creating affiliations that smother some and soothe others. Some faculty wrote to us or spoke of the good comradeship they share with their colleagues, others of the "backbiting," "cattiness," and "just plain meanness." The faculty culture has no real recognition; it exists in between the student culture and the official culture of the school. Teachers are, as one teacher put it, "essential nonessentials." The schools do not exist for them, but cannot exist without them.

Each year as the teachers wish the seniors on their way, a little part of their life also graduates; the most they can hope for from students is "thanks for the memories." Classrooms, hallways, dormitories, dining rooms, and libraries all hold memories for long-term boarding school teachers that even most heads cannot share. The returning student they cannot quite remember, the lessons that succeeded, and those that failed, the sudden awareness that ten or more years have passed almost without notice—all these fleeting glimpses into mortality can be poignant for the teachers who do "serve them all their days."

Older teachers are also faced with a number of practical problems. Unless they have a private income, they may discover that they cannot afford to send their own children to a private college; the years spent ensuring the educational futures of other people's children may leave their children unable to attend their first choice college.

Few schools have adequate pension funds, and because many boarding school teachers never bought a house, they have had little opportunity to build up equity. Some older faculty feel used; with the best years of their life gone they have no marketable skills with which to start a new profession. They become the victims of their own good intentions, and nobody is really interested in their problems. Most trustees and heads seem to have little inclination, time, or money to worry about the sins of the past.

One psychologist suggested to us that boarding school teachers unconsciously want to be institutionalized; they are drawn to the prep school because of their dependency needs. Certainly many heads complain that their teachers are childish and dependent. Not only are they "people who never paid a utility bill," but they need constant stroking and paternalistic advice. Teachers themselves speak of the "big, bad world" and the pleasure of living in a "cashless society." Whether or not boarding school teachers are more dependent than soldiers, sailors, ministers, priests, or others who have chosen to commit their lives to a total institution is open to question. Certainly those that wear the "golden handcuffs" of corporate America are as dependent on their multinational companies as the prep school teacher is on his or her school.

The life of service, even service to the rich, however, has its intangible rewards; giving to others can be its own satisfaction. Teachers "are involved in the lives of young people at turning points in their lives, as they make choices about drugs, alcohol, sex, and living with other people," said one. Pride in service is an old-fashioned quality that captures more than a few boarding school teachers. There may not be many Mr. Chipses left in prep schools, but there are a good number of men and women who have devoted their lives to the young with a level of dedication that elevates their calling, even as it reinforces among their students the perception that their teachers are akin to the family retainer—unobtrusive, hard-working, and ultimately expendable. As one teacher powerfully captured these sentiments, "The kids go off to Gstaad and you're left to write the college recommendations for them (or grade their term papers, or whatever)." We asked how this teacher felt about that. "I feel beleaguered, like I sacrificed my life, like a functionary rather than a mentor. The psychic rewards of teaching are seriously undermined by this."

The greater power and wealth of many students, their relative lack of interest in getting involved with their teachers, and the tendency for them to see their teachers in the role of doing for them, means that some tend to resist demands to do more for themselves. Such a situation creates frustration for teachers, who may take it out in subtle or not-so-subtle ways on their students. Hence, this structural discrepancy contains the potential for tension. Teachers may, perhaps even at an unconscious level, feel more affinity for the "scholarship student"[1] and in subtle ways do more to encourage him or her than they do for more advantaged pupils. One countervailing force to this possibility may be the hope for favors from very prominent or wealthy families. Children of wealthy or powerful families, on the other hand, may worry, "Did I get these grades because of my work or because of my parents?" (Coles 1977, part 7). The discrepancy between the social class backgrounds of teachers and students is a potential source of frustration and tension underlying the teaching situation.

1. Compare Coles (1977, part 7), Hoggart (1957), and Rodriguez (1982, chap. 2) on this subject.

5

*Academic Climates,
Teaching Styles,
and Student Stress*

THE QUALITY of teaching we observed in most boarding schools is exceptionally good. Cultural capital is of only limited use if it is neglected, and certain prep school teachers excel at transforming curricula into educational excitement. Four out of five boarding students believe that "teachers here encourage students to value knowledge for its own sake." In fact, compared to many public high-school classrooms, most boarding school classrooms are alive with intellectual intensity. When boarding school students were asked in our survey of twenty schools whether the statement "Many classes here are boring" was true or false, nearly 70 percent answered "false." When 426 high-school students attending three public schools in middle-class school districts were asked the same question, only 25 percent indicated the statement was false (Cookson 1981). Studies show that students at many public schools are bored and undermotivated (Adelman 1983; Csikszentmihalyi and Larson 1984, 202–14).

At prep schools education is still a cottage industry, where learning experiences are hand crafted. More than 90 percent of boarding school students believe that "teachers here are very interested in their students." The craft of teaching is taken very seriously by most boarding school teachers and some are masterful in their ability to transmit high culture with a gracefulness, enthusiasm, and style that may not always make learning easy or fun, but generally does not equate learning with pain or failure.

Perhaps this is why the academic climate scores of boarding schools are so high when compared to other secondary schools. (See McDill and Rigsby 1973, for an explanation of how academic climates are measured.) In our questionnaire, students were asked to respond to a number of items on how they perceived their schools' academic climate. Statements such as "Few students try hard to get on the honor roll," and "There is a lot of interest here in learning for its own sake, rather than just for grades or for graduation credits" were designed to tap an underlying attitude toward academics. Eighty-four percent of all boarding school students believe most students "try hard" to get on the honor roll and 60 percent report that there is "a lot of interest here in learning for its own sake."

By combining a number of statements for evaluation, much like those discussed above, a scale was created by which the academic climates of public and boarding schools could be compared. Not surprisingly, it was found that boarding schools score much higher on the academic climate measure than do public schools, and select 16 schools receive the highest scores on the scale. Not only are the mean differences substantial, but as a group, boarding school students are much more homogeneous in their attitudes toward academic excellence than public school students (Cookson 1981, 114).

Being among other students who are academically interested and ambitious can have an impact on even an indifferent student, especially because adolescents are easily influenced by their peers. As one boarding student said, "It isn't cool to be dumb around here." Another told us, "Here even smart students ask for help, there's no stigma attached to going to your teacher if you don't understand something, while there was in my old school." Several students suggested that there were "better intellectual mores" at boarding school than in their previous school and that they had found others who shared their intellectual interests.

One on One: The Socratic Method

It is January in California and the rain will not stop. The school which believes in self-sufficiency and simplicity has few heated buildings; many classrooms are open to the air on one side, placing teachers and students at nature's doorstep, if not directly in her lap. At 7:45 A.M. a young English teacher looks up from his poetry book and scans his students, all six of them. They are cold and damp and they huddle over their books as though literature could heat the body as well as the mind. Each student is wearing a coat, a hat, and gloves. The fingers have been cut from the gloves to make page turning possible. Several dogs are wandering about, two appear to be facing off for a canine quarrel.

The teacher, who also wears a coat, hat, and cut-away gloves, watches the rain fall for several seconds, apparently lost in thought.

"Frank," he says at last, "What does Yeats mean by 'the center cannot hold?' "

"He means things are messed up."

"What do you mean messed up?"

"Nobody believes in anything."

"Too vague, Frank. Don't be lazy. Gretchen, what other poet reminds you of Yeats?"

Energy levels begin to rise; Gretchen's statement that Yeats is similar to T. S. Eliot is challenged by another student, and like a ripple effect it is not long before everyone is "thinking poetry." The rattle of the rain as it hits the tin roof is muffled by the sounds of the students who begin to raise their voices to make their points. The teacher puts his feet on the desk and checks his watch; he's done his job with this class.

The central classroom metaphor of the boarding school is the seminar table, even when students do not sit around a common table. In these classrooms, personalized, individual instruction creates the possibility that the actual meaning of the verb to learn—to draw out—can be realized. It was Lewis Perry of Phillips Exeter who was most responsible for shifting the teaching emphasis in boarding schools from rote and memorization to participation and expression.

At the center of an Exeter education is the Harkness classroom—twelve to fourteen students and a teacher seated around a table for the purpose of forming and expressing ideas rather than dispensing and receiving information, a classroom in the Socratic manner where maximum participation is encouraged, pretense and careless preparation readily perceived. In an age given more to manipulation than to understanding, Exeter stands for the values summed up in the Harkness plan and is determined to preserve them. (*Exeter Catalogue* 1982, 35).

Today the Socratic method lies at the heart of the boarding school teaching craft. The dialogue of a seminar implies a certain amount of intimacy and sharing among teachers and students that in turn suggests small classes. On average, the class size in boarding school is 12 to 15 students, with some being as small as 4 or 5, compared to 32 students per class in New York City, for example. Most public high-school teachers have five classes each school day in which approximately 30 students are enrolled, a total of 150 students a day. Boarding school teachers usually have four classes of 15 or fewer students, totaling 60 students or less. The debate as to how class size is related to achievement is unsettled at this point, but some research suggests that some forms of learning, particularly oral and written expression, are more likely to occur in classes of fewer than 15 students than in larger classes (Persell 1977).

Boarding school teachers have high expectations for their students. In the ideal, students are expected to think and to explain their answers, not just state them. Small classes enable teachers to tell individual students "Good," "You have the idea," or even, "A very good guess—I admire your logic, but it's wrong," or "That's such a good metaphor." These comments help to personalize learning and to develop the individual learner. Teachers stress the relationship between ideas and encourage students to play with them, pushing their students to be clearer in their expression of them. A teacher will ask probing questions like "What is your conception of his character?" referring to a character in a novel the class is reading. They will probe further after several people have answered, "Any other ideas about his character?" Students are taught to reflect on the people in the literature they read, and asked to provide reasons for the ideas they put forward. The teacher will often press further: "Why do you say, 'he's a fake?' "

One teacher at a select 16 school conducts a discussion of the French Revolution the way a college teacher would, using the Socratic method, asking leading questions and guiding the discussion. He keeps the students returning to the central question, suggesting that he expects them to push their thinking in a focused way. History students are continually advised to be specific in their use of evidence. At a New England school another history teacher is trying to make her discussion of Oliver Cromwell relevant. "If you were Oliver Cromwell and head of this school, how would you change the weekly schedule?" Artfully, the teacher directs the ensuing debate back to the Puritan Revolution, the imaginations of the apprentice Lord Protectors having been stimulated by visions of absolute power.

Students who haven't read the day's assignment have little hope of escaping detection. There is no back row at prep school, as almost everyone sits around a table or in a circle. Monarch Notes and other study guides are generally not available in boarding schools; a student who substituted reading a synopsis for an original work is likely to be discovered in the intense atmosphere of the boarding school classroom. Excellence and ignorance are constantly up for public display, although compared to British schoolmasters American teachers seem meek. Teachers at girls schools may be delicate but nonetheless quite definite in conveying their expectations. For example, "Why didn't you say all those wonderful things before?" a teacher asked her class, suggesting that their prior comments were not up to standard, but doing so in a positive way.

Writing is one of the hardest skills to develop, as it requires the ability to express ideas, mental organization, logic, and a grasp of grammar, punctuation, and spelling. Compared to public high-school students, prep school students are asked to write a great deal. Two-thirds of boarding school students at twenty schools report having to write essays, themes, poetry or stories "frequently" in their courses as compared to public school students, only 27 percent of whom report having to write frequently (National Opinion Research Center 1980, pp. 8–9). Most prep school students complete several long papers, one or more research projects, as well as book reports, essays, stories, poems, and perhaps even a play in the course of a school year. History and English assignments are often coordinated, requiring students to use their language skills outside of the English class.

At a select 16 New England school, tenth and eleventh graders sit in a required English class. The course centers on how to write, taught in a systematic, well-conceived way. We observed a lesson dealing with ways of suggesting cause and effect in writing. The teacher asked, "Are there word clues that help suggest causality?" Students suggested several: "If . . . then," "Thus . . ." "because," "due to," and "therefore." "These enable you to move your writing forward," noted the teacher, and they also help students to read material more thoughtfully.

In addition to encouraging writing, the boarding school curriculum is permeated with features designed to stimulate the development of other verbal skills. Eighty percent of boarding school students participate in student-centered discussions "fairly often" or "frequently" compared to 55 percent of public school students. Most boarding schools offer public speaking courses, and public debates are held regularly. We observed many English classes where students were assigned a part in a play (usually Shakespeare) and, while their enunciation and stage presence is generally modest compared to the British public school boys and girls who devour Shakespeare by the stanza, the fledgling American actors are nonetheless expected to make Shakespeare come alive. When students were reading aloud from a Shakespeare play, one teacher gave a running commentary on how they were reading, "I didn't like that line, do it again," or "excellently read," as well as interpreting what they were reading.

Students are also asked to think about what they are doing. For example, when they are asked, "If you were the director of this [Shakespeare] play, and had to defend your decision, how old a person would you choose for this role?" These experiences teach public poise and confidence, we suspect, as well as verbal skills. Students also begin practicing for their future roles in power. "Why does Brutus decide he must help in the murder of Julius Caesar?" a teacher asked a ninth-grade class. "What justifies murder?" he continued, implying that the exercise of ultimate power is justifiable under certain circumstances. Similarly a ninth-grade history teacher helps students understand Alexander the Great's charismatic leadership, resourcefulness, and ambition by having them read *The Nature of Alexander* by Mary Renault.

Students who need individual attention can find it at prep schools; about half report getting individual instruction from a teacher either "fairly often" or "frequently." The sense that teachers are there to be consulted was expressed by one student who said, "It has given me an even more aggressive attitude towards my education, meaning if I want something I'm not likely to give up trying to get it (for example, extra help or answers to questions I can't answer on my own)." For another, boarding school "pushed me to achieve my goals."

Part of helping students to reach their goals is making them do their homework. On average, a boarding school student is expected to do an hour of homework per subject per night. Even at a relatively competitive suburban high school, only a half hour of homework per night is expected; how much is actually done is another question (Cookson 1981). Seventy-three percent of public high-school students report doing five hours or less of homework per week compared to 82 percent of boarding school students who report doing ten or more hours of homework a week. Twenty-six percent of the students at boarding schools claim to spend more than twenty hours a week on their homework. (See Coleman, Hoffer, and Kilgore 1982, 104, for public school data.) At one of the select 16 schools, everyone had identical red books in which to write their homework assignments.

At many boarding schools, getting homework done is supported by a school requirement that students be in their rooms studying, usually from

7:30 to 9:30, with no talking and no radios or stereos playing. Students whose grades slip below a certain minimal acceptable level are required to report to a supervised group study hall, where a proctor watches them work. Most students prefer the comforts of their own rooms and are thus encouraged to keep their grades above the critical threshold. Weekend passes may also be contingent upon doing satisfactory course work. Thus schools use various rewards and restrictions to reinforce the desired behavior of study in students whose inner motivation needs fortifying.

It is not surprising, therefore, that boarding school students, compared to public high-school students, seldom watch television. Forty-eight percent of prep school students watch no television, and only 12 percent watch more than two hours per day during the school week. Among public school students, only 4 percent do not watch television at all during the school week, 38 percent watch between two and four hours per day, and 31 percent watch more than four hours per day during the school week.

Preparing for standardized tests is another key element in many boarding school curricula. Although some schools offer special review courses for the Scholastic Aptitude Tests, others simply integrate test-taking skills into their overall curriculum. Quite often prep school students take the PSAT in tenth grade to uncover weaknesses and develop strengths and experience. Learning to take a test is, of course, half the battle in doing well and many boarding schools leave few stones unturned in helping students through the intricacies of multiple choice exams.

Advanced Placement (AP) exams are also taken seriously. Students are given very explicit instructions on how to take the exams, often by teachers who have graded them in the past. In an AP American history class, students are told, "You must use concepts correctly, for example, the terms 'loose construction' and 'strict construction' of the Constitution. Actually there was a question about that on a prior AP exam."

At one select 16 school the coaching the students received for an AP history exam was designed to motivate their desire to "win" as well as pass along important test-taking skills. As we sat and observed the class, the teacher exhorted:

> You don't want to read the question more than once in the exam. Know what topic they are addressing and isolate the categories. Know the date and location of the documents, and whether they are primary or secondary sources. There's a statement at the top.
> Number the documents and refer to them by number. Make marginal notes on the documents as you go along. Then write an outline or a plan for your essay. When writing the actual exam, start with a good topic sentence, but do not restate the question. Avoid unsubstantiated generalities. If you are uncertain

about something, avoid it. If you don't, you'll drop into the 2 category on your score. You'll also get a 2 if you misunderstand the question. They're looking for the time setting. Decide what countries you will treat. Have the historical chronology correct. Get to the essence of the event. When your back is against the wall you may be brilliant.

Look for changes in attitudes in the primary documents. Why has a change occurred? What are the forces behind it? Try to find relationships among all the documents. The more you can tie them all into your thesis, the better.

Don't ignore the pictures if they have them. Look for similarities and differences and causes and effects among the documents and be able to explain them. Consider the frame of reference of the documents—if it is a speech what was its purpose and direction? Is it a private document like Nixon's tapes? Be strongly historical, avoid editorializing.

Do not introduce anything new into the conclusion. The readers want a well-written conclusion that relates to the argument stated at the beginning. Avoid one or two sentence paragraphs. Write like hell. The length of the essay is positively related to the grade. We'll do a practice DBQ [document-based question] in class. Not to do one would be irresponsible on my part. After that, we'll see if we need to do another one. I have copies of all of them.

A good coach doesn't simply tell the team to "go out there and win," but shows the players strategies and procedures. Similarly, this teacher was giving very concrete advice on how to do the exam.

Given this massive academic assault on indolence it is little wonder that many boarding school students report that the prep experience changed them intellectually. Among the ways they felt changed, some indicated they had learned to write better. Compared to freshmen, seniors write longer, more complex essays, with fewer grammatical, spelling, and punctuation errors. Others indicated, "I have become a more effective speaker," "The work has changed my mode of thinking," "My mind has been stretched," "It taught me to think," "I think differently," "It taught me to think critically and independently," "I have learned how to question and analyze," and several felt it had made them "smarter."

Other students said that boarding school "has made me appreciate the depth of knowledge to be had"; "It has convinced me of the importance of having broad knowledge and a clear mind"; "I feel I have academic preparedness"; "I'm more knowledgable"; and "It has given me a different perspective toward the process of education; before education was merely going to eight periods a day and getting by, whereas here education becomes more important and more interesting." As one student succinctly put it, "My education has been superb."

Students also mentioned that they felt boarding schools prepared them for college. Because of their rigorous academic training and the development of better habits, they learned to work hard, how to manage their time effectively, and to live on their own and be independent away from their parents. One wrote, "My study habits, scores, and motivation have all improved."

Miller, Kohn, and Schooler (1985) have measured the substantive complexity of schoolwork by assessing the intellectual difficulty of courses, the length of a complete job, and the complexity of an out-of-class project (for example, whether it involved the independent evaluation or analysis of professional, technical, or other primary source material, or data the student gathered). They also measured how closely teachers supervised the work that students did and found that the two had a strong negative relationship. Students who experienced greater substantive complexity in their schoolwork and less supervision by their teachers scored higher on what they called educational self-direction. These students used more initiative, thought, and independent judgment in their schoolwork. The complexity of their schoolwork in particular had a decided impact on their problem-solving ability. Their mental performance, in turn, seemed to increase the exercise of educational self-direction. These findings suggest that the quality of a student's secondary school experience makes a positive difference in their reasoning and problem-solving ability.

Although we did not systematically rate the substantive complexity of the schoolwork performed by boarding school students, our observations of classes, examination of some of the papers and projects they were assigned, and of course the content of the courses themselves all indicate that the work students are given is complex and demands a considerable amount of independent analysis and effort on their parts. Therefore, the research of Miller, Kohn, and Schooler means that the curriculum studied by boarding school students is well designed to develop their reasoning abilities and to encourage them to become even more self-confident in their future educational efforts, namely college. The pressure for academic success is also part of the stress of living in the status seminary and it can cause anxiety for many students mastering the demanding program.

Academic Pressure and the Prep Learning Style

Not every prep school teacher succeeds in setting students on fire, and the pressure to be successful in school can lead to a kind of teenage indifference to learning. One spring day at a select 16 school, an English teacher is teaching a poetry class. The subject is Emily Dickinson. Sitting in front of him is a semi-circle of boys in jackets and ties. They sit quietly, glancing at the clock, trying not to look at the green fields that stretch beyond the colonial windows of their elite boys school. They are tall and good-looking as a group; most of them are athletes.

"You were to read the five poems I assigned on Monday. Can anybody tell me why Emily Dickinson is a genius?"

Silence.

"Jackson, did you do the reading?"

"Yes, sir."

"Well?"

"She didn't use any titles, sir."

"Does that make her a genius?"

"No, sir."

The teacher, as it turns out, does have a theory of Emily Dickinson's genius, a theory he proceeds to elaborate. Two minutes before the end of the class he is interrupted by a boy raising his hand.

"Yes, Anderson."

"Excuse me, sir, will this be on the test?"

The drive for academic performance, however, can put enormous pressures on students for whom learning is a struggle. Even students who enter boarding school after graduation from a prestigious and demanding day school may find that they are struggling just to keep up with their teachers and other students. Straight "A" students in grade school may find themselves pulling "D's" their first semester at a select 16 school.

Grade inflation has not occurred in boarding schools to the degree that it has in the public sector. Approximately 2.5 percent of boarding school students are able to maintain A or A-minus averages compared to suburban public high-school students, where as many as 14 percent of the graduating class will have average grades of A-minus or better (Cookson 1981, 117). At one suburban high school, 20 percent of the seniors were A students. At one prep school, 46 percent of the graduating class had a C average or below; 10 percent graduated with a D plus average. Only 14 percent of public school graduates earn less than a C average and rarely does someone graduate from a suburban high school with a D plus average or below (Cookson 1981, 117).

The stringent grading practices of boarding schools have two important consequences, besides being part of the toughness of the prep rite of passage. First, they keep the students working hard, as it is not easy to get good grades. Second, the demanding standards of these schools enhance their credibility with college admissions officers. The prep schools can say with confidence that "we work them hard here."

If we think of an ability curve that takes in the whole of the high-school age population, it seems apparent that most prep school students are clustered at the upper tail of the curve. The ability curve at boarding schools is not normal in the statistical sense. There are few weak students, and even average students need something extra to be admitted to an academically competitive school. At the select 16 schools, in particular, the competition can be fierce; a school full of academic race horses can charge the atmosphere with a sense of competition that can cause even the swiftest thoroughbreds to stumble.

At one select 16 school, we interviewed the school psychologist. After being asked if girls and boys had different psychological problems adjusting to life at boarding school, he paused and then almost absent-mindedly reflected, "Well, I guess girls are more likely to attempt suicide than boys." Before we could follow up with another question the dean of students whisked us out the door to lunch.

At other schools teachers talk of "corks popping" and "freak-outs." At one school, students show their displeasure at too much intensity by "treeing," a form of protest in which the entire student body climbs into the trees and screams and refuses to come down until the administration is willing to negotiate differences. Lest one thinks the school could simply leave the students up in the trees until they got tired, consider how one explains the situation to a visitor or a parent who stops by.

Despite the fact that they have been carefully selected, some students leave school before the end of the year; others simply run away. Students will sometimes run away from school for a night with little purpose other than escaping from the confines of the total institution for a while. In one case, two boys ran away to go into town for a cheeseburger. The town in question was nearly twelve miles away, so by the time the boys returned, dawn was breaking and they were apprehended by the night watchman. Naturally the head was skeptical about their cheeseburger story, but after several question and answer periods, they were "only" punished by forty hours labor and twenty laps around the track.

Crack-ups are more common than most heads will admit, and escapism is stylized and abetted by drugs and alcohol. The pressure for perfection and performance can cause even the most stable youngster to "bail out," either by "acting out" or withdrawing. The student underlife, which will be discussed in Chapter 8, is in part a rebellion against the pressures that family and school place on students to achieve.

Prep schools recognize these problems, and offer students psychological as well as academic counseling. Students seem to fear the stigma of going for psychological counseling. As one teacher put it, "These [boys] need to present themselves as being in control. It goes with the nature of the breed. If he shows he's in trouble, what will his faculty or college counselor think? It might screw up his chances for college." Thus, despite the efforts of schools to provide counseling or other interventions, students may resist those efforts until they explode from internal pressure.

Academic advisors are usually faculty members who, in addition to their other roles, are also specially responsible for a small group of about ten students. As advisors they are the primary adult with whom a student is supposed to maintain contact. Regular meetings are scheduled and a good advisor will meet with a student informally and as the student needs it. If a student's problems become too acute or chronic, the advisor may suggest a peer support group, or a drug and alcohol counseling group. If the situation appears to be getting critical, an advisor may suggest a student see the school psychologist or psychiatrist. If students fail to be helped by this supportive safety net then they may be sent home either temporarily or permanently. In the end, it is the student who is held responsible for failure to adjust to the pressures of the prep academic rite of passage.

For a student to challenge the curriculum and the pressure for academic success is to be labeled deviant. On the other hand, while schoolwork needs to be done, it doesn't need to be loved. Thus, at most schools there is an unspoken but recognized norm among students that studying too hard is considered poor form. At one school, too-intense students are referred to as "Embryo Joes," an expression that evokes images of infantilism and the shape of the brain simultaneously. A teacher at another school noted, "their peers here don't understand academic grinds." "Sweats"—students who show they are working hard—are much like Embryo Joes, treated by other students with a certain amount of disdain. In the end, the adaptation chosen by most students is a compromise between parental and the school's expectations, student resistance, and themselves. "No Sweats" are those who conform to the institutional means and goals, while at the same time avoiding the appearance of trying too hard. Many students are consequently placed in a difficult bind where they must succeed without appearing to try, a dilemma which has caused more than one prep school student to "freak out."

The prep learning style, then, is the maintenance of a dynamic tension between mastering the college preparatory curriculum, placating one's friends who disapprove of too much studying, and meeting one's own needs. In effect, prep school students say, "I agree to meet the academic requirements, but don't expect me to love the process." Some students feel that self-directed learning was cramped by their boarding school experience. Speaking of the future, one student wrote, "I feel that finally there will be a time when I can learn on my own, on my own time, in an environment of my own choosing, where my decisions are mine and mine *alone.* (And my *responsibility!*)."

Apparently, the academic pressure for success contributes in part to the general loss of innocence that is part of the prep rite of passage. Freshmen in our sample, for instance, are much more likely (74 percent) than seniors (49 percent) to agree that "there is a lot of interest here in learning for its own sake, rather than just for grades or for graduation credits." Seniors are much less likely than freshmen to see the "education they received" as the most valuable part of their experience for the future, while freshmen are less likely than seniors to recognize the social value of their experience. Fifty four percent of the freshmen come expecting that the education they receive will be the most valuable part for them in ten years, but only 30 percent of the seniors think that it will be the most valuable part of the experience in the future. Seniors are much more likely (31 percent) than freshmen (13 percent) to think that ten years from now the most valuable part of boarding school will be the "experience in relating to people."

For students, the major aspect of their education seems to be social, not simply academic. One senior wrote, "I strive to have better relationships with others, and to look at the world around me instead of just concentrating on studying, as I used to. I am grateful to———for making me realize the importance of life outside academic studies."

The prep rite of passage is not intended to produce divergent thinkers. Intellectual convergence is a prerequisite for collective identity. Academic ability and social ability become merged in the minds of students. Writing about the future a senior says, "I am attending this school to enrich my academic and social future." In a similar vein, a girl writes, "I think that I am preparing myself well for the future by receiving a good academic and social education."

A major feature of the prep rite of passage is its intense, unremitting social quality, which is perfect preparation for upper-class life. The intense pressure to get into the "right" college coupled with the collective demand for conformity creates academic atmospheres where excellence is most highly valued for its practical rather than its intrinsic worth. Life in the status seminary leaves little time for solitary pursuits or individualistic intellectual voyages.

As we shall see, however, the loss of individuality is thought of as part of the price students must pay if they are to be prepared for the exercise of power. The socialization processes that go on in boarding schools include both the visible curricula, as we have just discussed, and an invisible curricula that is designed to mold students into certain kinds of people. Leadership training has been a central mission of the schools since their founding. Teaching the young status "novitiates" that the price of privilege and power is self and social control begins with the head. He or she is the symbol of authority within the school and the students' primary power role model. The head must implement a treatment to ensure that by the time the chosen ones graduate, they will be united in a common consciousness.

6

The Iron Hand in the Velvet Glove: Trustees, Heads, and Charisma

MUCH as Aristotle sought to civilize and educate the young Alexander the Great for his role as world conqueror, prep school educators often depict themselves as mentors to the next generation of the power elite. The classic values of duty, honor, and loyalty are central to the ethos of the schools, and much of the physical, psychic, and intellectual training that goes on within the status seminary is directed toward creating a class of leaders who have the character to shoulder the burden of leadership and the talent and courage to protect their own class and status interests. A key component of the prep rite of passage is the acquisition of the moral authority to exercise power without remorse.

Students in the total institution need not look far to find examples of how power can best be exercised, because the leadership patterns within the prep school world serve as examples of how the world really works. Like other power structures, the prep power structure is hierarchical, but unlike many public power structures much of the real decision making at boarding schools is conducted privately and according to an informal set of rules known best to the participants. Certainly, by cloaking power relations in moral authority, leaders often encounter less resistance than if they simply imposed themselves on others. To make this style of leadership work, however, some leaders themselves may undergo a psychic transformation, in which perception becomes progressively more selective until at last, in sociologist Dennis Wrong's (1979, 109) phrase, they can function with a "disciplined self-deception" that makes self interest and the larger public interest inseparable.

The Three W's

At the top of the prep school power hierarchy is the board of trustees. Taken collectively these individuals are legally responsible for the school and assume the financial responsibility for the school's well-being. The vast majority of trustees are male, and few reside in the community in which the school is located. Hence, the locus of power in a private boarding school is in the school's position within the larger society, rather than in its geographic location. These trustees are not elected by the residents of a given community or school district, as in a public school board. Instead, trustees select their own members from alumni, current or past parents, or from individuals who have shown a continuous interest in advancing the welfare of the school. Most board members are successful in some area of the business world, although boards usually will include ministers, college administrators, and other prestigious but relatively nonpowerful individuals. Most boards are created by fusing together power and influence with morality and education.

The real power of most boards is exercised by an executive committee, which includes the president, the most influential board member. Trustees bring to their job one or more of the following W's: wealth, wisdom, or work. While work and wisdom are important, a board of trustees must also have considerable collective wealth, as they are expected to set an example in terms of gifts to the school. Trustees also select new heads and, on occasion, intervene in school affairs if a major problem arises.

An ideal trustee also provides an essential intangible to the school— social visibility. Men who have been successful in business, in particular, are likely to be asked to become board members because of their connections with the world of finance. Even at girls schools, a third or more of the trustees are often male.

There are two ways to assess a trustee's social visibility. Being listed in the *Social Register* is one reliable measure of membership in the upper class, while inclusion in *Who's Who* indicates personal achievement or the attainment of an important position. While we did not have information about all the trustees of the schools in our sample, an analysis of available data on 538 trustees from 22 schools indicated that 41 percent of the trustees of these schools are listed in either the *Social Register, Who's Who,* or both. Trustees are more likely to be listed in the *Social Register* (23 percent) than in *Who's Who* (18 percent), emphasizing the schools' continuing connection to the upper class. Thus, at a socially elite school like St. Paul's in New Hampshire, 63 percent of the trustees are listed in the *Social Register* compared to 26 percent in *Who's Who.* Not surprisingly, we found that the trustees of the select 16 schools are twice as likely to be listed in either *Social Register* or *Who's Who* than are trustees from other leading boarding schools, again emphasizing the select 16 schools' connection to the world of high social status and achievement.

Board members not only come from influential backgrounds, but a great many are also alumni of the school they serve. Seventy-seven percent of both the Taft school and Choate-Rosemary Hall's trustees were alumni as of 1982–83, and 95 percent of Phillips Andover's board members were alumni in 1982–83. For reasons of loyalty and continuity, most boards recruit alumni to fill vacancies when they occur among the trustees; if too many outsiders join the board, the "old boys," and "old girls" stand a chance of losing control of the school's present and future direction. Smaller, somewhat less elite schools are more likely to have boards with a majority of non-alumni trustees.

During the late 1960s and early 1970s, when it was popular for boys and girls schools to merge, there were organizational and social problems about how the new boards were to be composed, because merger carried with it the threat of losing power. One consequence of coeducation was that male trustees at the former boys schools were required to share power with at least some women. As there were no women alumni from these schools, it meant that the percentage of alumni on the board declined. Boys schools that chose to remain single sex, such as the Lawrenceville School, the Hill School, and Deerfield Academy still have boards composed almost entirely (93 percent on average) of alumni. One hundred percent of the trustees at the Hill School are alumni.

Presumably, one of the qualities that trustees bring to their positions is perspective. As guardians of the future, they hold the fate of the school in their hands; they must set the long-term goals of the school and devise strategies for attaining them. Trustees must also be shrewd tacticians to deal with the highly developed political infrastructure found in most schools. For example, they must determine how to deal with senior faculty members when searching for a new head, because it is to these teachers that other teachers look for leadership (Cookson 1980). Yet, trustees cannot be controlled by the faculty, and quite often they will take the opportunity during a change in leadership to root out difficult cliques or individuals. Part of looking to the future is knowing when to clean house. Because of their importance, the quality of a board of trustees has a direct relationship to the quality of the school.

Much of the power of the trustees is difficult to detect within the school community because they tend to keep low profiles. Their representative is the head, who both directs and is directed by the board, and is often called upon to translate the board's wishes into school policy that will not ruffle too many feathers among the teachers and students. The unobtrusiveness of most boards is an example of how power can be exercised without publicity; they are indeed the power behind the throne, and many students may only be dimly aware of the board's importance or even presence. To the students it is the head who represents the final authority within the school. As the headmaster of an illustrious British public school said to us, the head must make sure the school "ticks over with the right sort of heartbeat."

Charisma and Common Sense—The Head

When one thinks of boarding school headmasters, certain images percolate up from the imagination. Based on fiction, movies, and television, the people who run boarding schools seem a bit behind the times, slightly eccentric, or at the least, unusual. The good headmaster is moderately handsome, vaguely sentimental, quietly clever, and very, even painfully, sensitive. More often than not these heads are found in romantic rural schools, such as the school portrayed in the public television series, "To Serve Them All My Days." Bad headmasters are the good head's opposite. Enamored of cruelty and efficiency, these headmasters beat boys and make a fetish of "building character."

The image of the headmistress is less vivid in the public mind. There is the austere and proper spinster who has given up her life for the girls, but that is a rare breed. In fact, headmistresses themselves are becoming increasingly rare as girls schools either close or merge with boys schools. The recent and tragic case of Jean Harris, former head of the Madeira School in Virginia, has probably done more to shatter the stereotyped image of the headmistress than anything else.

Headmaster and headmistress are ancient titles, the former stemming from the thirteenth century when the Winchester School in England was founded as a center of medieval learning. To be a headmaster at one of the great public schools such as Eton, Harrow, or Winchester was a position of great power, great importance, and sometimes great corruption. Absolute masters of their schools, British heads were close to being a law unto themselves, beating their students with such regularity one wonders what, if any, time they had left to teach, study, or even sleep. No one knows for sure who was the greatest flogger in the history of the British public school, but Dr. Keate of Eton must be among the foremost, having caned eighty boys on the single evening of 30 June 1832 (McLachlan 1970, 152). Some heads might have argued that caning was too good for their students, as public school boys up to the middle of the nineteenth century lived in a Hobbesian state of anarchy that makes the society established by William Golding's boys in *The Lord of the Flies* seem tame by comparison. Brawling, drinking, gambling, and licentiousness was the preferred curriculum among the sons of England's aristocratic class.

Thomas Arnold of the Rugby School is traditionally credited with bringing morality and a proper Victorian respect for bourgeois values to the British public school. An evangelical Anglican minister, Arnold was appalled at what he found at Rugby when he was appointed head in 1828. Boys will be boys, but at Rugby the roughhousing had reached such monumental proportions that Arnold had little choice but to turn the chaos into sport, surely one of the greatest organizational sleights of hand in school history (compare Mangan 1981). Rugby, or rugger, caught on at other schools and before long pietistic heads were turning young aristocrats and roustabouts into "proper" gentlemen.

George Shattuck, the founder of St. Paul's School, was deeply religious and influenced by early nineteenth-century nature worship. Shattuck believed that "boys ought to be trained not only for this life, but so as to enter into and enjoy eternal and unseen realities" (McLachlan 1970, 143). To find his first head, Shattuck might just as well have canvassed the immortal community of saints rather than the list of available candidates, his standards were so high. The new head had to be a gentleman scholar and a Christian (that is, Episcopalian), as well as possess an "aptness in teaching" and an impeccable personal life. Shattuck was aware that earthly perfection was rare and was quite willing to postpone opening his school until the right man was found. The single most important qualification upon which a successful application rested was personal virtue. "Sinful and frail men are all that are to be had. We may know the faults of some, and others may appear better, because we do not know them" (McLachlan 1970, 147).

At last Shattuck settled on Henry Augustus Coit, a young Episcopalian clergyman engaged in missionary work in New York state. Coit was only twenty-six, stuttered, had no experience in running a school, and, in the words of his own father, his "money gumption" was untested (McLachlan 1970, 148). But Coit was deeply religious, properly married, and believed that "the training of conscience is the highest part of education" (McLachlan 1970, 164).

Coit's piety and dedication set the tone for subsequent generations of aspiring heads. A quick review of official and semi-official biographies of great American heads, such as Louis Perry of Exeter or Frank Boyden of Deerfield,[1] leaves the reader with a firm impression that the sagacity, wit, and patience of these headmasters has no known parallel. Perhaps the most prodigious of all boarding school patron saints was Father Diman, an Episcopal minister who founded St. George's School outside of Newport, Rhode Island, in 1896, and then, after converting to Catholicism, founded the Portsmouth Priory School in 1926 not far up the road from St. George's. With this evangelical tradition, it is perhaps not surprising that when heads were asked which of several qualities are most important for the development of an outstanding head they chose moral character first; tolerance, consideration, and the ability to deal effectively with students second; followed by resourcefulness, ability to deal effectively with parents, efficiency, and last, intellectual acuity (Cookson 1980).

Sanctimoniousness, however, is not the contemporary boarding school style. The modern head is more apt to be low-key, unpretentious, and wear his or her religion lightly. Humor and self-depreciation are much more in keeping with the prep style. Perhaps it is the job itself that has fashioned the present generation of heads, when the route to success lies in organizational management and human relations rather than religious devotion. To survive, a head must be tough. John Verdery, who was headmaster of the Wooster School in Connecticut for 33 years, wrote of a veteran teacher who offered this evaluation of him during his first year: "You know, Verdery, you're the best Headmaster I ever worked for. But I suppose in a couple of years you'll be a son of a bitch just like all the rest of them" (Verdery 1981, 10).

1. See, for example, Conover (1906), Drury (1964), McPhee (1966), and Saltonstall (1980).

The Right Stuff

Sociologist Max Weber has suggested that authority must be perceived as legitimate if it is to be effective. Establishing legitimacy cannot be taken for granted because by its nature power implies a certain amount of coercion. Weber believed that legitimate authority can take three different forms (1978).

The first is charismatic authority, which rests on the personal qualities of an individual who is believed to have extraordinary powers. Historically, the great heads have had charisma; Endicott Peabody, for example, is recorded to have been referred to by some of his contemporaries as the "Sun God" (McLachlan 1970, 246). The cult of personality is not entirely absent from boarding schools today; powerful heads may indeed need to possess magical powers to survive beyond the average length of tenure, which is roughly seven years. Those heads who have been in office for longer than twenty years strike us as having unusually high amounts of what might be called tenacious charisma.

A second type of authority, according to Weber, is tradition. Domination in this authority system relies on "piety for what actually, allegedly or presumably has always existed" (Coser and Rosenberg 1976, 133). Boarding schools place great stock in tradition. How things were done at any particular school determines in large measure how they are done and how they will be done in the future. Boarding schools represent a sizable number of collective biographies, and maintaining the outlook of previous generations is an important aspect of the head's position. When we asked a new head what changes he foresaw at the school during his tenure he appeared to be somewhat uncertain, as though the question had not really occurred to him before. After a few moments of soul searching, the most radical change he could think of was strengthening the English department.

Weber's third type of authority is bureaucratic. Bureaucratic legitimacy rests on the acceptance of certain rules and laws that are considered to be rational and impartial. Bureaucracy is believed to create an impersonal environment, which, we might add, is just what the parents of boarding school students do not want. Not that boarding schools, especially large ones, are not bureaucratic, because in some ways boarding schools are model bureaucracies—efficient, unobstrusive, and systematic. It is just that they must not look, smell, or feel bureaucratic. Internally, a head may gain legitimacy by mastering the school's bureaucracy; externally, the head must avoid the taint of seeming to be impersonal or formal.

A head's legitimacy rests on all three of these types of authority; but the authority that makes the school work is ultimately charismatic. People have to believe in the wisdom and strength of the man or woman in the head's office. Not only must the aspiring head have the right background, the right education, the right marriage, the right balance between academics and sport, and the right looks, but he or she must be charming, thoughtful, resourceful, and shrewd. Yet that is just the beginning, because a successful head must also have the right connections.

If the life cycle of a boarding school could be charted, it is probable that the turning point in the organization's evolution could be traced to those periods when there is a change in leadership. When change is in the air, the strengths of any school are tested as the tensions suppressed by the outgoing administration rush to the surface. Reminiscent of the Italian politics of the Renaissance, forces compete openly and sometimes covertly to push their agenda forward. Students, teachers, other administrators, parents, and alumni all become involved in the process.

Image Management

The whole drama of selecting a head is highly politicized. Even the formation of a search committee is not without political overtones. The trustees, teachers, and sometimes students who compose this committee create the pool of candidates from which the head will be drawn. Their points of view, attitudes, and prejudices form the first hurdle an aspiring head must clear. Search committees operate in different ways; some invite outside input, others are more secretive. In recent years searches have been extended far beyond the school itself. There are a number of educational management consultants who gather information about potential heads and pass their findings on to search committees. Aspiring heads do well to be connected in the world of these "head hunters." The search committee's reach usually extends beyond formal information channels—rumor, gossip, and chance are also part of the process. A talent search of this nature quickly becomes public knowledge.

The trustees and the search committee have a number of options. Do they want an inside or an outside candidate? More often than not there is at least one individual already at the school with some political backing. Interestingly, these individuals generally do not come from positions where a certain expertise is called for, such as admissions, or college guidance. They tend to be assistant headmasters or teachers. The days when the trustees reached into the faculty to find their new head are largely gone, but dynamic young faculty members are still considered the basic raw material from which to create a head. The problem with an insider is just that; they already have commitments and alliances that might inhibit them from cleaning house, and there is always the possibility of dissension and jealousy from other faculty. One teacher who rose from the ranks to become head of an elite school said that the day he became head was the day he lost his friends.

Outsiders may have the opposite problem. Unaware of the delicate balance of human relations at the school, they may crash about like a bull in a china shop. If the trustees are really intent on giving the school a new direction, however, they may have to choose an outsider. A head at an elite academy reported that he was convinced he was hired as an outside candidate because at a particularly somber, self-conscious moment in the selection process he asked, "Doesn't anybody around here laugh?"

This remark touches on a key ingredient in the byzantine process of head selection. Self-deprecation and quiet assertion is more likely to warm a trustee's heart far faster than unseemly displays of self-importance, not to mention outright self-advertising. To push oneself forward in an obvious or brash way is considered very bad form in the prep school world. Ambition, though it may be burning, cannot be seen as white hot. The feeling that heads are born, not made, places special burdens on those who seek the position. In the private school world you either have charisma or you don't, and no amount of good intentions or effort will turn a frog into a prince.

Much like good actors, aspiring heads need to have a quick and intuitive grasp of their audience's expectations, needs, and frustrations. The ability to be sensitive to and then manipulate the audience is part of the formula for stardom. What the clever actor or head knows is that behind the ease of the public performance lie many hours of training and rehearsal so that virtually nothing is left to chance when the curtain goes up. Several new heads told us that the key to their success in getting hired was doing their homework. They had read everything they could about the school weeks before being interviewed. Showing such interest in a school subtly suggests that one does want the job, a feeling that many trustees want to find. The attainment of power within the prep school world depends, in Machiavelli's words, "Not wholly on merit, nor wholly on good fortune, but rather on what may be termed a 'fortunate astuteness.'" (Machiavelli 1981, 33).

The appearance of being a natural leader requires careful and constant attention to image management. Confidence, self-deprecation, humor, and seriousness must all be put into the right package. The formula for success is composed of many subtle elements, the most elusive of which is that extra charismatic dimension best captured in what we have come to call the legend. It was told to us something like this:

> Interviewer: Can you tell us how you were selected for your job?
>
> Head: Well, gee, that's hard to pin down, exactly. When I was in college I did crew with a couple of graduates, and while I was in Divinity School I spent some time here on an internship. The funny thing is that it all happened by chance. A couple of years ago my wife and I were backpacking in the Andes, and I'll be darned if we didn't bump into Bill Jones, who is on the board here. We had a great time. I certainly wasn't looking for a job, so you can imagine how surprised we were when I got a call from Bill. I told him I didn't think I was really ready for a change, but a couple of days later I got a call from another head, whom I admire a great deal, and he said that the school here really needed new leadership. It seemed a real challenge, so when Bill called back I said I'd consider the opportunity but I'd have to talk to my wife first. Bill understood completely.

The key element in the legend is chance; charisma cannot be tarnished by petty calculation. Another important element is the emphasis on having a close and happy marriage. Marriage may not be proof positive that a head is without any eccentricities, but it at least certifies that he or she publicly upholds the conventional beliefs on questions of love and sex, and having children is even better.

The importance of the head's wife should not be underestimated. Upon her shoulders, especially at the smaller schools, rest a number of responsibilities of which virtually none have been codified, but all of which bear the weight of great tradition. Not only is she expected to be devoted and discreet, she is also expected to lead the social life of the school. One head told us that he was convinced that he was hired primarily because of his wife.

Today the traditional activities of flower arranging, tea serving, and party giving have fallen into some disrepute as they appear to relegate women to a decorative role. Some heads' wives still do perform such functions, and a few have expanded these activities to such a degree that they maintain a separate office on campus to organize social activities, many of which are directed at fund raising. This custom of taking charge of the social aspects of communal living is being redefined by some younger wives who feel uncomfortable in the traditional role and seek professional identities. In at least one large eastern school the head's wife works off campus.

The work of the head's wife is not as decorative as it may appear; in fact, it is a highly political position. All manner of informal information can flow to and from the head through his wife. For example, a boarding school faculty couple who were on the verge of separation might well tell the head's wife before the head himself, on the assumption that a woman can handle personal problems more sensitively than a man. As confidant, organizer, and intermediary, the head's wife provides much of the glue that holds a school together.

Women who aspire to be heads have a disadvantage in this regard. Few men would be willing, or able, to become the "headmistress's husband." In some cases where schools have hired a woman head with a husband, the marriage has dissolved. In other cases, the husbands simply refuse to have much to do with the school. After all, within the school his wife is the authority figure and our sense is that most men, despite some rhetoric to the contrary, find it difficult to be in an environment where their wives are the boss.

There is more than one reason, however, why women have a great deal of difficulty in becoming heads. As our legend implies, heads and aspiring heads belong to a network of colleagues, friends, and mentors who can move a career along—the old boy network in action. As our data show, boarding schools are still a man's world. In the Porter Sargent sample of 289 schools, 92 percent of the heads are male; even at girls schools, 64 percent of the heads are male. Of the nine girls schools we visited, four had male heads. Among the other 46 schools we visited only one had a woman head; at this school the president of the board of trustees was also a woman. None of the select 16 schools has a woman head.

We asked heads we interviewed about the lack of women in positions of leadership. The answers were quite similar. Aside from the questions of tradition, and the headmistress's husband, most boards worry about whether a woman will have business sense, or be tough enough to enforce discipline and fire teachers.

Male authority is a deeply entrenched tradition of prep school life; a charismatic woman might be viewed with suspicion not only among men but among some women as well. After all, power has traditionally been a male prerogative. Until very recently the idea of women being socialized for power would have seemed incongruous, and even shameful, in a world where a woman's place was in the home. There have been, of course, strong women leaders throughout history, but in the prep school world strong women usually find their mobility blocked. Leadership positions within the elite schools are something like a men's club, where women are not made to feel particularly comfortable nor considered truly acceptable for membership (Cookson and Persell 1985a).

Most women administrators spoke to us with a great deal of feeling on this subject. Men need only be men to be successful; women need to be superwomen to be successful. The list of available candidates for headships seldom includes a surplus of superwomen; even one might be considered a rarity.

A Head's Career: Artfulness and Heartache

Once the search committee has processed the long list of candidates and arrived at a short list of definite possibilities, candidates are invited to a meeting of the board where they are questioned, scrutinized, and evaluated. Some boards treat the process with tact and diplomacy; others are less thoughtful. For instance, the board at a small school invited two candidates to an interview, chose one, then had to pass the hat in order to fly the loser home.

Eventually several candidates, and their wives, are invited to visit the school. Here the candidates' stamina is put to the test. Endless meetings are scheduled so that all major constituencies can have, in the jargon, input. The aspiring head must suffer fools lightly, remain crisp, sound enthusiastic, and ask lots of questions. If the candidate feels that the board is serious, he or she must make a few demands as well. Certainly a shrewd candidate will want a place on the board, and there are questions of salary, security, and housing. There are also critical issues about policy, employee practices, and school finances. Finally, vacation time is important. One head remarked that his vacation time was an essential part of his job description. This was the same head that when asked, "How do you resolve differences between you and your trustees?" answered, "I don't have differences with the trustees." End of story.

After all the input is collected, a new head is chosen. Like his British counterpart, the new American head is unlikely to have studied administration. But in contrast to his British counterpart, the American head is less likely to be a published scholar. Most heads are in their late thirties or early forties, have graduated from an Ivy League or other acceptable college or university, have earned a master's degree in a liberal arts subject, and have taught humanities. History is still the most fertile nursery of heads, with the English department a distant second. Some heads have divinity degrees, only a few have Ph.D.'s, and fewer still have experience as college teachers.

THE PREP RITE OF PASSAGE

Like effective public school principals, the effective boarding school head is likely to be forceful, dynamic, and have a high energy level (Persell and Cookson 1981). Unlike most public school principals, however, the elite school head must also understand the uses of charisma because he, and occasionally she, is a role model for students who are being socialized for power. Charisma mobilizes and mesmerizes simultaneously; the relative youth, good humor, and "innocence" of most heads camouflages the toughness that the exercise of power requires. As one head remarked, "You can't be afraid of being hated." Preps are taught by the head to camouflage their interests in the rhetoric of morality and community service, and they learn by observing the head's independence and autonomy that power requires dedication, and to some degree the loss of freedom. To be effective, heads must be on public display almost continuously and discipline themselves against showing public weakness. Self-assured, discreet, and above the fray, the ideal head acts as a stylistic guide to those destined for leadership.

As the symbol of authority in the total institution, the head must insure that the school forms a true collective, not merely a collection of individuals; he or she is the community's emotional lightening rod as well as the school's chief executive. To be successful the head needs to have a talent with young people, taking their problems seriously and not condescending to them. Without this commitment, relationships can become strained.

The head deals with a number of disparate constituencies whose circles of interest do not always overlap. Students, parents, teachers, administrative staff, service staff, trustees, alumni, and the public at large all want the head's attention. The stress involved in trying to be all things to all people is apparent, and it can become accentuated by the many tasks a head must perform. Some tasks are lofty, like revising the curriculum; others are prosaic, like getting a broken boiler repaired. There is no part of school life a head can afford to ignore, and a good head is nimble in switching from one task to another.

Heads also act as mentors to some faculty or staff members, often finding a headship in another school for an ambitious assistant head or dean. Asked what they liked most about their jobs, heads replied, "Working with students." What they liked least was "dismissing teachers." Heads can accomplish many of these tasks because they have nearly absolute power within the school. Everybody serves at the pleasure of the head. There are no bureaucratically protected enclaves at boarding schools, no unions, and in most cases no tenure. In some schools, there isn't even a written contract. Teachers are simply invited back or not invited back, usually in the form of an informal note from the head. To bicker about conditions or salary would be gauche. Such dependency relationships cause their own set of problems, especially when the head abuses his or her power.

Management skills have become survival skills for most heads. A smart head will have a smoothly running development office for fund raising and alumni relations, a dean of faculty, a dean of students, a business manager, a maintenance manager, and an assistant headmaster to handle much of the paperwork. By delegating authority, the head is left time to polish the school's public image, talk to students, teachers, and parents, travel on major fund-raising expeditions, and in the words of one successful head, "just hang out."

Making their presence felt is an important management task for all heads. Administrations are sometimes evaluated as to whether they are "open door" or "closed door." A head who tries to run the school by remote control is likely to lose control, a serious problem in a total institution. The open-door policy is an invitation and a message—"I am available." Heads make a point of getting out of their offices to be seen around campus and to be open for informal contacts. Some heads visit classrooms, others prefer less direct methods of faculty evaluation, such as assessing the amount of damage in certain teachers' dorms. As they tour their campuses, heads keep their eyes and ears open looking for signs that the tone of the school is slipping. Vandalism must quickly be repaired, a scrap of paper is immediately picked up—is the grass as green as it should be?

Attentive heads do not ignore their local communities, contributing to them at least part of the funds the schools save by being tax-exempt. Heads will attend town meetings as well as establish good relations with the local police. Having a friend in the police department can save a great deal of embarrassment and bad public relations—when students are caught shoplifting, for example. Some heads become well known locally; church groups, country clubs, and volunteer efforts are fertile grounds for enhancing the school's and the head's reputation.

Because of their power and position heads can become lonely and isolated. They are not allowed to "break-out" or break-down. With the exception of their wives, few heads can afford to be totally frank with anybody. Oddly, this sense of isolation can be intensified within the total institution because so few non-school outlets are available. Few heads can expect to have a night on the town and not pay serious consequences. They must be a model of behavior at all times. This can lead to a certain amount of heartache as the private self is constantly giving way to the public persona, a model for the students of their public lives to come. The head must bear disappointments stoically; anxieties are not for public display.

Some heads burn out. They lose their grip, become hostile, argumentative, or depressed. At times they find more and more reasons for being off campus, or they simply close their doors. They begin to look for other jobs and some suddenly see prep schools in a new, negative light. Trustees can be tough, and a depressed head may find himself or herself looking for a job sooner than expected. A head who is drinking or sexually provocative is quickly shown the door. Heads can also be scapegoated if something goes seriously wrong at a school, and be terminated for the "greater good" of the organization.

Even the best head is going to make some enemies, and in the final analysis even the most successful head is expendable. The ever-present fact of life for the head is that he or she is vulnerable, a condition not conducive to peace of mind or relaxation. To be seen as defeated can cause a decrease in credibility, and at some point charisma can turn to catastrophe if a head loses his or her special authority. Yet, by nature most heads are adaptive and conservative, and adroit at diffusing disaster. Their survival instincts are generally advanced.

In part, what makes heads able to cope with the complexities of their position is that they are individuals whose perceptions of the world around them are somewhat limited. Recall that heads chose "intellectual acuity" as the least important quality necessary for the development of an outstanding head. Questioning or radical change has little place in their view of the world; tradition and continuity are prized far above experiment and chance. Most heads come from middle-class or upper-middle class backgrounds in which a guiding principle is to enhance one's status, not change the rules of the game. Within the rules of the game a certain amount of change is accepted, even appreciated, but to change the rules themselves would seem not only dangerous but unnecessary.

Charisma provides its own set of limitations, including, perhaps, self-deception. In the "Tory" world of the prep school, personal qualities and legitimate authority become merged. This marriage between idealism and self-interest can give rise to a belief, seldom openly stated but generally held, that power and privilege is given or taken by those who deserve it; morality often conceals the operation of power.

Preps learn from the head that power is less obvious if no less intrusive when the mantle of authority is worn lightly. Henry Coit's observation that "the training of conscience is the higher part of education" was an astute summary of the primary purpose of the elite total institution. Like the heads that followed him, he recognized that the discipline and self-denial required for effective leadership could not be imposed on students without controlling their consciences. The forging of a collective identity among elite students requires a dramatic intervention in their lives so that they will be transformed for life. As the high priest of the status seminary, the head presides over the prep rite of passage, ensuring that the school's program and personnel are committed to the goal of producing an elite cadre of patricians and parvenus.

7

The Prep Crucible

L IKENING prep schools to crucibles may seem incongruous or exaggerated. After all, most prep schools look more like playgrounds than industrial blast furnaces, and coolness, not heat, is the popular perception of prep style. However, the crucible metaphor is more apt than it might at first appear, for since their inception the elite schools have had the responsibility of melting down the refractory material of individualism into the solid metal of elite collectivism. By isolating students from their home world and intervening in their development, it is hoped that they will become soldiers for their class. A good many soldiers, however, also run the risk of being prisoners of their class. The total institution is a moral milieu where pressure is placed on individuals to give up significant parts of their selves to forward the interests of the group. As one admissions officer said, "We don't want selfish learners here." What should be remembered is that while outward conformity is required, more importantly, treatment is designed to penetrate deep below the surface of student behavior into their very consciousness, so that values and even somatic needs are subject to standardization and regulation. Thus, the requirement that students eat, sleep, and study together creates and continuously reinforces a sense of collective identity. As we shall see, at one girls school, the students all sleep together on a sleeping porch, virtually eliminating any sense of privacy.

The fledgling prep school student embarks on a "moral career" that is difficult and complex. Much of the socialization that goes on in prep schools is done by other students. They teach each other how to dress, think, and often what and how to study. They also share alcohol and drugs, and protect each other by a code of silence. Giving information to the administration that is detrimental to one's peers is considered a form of treason by nearly all prep school students.

While many students report that they found their prep school experience rewarding and positive, too many report that their experiences have made them cynical and unhappy not to conclude that the prep crucible does take a toll. Caught between the demands of parents, school, and peers, prep school students are forced daily to make decisions about life and themselves that are immediate and often poignant.

Since the 1960s the "totality" of most prep schools has somewhat lessened. Students have more freedom than before, and many of the most repressive aspects of life in boarding schools have been modified or abandoned. The requirement, for instance, that students all dress alike has been dropped by a number of schools, although almost all schools require students to be "neat and clean." Some schools are organizationally and philosophically more open than others, and coeducation and the admission of a significant number of day students have also brought new, less inward-looking elements within the walls of the status seminary.

But while the style of the schools has changed, their missions have not. If they abandon their goal of socializing students for power their very purpose is open to question. After all, why should students be deprived of significant parts of the self if the reward of empowerment is withdrawn? Leadership training is as much a part of the prep school mission today as when Endicott Peabody founded Groton to train leaders in 1884. Whether or not prep schools are successful in producing great leaders is debatable, but their primary purpose has been basically unchanged in their long tradition.

Privilege must appear to be earned, because the only real justification for inequality is that it is deserved—in payment for sacrifices, the powerful must endure in the name of the common good. Thus the prep rite of passage aims not only to transform individuals into a collective identity, but also serves to legitimate the maintenance of privilege. To achieve this end, the prep school administrators and teachers must tame their high-spirited, hedonistic charges both in the sense of demanding outward conformity and in the deeper sense of internalizing the school's value system.

"Habit formation is the basis of freedom," one head said to us, a remark that says worlds about the true nature of the prep rite of passage. In order to complete their missions, boarding schools cannot afford to let adolescents develop naturally; they are required to intervene in the growth process. They must control their students if they are to transform them. In this chapter we explore some of the mechanisms employed to intervene in students' behaviors and inner lives in the schools' attempts to mold them for the responsibility of power.

"Fitting In" at the Total Institution

According to Erving Goffman, a key organizational prerequisite of the total institution is to detach entering "inmates" from their previous or "presenting" culture (1961, 37). This is the beginning of the "mortification process," in which individual identities and past loyalties are abandoned, or at least temporarily stored away. The beginning of a "moral career" within a total institution is the "'stripping away of the self." This is not an easy process, and for some students who enter boarding school at the age of thirteen or fourteen, leaving home can be quite difficult; many parents as well suffer from the shock of separation.

Homesickness is a common experience among new students at boarding schools. One student described how he felt his first day at the status seminary: "I kissed my sister, mother, and father goodbye. When I heard the car door slam shut, that's when I realized I was alone. Would my roommate like me? Would I like my roommate? My heart started to pound, and my stomach got tight, as I climbed up the stairs to my room."

The schools tend to downplay the importance and extent of homesickness, but also recognize that left unchecked the empty feeling of abandonment and isolation can quickly spread throughout a dorm or class, in part because homesickness is highly contagious. One dean told us that he saw homesickness as a fear that things were "sick at home," perhaps the parents were getting a divorce, and the child felt uneasy being away from such momentous events. Another common interpretation of homesickness is that the students miss the comforts of home, but surely the real causes of this melancholy must begin with the sense of loss and perhaps rejection many students may feel as they are deposited at the school door by parents who, in effect, are saying, "I love you, but it's better that you go away." When all is said and done, the child has been left in the hands of strangers. It is, of course, not unusual in our society for an eighteen-year-old to go off to college alone. But there is a considerable difference between an eighteen-year-old and a thirteen-year-old.

To avoid homesickness, the schools focus a great deal of attention on integrating students into their new environment; faculty, for instance, must be in evidence in order to smooth the way and provide a comforting shoulder. Usually a new student is assigned a "big brother" or sister who is responsible for showing the new student the ropes. Through a series of seminars, teas, parties, and structured bull sessions, students are introduced to the school's stated standards and objectives. Often, a small school will organize a camping trip for the entire student body and faculty in order for them to get better acquainted.

To anyone who has noticed the many times a day some boarding school students check their mail boxes, it is clear that homesickness can linger well past the initial shock of separation. According to our student survey, girls at girls schools dislike being away from home the most, and girls at coed schools find separation the easiest. Perhaps teenage girls at coed boarding schools find boarding schools more liberating compared to boys, who may have more freedom at home and thus find boarding school more constraining. Boys also miss home cooking more than girls do.

Certainly not every student suffers from the pangs of homesickness. Older entering students will have less sense of loss than freshmen. Some of the more elite schools, in fact, will not admit students after the ninth or tenth grade because they believe that older students are more impervious to the "school's message" than younger students, who tend to be more vulnerable and thus receptive to their new surrogate parents.

In recent decades the harshness with which entering students were initiated into boarding school has softened considerably. Hazing and physical debasement have been outlawed; today most schools are more likely to try to love, rather than beat, students into submission. Yet boarding schools can still be very strict. Students are instructed on what to wear, how to eat, when to study, when to relax, and where to sleep. At one school a freshman was berated at some length because he held his fork wrong. Hair length can still be a bone of contention on many boarding school campuses, and a boy who refuses to get a haircut may be sent to the barber involuntarily.

Accepting the rules of the schools and being submerged in the group, however, is not exactly the same. The regulation of hair length is a superficial form of social control; a more important form of control is the requirement that virtually all activities be performed in the presence of others. The transfer of attachment from parents, to school, to classmates is an essential process if students are to become part of a larger collective. The schools do not expect or desire a complete transference of loyalty; that would be unreasonable and, in any case, unworkable, as students are in the total institution for only half the year. But loyalties do shift. At one select 16 school, we asked a group of boys if they found the transition from home to school and back again difficult. Almost all of them reported that they found it difficult to adjust to home after being away. They felt "funny" or "like strangers," and that they found it easier to readjust to school life after vacation than to readjust to home life after being in school.

The bond between parent and child is probably weakened when children are sent away to school. From the child's point of view, he or she has little choice but to forge new loyalties to survive. The vulnerability caused by detachment is magnified by the assault on privacy in the total institution; the compulsory social intimacy that prep schools require of their students is, from an outsider's point of view, extraordinary. Like privates in army boot camp, prep school students must grow accustomed to eating, sleeping, studying, and playing together. As one student wrote, "The art of living close to other people is part of the education. You learn not only to face ten people in the shower in the morning, but you get a full picture of a friend's character."

From a student's point of view, the focal building on a boarding school campus is not likely to be the chapel, classroom, or library, but the dormitory. It is in the dorms that the real action is, where students must learn to join the group if they are to survive. Schools vary on how they house their students. The large brick dorms of many eastern prep schools, for instance, remind one more of a cell block than a home away from home. Most rooms open onto a central corridor, and there is a community bathroom at the end of each corridor. One room is like the next including the institutional beds, chairs, and tables. Girls' dorms tend to be less spartan than the boys, and in some cases girls are boarded in converted homes rather than dorms. Dormitories that have been built recently tend to be more like motels than barracks. As part of the concessions the schools have had to grant to teen culture since the 1960s, modern dorms usually include lounges, open spaces, game rooms, laundry rooms, and occasionally some cooking facilities.

While few dorms could be described as plush, most are reasonably habitable, although economically marginal schools often have difficulty maintaining their dorms. Windows get broken, chairs dismembered, and bed springs sprung. Students, especially boys, are not renowned for the care with which they treat furniture, fixtures, or plumbing. Breakage can be accidental (that is, a by-product of horseplay) or deliberate (that is, an act of rebellion). The faculty who live in the dorms are required to protect the school's real estate. Yet even the most well-run, well-maintained dorm has an institutional feeling to it, and some of the more austere dorms can seem forbidding. Even in schools that have acquiesced to the teen culture by allowing students to decorate their rooms, the impersonality of living in a total institution is inescapable.

But this pervading sense of uniformity is essential if students are to form a collective whole. If individuals were allowed to live in small private buildings and decorate their living quarters totally to their own taste, there would be little pressure to join the group. Indeed, most younger boys at Groton live in cubicles, which are nothing more than wood-paneled stalls where personal possessions and furniture are kept to the bare necessities. Privacy in the everyday sense of the word is virtually nonexistent. There are few secrets that the boys can keep from each other, and sharing is compulsory. Today most boarding school students have at least a room, although in most cases they must share it with one or two others.

At some schools students are still required to live in public view constantly, as at the eastern girls school where they all sleep together on a screened porch with a long row of beds in it. In those schools where there is less socialization for power or less pressure for collectivism, sleeping quarters are often separated and more personalized. Thus western and progressive schools are more inclined to build "huts" rather than new dorms, and the dorms that are built are more likely to open out than in. At some of these schools students have been allowed to build their own huts, a form of individualism nearly unthinkable in a socially elite school.

As one might expect, dorm life is highly regulated. If students were allowed to do what they wanted in the dorms, the corridors and rooms would be expropriated by the teen culture, rendering the school program virtually ineffective. Thus students are told when to be in their dorms, when they can have visitors, when they must turn off their lights, and how loud they can play their music. Regulations can be very detailed. For example, some schools will not allow students to use thumb tacks to put up their posters as this would damage the walls. Most students have clean-up jobs in the dorms, and room inspections are done regularly. Students who fail to abide by the rules are disciplined, sometimes by being confined to their dorm or doing extra clean-up. Being restricted to one's dorm is a particularly painful punishment, especially in the afternoon when everybody else is at sports.

Dorm supervisors often vary about how strictly they enforce the rules. Students are quick to find out who is strict and who is easy, and students in "authoritarian" dorms may try to transfer to more permissive dorms.

Usually the job of monitoring a dorm is too difficult for a single or even two adults. One or more dorm senior prefects (called "whips" in one school) are appointed to help ensure that law and order is maintained. Often prefects are allowed certain privileges like private rooms. The lesson that with the exercise of "responsible" power comes privilege may not be lost on the other students; a modicum of privacy in the total institution is perhaps the greatest privilege of all.

Most students must share their quarters with a roommate whom they may or may not like. Roommate relations can be intense because sharing usually extends to clothing, books, records, and sometimes friends. Occasionally, roommates have a hard time distinguishing borrowing from stealing. A dominant roommate can also make a passive student's life difficult. Holden Caulfield's relationship with Stadlater in J.D. Salinger's *Catcher in the Rye* is an example of a boarding school odd couple. The dominant Stadlater even has Holden do his homework for him, and when Holden "messes up" by writing an essay on the wrong topic, Stadlater lets him know about it: "No wonder you're flunking the hell out of here. . . . You don't do one damn thing the way you're supposed to" (Salinger 1951, 53).

Bullying brings attention to a critical aspect of boarding school life, especially in terms of the difference between what is taught and what is learned. The sense of orderliness and solidarity that the school hopes to instill in students by making them share nearly identical living situations is often undermined by the student culture that mushrooms inside dormitories. The student culture is more likely to be competitive than cooperative, and power tends to flow to those, like Stadlater, who are strong and aggressive.

In one sense, students learn the real lessons of power and privilege from their fellow inmates. At a deeper level, however, the competitive student culture that often thrives in the dorms may not be in as much opposition to the socialization objectives of the school as it might appear. After all, heads since the time of Endicott Peabody have known that students who lack the stomach or muscle to fight and win make unreliable soldiers in the struggle for social position. The rhetoric of cooperation is useful in this struggle as a kind of verbal smokescreen, but is not intended to be taken as an article of true prep faith. Greatness has seldom gone to those who are passive or, like Holden Caulfield, indecisive.

In other words, students socialize each other for power in the total institution, and as long as the competition does not become too intense, the schools give their tacit approval by allowing them to continue. The new teen culture that many first-generation students bring with them is in opposition to the asceticism required of Peabody's gentleman warriors.

At some schools today, students seem more like an occupying army than docile novitiates. The asceticism and inverse snobbery so beloved by patricians has been replaced by rock, suggestive posters, and truckloads of paraphernalia that includes banners, rugs, drapes, bedspreads, and electronic gear.

When schools try to regulate how students customize their rooms, trouble can erupt. One school we visited was locked in a battle between administrators and students over the issue of tapestries on their walls. The local fire department had declared that the tapestries were not safe, but the students were determined to keep their wall decorations. The intensity of student reaction was startling even to the school. The students seemed prepared to defend their Alamos to the bitter end, an indication of how well entrenched the teen culture is in some schools.

One of the clearest ways adolescents mark out their territory is through music. One boarding school teacher in the 1960s described student music in the following terms:

> They will turn on their record players full blast, *and then go into a room where there is no record player and talk.* So what they've done is provide a curtain of noise for the background. They don't care about listening to music. It's a drug. They don't care anything about the nature of rock 'n' roll. It's a wall between them and the school. Every student possesses a record player. It has become for me a kind of symbol of the student mentality. A symbol of trying to shield oneself from the processes of education. (Prescott 1970, 157)

Just as wire taps are rendered less effective by the creation of background noise, administrations are rendered less intrusive by student rock. One British head said that if he were head of an American school he would spend many "sleepless nights" knowing he had so little power to intervene in situations he found destructive or distasteful.

Unlike British heads, however, American heads cannot count on filling their beds with the children from upper-class families for whom a ritualistic period of self-denial is *de rigueur.* Some American heads have had to make concessions to the teen culture to keep their schools in operation. The détente established by the students and faculty at many schools may have halted the shrinking of the applicant pool. Thus, while few students in our study think of dorm life as boarding school's best feature, even fewer consider it boarding school's worst feature. Students at the large eastern schools did not seem to think that dorm life was any better or worse than students at western or progressive schools. In general, however, students at single-sex schools dislike dorm life more than do students at coed schools, which makes sense because the single-sex schools, by and large, have made fewer concessions to the teen culture than have the coed schools.

The loss of self that is required by the school and the student culture can be a difficult experience for some students. For these adolescents individuality is constantly at war with the pressures to join the collective. Some students withdraw—one said, "I've become more fond of spending time alone." Several others put it more strongly, one saying that boarding school has "shaped me into an introverted selfish person who doesn't get out and meet people," and another that "I've turned into a recluse." Yet another went so far as to say, "I had to create another personality," and a senior stated that boarding school "caused me to hate institutional life."

The strength of these students' responses to the total institution, however, may have less to do with dormitory life per se than with the entire fabric of life in the total institution. The loss of self and enforced social intimacy are in a sense only the beginning of the social control the schools try to impose on students. Total educational institutions are designed to get below the surface of behavior and regulate the students' inner lives.

Compromising with Modernity

Behavior modification in the prep school context generally takes on three forms. Through discipline schools try to enforce certain types of outward behavior, through the manipulation of ritual and symbol the schools try to instill certain collective loyalties, and by what we call "deep structure" regulation they try to regulate the students' emotional and somatic needs. By intervening in the students' growth the schools hope to mold certain types of individuals who will internalize the school's values, making more blatant forms of outward social control unnecessary.

Royston Lambert, who, along with Spencer Millham and Roger Bullock, spent years studying the effect of British public school life on students, wrote this about life in the elite total institution:

> The key to the public school ethos is that its ends and means are one. Its values are embodied in a total social system; divesting its pupils of many of the roles and attributes they possess in the larger society, the school provides them with its own structure, role patterns, relationships, style and norms. It is in living out its subtle, complete and all-inclusive way of life that the values are so effectively and permanently imbibed. (Lambert 1977, 67)

As mentioned earlier in this chapter, in the contemporary American context the "totality" of the total institution has lessened, particularly with the widespread move to coeducation and the admission of day students. Compared to most day schools, however, boarding schools try to regulate many more student behaviors. Outward conformity is less important than it was two or three decades ago, but it still matters on most campuses. Some of the most traditional schools still require jackets and ties for boys and demand that students comport themselves in a gentlemanly manner. Whether a school is traditional or not it is likely to have a stringent disciplinary code. As one school handbook put it, "It is expected that in becoming a student at the Academy the student will have the integrity and self-discipline to accept that which is asked of him, even while working for change if he feels that to be necessary. We recognize, however, that there are those who will want to test the system—to go their own way" (*Deerfield Life* 1982–83, 18).

The ubiquitous social control takes its toll on students and teachers alike. We had this conversation with a teacher:

> You know what I don't like about teaching at this school, really? I get so damned tired of being a policeman, it's awful. I feel like a warden. If I enforced half the rules that are in the student handbook, I'd spend my whole time bringing kids up before the discipline committee. Look, these kids do everything. A couple of weeks ago I caught a couple of seniors in the ravine behind the gym—I mean I caught them. It was embarrassing. I was especially embarrassed for the girl, she's in my advanced writing course. I never reported it. What are you going to do? Wreck a couple of kids' lives because they're playing touchy-feely after dark?

The teacher pours us another glass of wine. He is tired. "The only thing I don't mess with are drugs. Drugs can destroy a school worse than liquor. Liquor you can't hide so well. Druggies are like another race, you know, real isolates.

"Listen, I've got to patrol for a while. It's after curfew. Feel free to help yourself to the jug." Paul disappears into the bathroom and emerges with a bottle of mouthwash.

"Can't have liquor on my breath," he says lamely before rinsing out his mouth. Grabbing his hat and coat, Paul, who has a stack of student essays to grade, ventures out into the night again, completing his second tour of duty.

At another school, students are startled when a squad of administrators descend on their rooms looking for drugs—bars of soap are cut open, talcum powder cans are emptied, and their rooms are searched for contraband.

The great fear among boarding school authorities is the loss of control. The structural relationship between student and school shares many of the characteristics of that between prisoner and prison—with a few important exceptions. Prep school students are volunteers or semivolunteers, their term is relatively short and fixed, the potential benefits of enduring the school's program can be substantial, and sometimes students are given a voice in how the school is run.

Yet many students still feel trapped. Just getting off a boarding school campus can be an ordeal. Detailed attention is paid to how, when, and with whom a student can leave campus. The dean of students at one girls school had a three-inch ring binder containing lists of the various kinds of permissions a girl could have for leaving school. At one coed school, students invited somewhere (even home) for the weekend must sign up by the previous Thursday. Later requests are denied. As one student wrote us, "Teachers and deans monitor every breath you take." Another wrote that boarding school has "soured my personality and made me watch my every move." The intense, almost manic, daily schedules of most schools are in themselves forms of social control. Students complain about "binding rules," "the very controlled life," and "the confining, too restrictive rules."

Schools vary on how much control they try to impose on students. Military schools try to control nearly every iota of behavior; progressive schools hope that adolescents will establish their own regulation. Entrepreneurial schools and academies tend to be somewhat less intrusive than military schools, and expect students to be relatively self-regulating. Western schools are constantly battling the allure of nature and balmy weather in their efforts to exercise control over students who are not driven indoors by the winter winds.

Catholic and Episcopal schools often equate social control with inner grace. At one elite Catholic school the boys were called together to discuss the low and rough manner in which they referred to each other. Apparently the larger, more muscular boys had fallen into the habit of calling their weaker brethren "wimps" and worse. As one adult after the other chastised the boys for their lack of charity, the smirks on the boys' faces grew wider, until at last, the young dean of students jumped from his seat, and shouted, "Was not our Lord a wimp? Did he not say 'the meek shall inherit the earth'!"

DISCIPLINE

Usually boarding schools make a distinction between minor rules and major rules. A minor infraction might be failing to wear a necktie, being late to class, leaving a bed unmade, or failure to show up for a work assignment. These infractions are not punished too severely unless they become repetitious.

Major infractions usually include: dishonesty and cheating, stealing; possession or use of drugs, alcohol, firearms, or automobiles; unapproved interdorm visiting; inappropriate sexual behavior; any offense against state or federal laws; and compromising the reputation of the school. Aside from these major infractions a careless student can violate dormitory regulations (including curfews), dining hall regulations, smoking regulations, permitted use of school facilities, bicycle regulations, and, at some schools, golf course regulations.

Some schools are candid about their expectations; one school emphasized that their school was not "an appropriate place for sexual intercourse between students," and "if you want to dress and act like a clown or like a slob, this is the wrong school." Most schools are less obvious in the declaration of war against teen culture, choosing instead to phrase the need for discipline in terms of creating a "healthy academic and social environment." Some schools, such as Choate-Rosemary Hall, Episcopal, and Taft, have honor codes that require students to uphold the basic principles of the school within the framework of faculty supervision.

Like most judicial systems, the pendulum of justice at prep school balances between the rights of individuals and the larger community. Justice must also be defined in terms of its primary objective—retribution or redemption. Virtually every boarding school tries to use discipline as a teaching tool, although they vary in how much time and effort they devote to redemption. Academies tend to be a bit more cut and dried in the administration of justice, perhaps because of their Puritan heritage. A student who leaves some academies without permission can be dismissed even if it is the first offense. Special pleading by family members is unlikely to reverse a dismissal decision.

The quality of mercy and the willingness to take extenuating circumstances into account are more likely to be found at the smaller schools, because they usually have a more family-like atmosphere. Too much forgiveness, of course, can cause the pendulum of justice to tip too far in the direction of the individual. Progressive schools have a tendency to emphasize the therapeutic value of discipline, implying that rule breaking is a symptom of sickness rather than sin. This tolerance can be difficult to maintain in reality, and more than one progressive school has found that adolescents can sometimes confuse forgiveness with softness.

As with most legal systems it is the administration of laws that matters most in the lives of people. There was a time when the head at most boarding schools was the law. Recalcitrant students were called into the head's office and dealt with in short order. The exercise of social control was personal, occasionally capricious, often merciful. Today, largely because of the student rebellions of the 1960s, most schools administer discipline through a complex committee system that includes students, teachers, and administrators. The Deerfield Academy has three separate discipline committees—the Ad Hoc Committee, the Rotating Discipline Committee, and the Standing Discipline Committee. The Hotchkiss School has one discipline committee composed of seven students and seven faculty members. The head may observe the committee's deliberations but not vote, although the head may fail to ratify the committee's decision.

The widespread use of discipline committees may have helped to diffuse some of the tensions between students, teachers, and administrators. Overall, 72 percent of boarding school students in our study believe that the discipline at their school is "effective." Episcopal, girls, and western school students rank their schools' discipline effectiveness well above this average, and academies and progressive school students rank the effectiveness of their schools' discipline below the average. Only 30 percent of progressive school students believe that their school's discipline is effective, although in an irony that might appeal to Rousseau, 75 percent of progressive school students believe that their discipline is "fair." Overall, 70 percent of the students in our sample believe their school's discipline system is fair. Episcopal schools tend to get a high rating on the fairness measure, academies and Catholic schools a lower rating.

Coeducational schools spend considerable time developing and enforcing rules about "intervisitation" between the sexes. This may help to explain why both girls and boys at coed schools are more likely than their counterparts at single-sex schools to see the discipline as unfair—34 percent of girls and 35 percent of boys at coed schools felt this way, compared to 23 percent of girls at girls schools and 22 percent of boys at boys schools. Coed school students are also less likely to see the discipline at their school as effective—67 percent of students at coed schools felt this way, compared to 83 percent of girls and 76 percent of boys at single-sex schools.

When students and teachers perceive discipline to be ineffective, unfair, or both, morale tends to go down. Balancing the needs of individuals and the community is in some ways less dependent on procedures (although they are important) than the sensitivity and firmness of those implementing discipline policies. Often adolescents believe that the punishment should fit the crime. The carefully calibrated system of punishment that most schools employ reflects their students' concern for fairness. Discipline categories can include first warning, restrictions, probation, suspension, and dismissal. Within each of these categories, or similar categories, there is a wide variety of punishments employed, including revocation of privileges, confinement, extra work, notification of parents, detention, community service, and laps around the track. At some schools good behavior is rewarded in an effort to emphasize the positive side of discipline. In one school, students who performed ten or more "constructive acts" in the past month were granted unlimited on- and off-campus sleep-overs.

Some heads and deans of students report that students are harder on fellow students than are faculty members or administrators. Motives for excessive punishment could be complex, ranging from revenge, to self-importance, to prudishness. It may well be that in interpreting the letter of the law, some adolescents are inexperienced in understanding its spirit.

Some adults, however, think that adolescents are quite responsible in the way they make decisions about discipline. For example, a dorm matron in a girls school said that the girls on the discipline committee were "thoughtful, careful, and quite just." The question of the ways adolescent boys and girls arrive at moral decisions has recently been explored in Carol Gilligan's book, *In a Different Voice* (1982).

Many British heads find the complexity of the American discipline system bureaucratic and excessively time consuming. The British employ more direct and personal forms of punishment, including, at some schools, caning. "Six of the best ones" to the bottom side is swift, painful, and "gentlemanly," but impersonal, as nobody is trying to pry into the student's soul, only informing him that certain behaviors will elicit a painful response. (It is a tradition that head and boy shake hands after a caning.)

Whether or not American boarding school administrations have successfully been able to co-opt student cultures by including them in the disciplinary process is a difficult question to answer, as schools often vary on how students perceive the administration's intentions. This is why the attitude of the head toward the administration of justice is so critical. If the head is considered too hard, too soft, or indifferent, discipline can break down, and when it does the amount of control the school can exercise over students is diminished (Persell and Cookson 1982). There have been schools that "got away" from the administration. In these cases students almost entirely withdrew into their own culture, flouting the school rules with impunity. At one school in the mid-1970s, faculty joined students in their rebellion against conformity by actually sharing their rooms with students. When the line between teacher and student becomes blurred, a school may find itself out of business.

In the end, no matter how complex the discipline system, it is the head, at most schools, who makes the final decisions on matters of real disciplinary importance. Dismissals are the head's prerogative. "Firing" a student, to use the British expression, is very difficult, most heads report. After all, expulsion carries with it a certain stigma that affects students and their families. For families with an investment in the prep style of life, to be excluded from a prep school can be shocking. One head told us that after he had dismissed a student, the boy's younger brother came to the head's house to plead for his brother. As touching as the boy's loyalty was, the head remained firm in his decision.

Occasionally, heads will soften the blow of expulsion by helping the student enroll in another boarding school. In one amusing case several boys bugged a head's office so that his private conversations became available to students in their dorms. Discovered, the boys pleaded guilty, were fired, and sent to another school where they were welcomed as unusually qualified transfers. Daring, initiative, and excellence such as that shown in the bugging incident are admired in the prep world, especially if it cleverly tweaks the nose of authority. And more than a few preps have ended up in the Central Intelligence Agency, including Andover graduate George Bush.

Sexual adventures can be used to tweak the nose of authority as well. At one small New England school the legend of the coed who fell in love with the head's son warms a number of hearts on a chilly winter's eve. A true story, this dauntless young woman used to scale the lattice work under the head's bedroom window. Once inside she and the son could frolic in the school's most, perhaps only, private room, until one day the head returned home early and discovered his son and the coed in his bed. The legend of their romance and the head's horror still lives in the annals of that school's history. Thus, at many schools there is a certain ambivalence about rule breaking; when done with wit and style it can become a mark of distinction; when done clumsily or meanly, it can become a mark of dullness, even dumbness.

RITUAL AND SYMBOL

The creation of a collective identity, however, requires more than outward discipline. Individuals must also be submerged in a belief system that guides their behavior and instills them with the proper values. The importance of religion becomes apparent, because through the use of religious ritual and the manipulation of spiritual symbols the young novitiates are expected to become absorbed in the brotherhood and sisterhood.

Chapel attendance until very recently was a way of life at many boarding schools, especially Episcopal and Catholic ones. Chapel could be held daily and twice on Sunday. At many Episcopal and Catholic schools chapel is still required and almost all prep schools have some religious service on Sundays. At the schools without formal religious ties, the service may be relatively casual and nondenominational, but at the traditionally religious schools the service may still be highly ritualized.

Like in the British chapel service, students are told how to enter and exit, when to stand, when to kneel, when to be silent, when to pray, when to sing, and when to listen. The heads at religious schools often hold divinity degrees and are role models for devotion. The hierarchical nature of religious ceremony also carries a subtle message; as John Wakeford said of the religious ritual in British public schools, "This daily service of worship, though based on moral egalitarism, serves to emphasize, or to identify, hierarchical levels in the school" (Wakeford 1969, 124). Thus power may be equated with religious authority in the minds of some preps and provide them with moral ammunition in the struggle for position.

Whether or not a boarding school has an institutional religious affiliation, preps tend to endure a great deal of preaching. Heads, in particular, are expected to lead students in the quest for "values clarification." Our survey data shows, however, that this preaching may have less effect on students than heads believe. Only 4 percent of the students feel that they will remember those hours and hours of chapel attendance, prayer, and bible study ten years from now, and no one thinks they will remember it as the most valuable aspect of their boarding experience.

Perhaps because of their aristocratic and military traditions the British are more fond of pomp and circumstance than Americans, who tend to be more puritanical and commercial in their outlooks. Thus the use of elaborate ritual in many American schools is at a minimum. In place of ritual, schools are apt to substitute collective games, such as dividing the school into teams in a year-long competition for points. Several girls schools, for instance, have school-wide teams, variously called Foxes and Hounds, Brownies and Spiders, or Reds and Whites. A frequent practice in girls schools is something called "Sing-Sing" in which two school teams move across a large field toward each other, each trying to out-sing the other. There are also elaborate "old girl-new girl" rituals, in which new girls are not allowed to walk on certain pathways and must memorize key pieces of school lore, like school songs. New girls at one school once had to shave their eyebrows.

DEEP STRUCTURE REGULATION

As with discipline, there is nothing about rituals or collective games that are intrinsic to boarding schools. Heads and teachers have been telling students what to do for centuries at all kinds of schools with probably very limited success. More permanent behavior modification requires that students be controlled at a deeper level. By definition, day schools are limited in their ability to regulate somatic drives, but a total institution is ideally organized for this deep structure regulation.

To control an individual's body is to have great power over him or her. The opportunities for socialization are increased when the subject is dependent on the "trainer" for substance. What better way to forge a collective identity than to compel individuals to eat and sleep in a uniform manner? How much more deeply can a school reach inside students' psyches than by regulating their sex lives? We might also wonder to what degree a collective identity is forged by the institutionalized collective repression in single-sex schools.

In one sense, social dominance starts with the repression of the self, and where better to learn the tactics of self-denial than in an escape-proof setting where temptation is removed and gratification is punished. In an earlier time, this extreme form of social control went unchallenged by most students; it was part of growing up. Today, however, teen culture is almost the polar opposite of the culture of repression. By accommodating "contemporary realities" the schools have had to give up some of their ability to regulate their students' physical lives, and thus we might expect that they have lost some of their ability to forge students into a collective. Regulations regarding eating and sexual behavior, for instance, have been considerably relaxed in recent decades.

The Importance of the Feed. Certainly one of the rudest shocks the new prep school student experiences is the loss of a full refrigerator. For most of these students, Mom or the cook has supplied them with an abundance of their favorite foods. The unconscious connection between nourishment and nurturing that is an important part of the meaning of home becomes severed upon entering boarding school.

In its place are group "feeds"—as some students and the British call them—in which the freedom to go to the refrigerator is replaced by standing in line, taking what is served, and eating with a number of relative strangers. At the most elite schools food is in great abundance, but at some of the less elite schools food can be simple, even scanty. Thirty-seven percent of boarding school students say what they like least about boarding school is the food. At one school, students are taught to "waste not, want not" by having to munch on the previous day's leftovers during midmorning break.

Schools pay close attention to the socializing effects of the feed. Many family schools and the more traditional schools still have two or three sit-down meals a day. These can be very organized affairs with assigned seats, monogrammed table settings, and firm rules of etiquette. Food is served and consumed within a prescribed time period. Very often the head will sit at the main table, and meals will begin with grace followed by announcements. The implicit assumption behind the highly ritualized group feed is that people who eat alike act alike and perhaps even think alike. You are not only what you eat, but *how* you eat.

Less structured schools have mostly abandoned central feeds for cafeteria-style feeds. Here students can often choose from a selection of dishes, sit with whom they like, and leave when they are finished. They may also skip meals, thus the socializing effects of cafeteria-style feeds are less pronounced.

No matter how plentiful the official food of the school, students almost always keep a store of "private" food. Packages from home and trips to town are the two main sources. Naturally, there is a widespread black market in private food; in fact, food can become a form of currency. Food exchanges can cement friendships as well as provide extra potato chips, cookies, and candy. Students may also try to heat foods by smuggling hot plates into the dorms. One school reminds students in their handbook, "Bedrooms are not kitchens."

The Management of Eros. We suspect that with the coming of coeducation some of the prudishness about adolescent sex has been softened. Students would have to be saintly, even inhuman, to live according to the high standards set by the more traditional schools. Certainly one of the main purposes of a single-sex school is to discourage sexual activity in adolescence, and it was not that long ago that many coed schools still enforced a policy of look but not touch.

The recognition that most adolescents develop strong sexual drives was one of the reasons that sports, cold showers, and incessant activity were built into the boarding school experience. Boys in particular were believed by early heads to be lustful. Unfortunately, the idea that removing the stimulus (girls) would make boys less interested in sex turned out to be naive. Faculty wives, in particular, could be the source of unending fantasy. Most older boys at boys schools complained of being "horny" and were generally only too glad to tell us that the thing they miss most about home is girls. Young women were usually more circumspect in openly discussing their sexual longings, but if the semi-erotic posters of rock stars and athletes that some put in their rooms are any indication of their feelings, we can safely say that their fantasy life is as rich as the boys'.

It was not until the late 1960s that many prep schools decided that the adolescent urge to be around members of the opposite sex was normal. Coeducation has brought with it new opportunities and new problems. Clearly, coeducation alleviates some of the rougher, even brutal, aspects of life in an all-boys school. On the other hand, new problems arise, most of which are obvious, including occasional pregnancies.

One alumna told of a girl who had a baby at boarding school. The baby was found under the bed. The girl had been home two weeks before delivery, and her father, a doctor, had not noticed her pregnancy, so it was not the school's oversight alone. The girl knew she was pregnant, but blocked it out of her mind. After the birth, the school closed ranks and kept her name confidential. The alumni tried to desensationalize it. The head later said that admission requests went up because of the school's excellent handling of the problem. The girl switched to another boarding school and went on to college. Pregnancies may be more infrequent today, if what a more recent alumna reports is at all typical: "There wasn't much pregnancy because the school, much to their credit, was liberal with birth control. Birth control or abortions were your two choices."

Today many coed prep schools take an enlightened view of sexuality, which means in effect that while they do not condone sexual relations, they do not condemn them. The bottom line is if you are going to do it, do it with discretion and taste. The prevailing norm seems to be that sex is an off-hours activity, done in privacy, and with little or no "public display of affection," or PDA. Compared to most public high-school campuses most prep school campuses seem almost asexual. More than a few prep observers have taken note that there is much in prep life that could be called unisex. (See Aldrich 1979, 65–66.) But in one California school, public displays of affection seem more the norm than the exception. The head was philosophical about adolescent sex; as he put it, "Girls do it for the experience, boys do it to tell their friends about it."

The amount of sex on boarding school campuses is impossible to measure. Alumni tend to fall into two camps when reporting on the subject, one claiming that almost nobody did it, the other that everybody did it. One suspects that sexual behavior varies by school, class, and clique. Some schools may be more liberal, some classes may "swing" a bit more than others, and some cliques may make sex a preoccupation while others may be prudish. For some, sex is the major issue of their boarding school experience. As one recent alumna said: "We struggled through in lurches. It was an attack issue. You had to confront it. If you avoided it, and some did, you paid a price. It was a part of everything that went on." Especially at coed schools, many students may feel pressure to spend lots of time with members of the opposite sex. Several alumni indicated that they think "girls grow up too fast at boarding school." As a result, some of these graduates will not send their girls away.

Homosexuality was mentioned by several students and alumni. An alumnus described how eight older boys left in charge of a group of younger boys in the lower school had been expelled for their homosexual activities. Other alumni describe mutual masturbation sessions among boys. Sexual frustration is common among adolescents, but in boarding school such frustrations can be used to forge collective identities. Masturbation, for example, seems to be the archetypal private solution to a universal problem, but in boarding schools even this lonely activity can become part of a group effort. Lacking privacy and driven by sexual desire, mutual masturbation is not unknown at the elite schools—"round-pounds" were a tradition at a number of former all-boys schools. This kind of sharing undoubtedly creates a quality of loyalty that is deeper than what verbal pledges of solidarity alone can provide. This kind of "legitimate" homosexuality is distinguished in the prep mind from the "weird" homosexuality chosen by an individual because of personal sexual preference.

Several alumnae mentioned that no one ever discussed the issue lest they be seen as peculiar by their peers, but that some lesbian teachers were dismissed from their school, and other alumni said that homosexual teachers had been thrown out when they were in school. These were considered major incidents at the time. But it is our distinct sense that homosexuality as a patterned way of life is less evident in American schools than in British boarding schools, and even there it may be on the decline.

As with so much about boarding school life, it is not so much what you do, but with whom you do it. For many parents the knowledge that their son or daughter is seeing another student with a similar background is more important than whether or not they are sleeping together. From a parent's point of view the relative lack of mobility their children experience at boarding school assures them that if they lose their virginity they will at least not lose their lives racing to a lovers lane in a car. Promiscuity is rare at boarding schools—the time and energy required for a major sexual career is simply not available. On the other hand, complete insulation from sex at most schools is also impossible, because at the very least, everybody talks about it. As with most aspects of life in the prep crucible, the issue of what is appropriate and inappropriate sexual behavior is forged by the heat of public exposure.

The Costs of Compromise

There can be little doubt that the prep rite of passage has an effect on students; 88 percent of the seniors in our sample reported that boarding school changed them. But while some report that their experiences were positive, many seem angered by having to undergo the rigors of the prep crucible.

It is also curious that the high percentage of students who report being changed by boarding school life is unrelated to the amount of social control that schools impose on students, and is unrelated to a student's perception of social conformity. It is also essentially unrelated to school type or degree of eliteness. Students claim to be changed by boarding school but it does not appear that the various intervention treatments the schools devise affect their perceptions of change (see table 7–1).

We learned that there is virtually no relationship between students' perceptions of "conformity" and seniors' perceptions that boarding school

TABLE 7–1

Boarding School Students' Perception of Change and Social Conformity

School Type	Seniors Who Feel Boarding School Changed Them (%)	Students Who Agree "Most Students Here Dress and Act Pretty Much Alike" (%)
Episcopal	92	75
Catholic	80	71
Girls	84	52
Entrepreneurial	86	48
Academy	90	44
Western	95	39
Progressive	84	19

NOTE: Data is based on questionnaires from 2,475 students at 20 schools, of whom 1,345 were seniors.

has changed them. Those at girls schools and progressive schools, for instance, have strikingly different perceptions of students' conformity, but seniors from both those types of schools have identical perceptions of change (84 percent feel they have been changed).

We also learned that schools historically associated with trying to exercise social control over their students—Episcopal and Catholic schools—are no more likely to produce perceived change than schools that have allowed students more individuality, such as western and progressive schools.

When we compared select 16 schools to other schools in terms of their seniors' perceptions of change, it was found that students at the socially elite schools were, on balance, no more likely to report change than students from other schools.

Thus while seniors perceive themselves to be changed by their experience in the total institution, their responses do not appear to vary significantly by major school characteristics such as type, degree of social eliteness, and student perception of conformity.

Schools can impose conformity, but they cannot legislate how students really feel about life in the total institution. The time and thought the schools devote to socialization may in fact have precious little effect on their inmates. Whether students like or dislike institutional living may only be marginally related to how they perceive changes in themselves. Human beings may be more resistant to behavior modification imposed from above than the founders of total institutions believed.

This finding leaves open another possibility—that student behaviors are modified by socialization from other students. In the enclosed environment of a boarding school there is no escape from other students, and schools may become less total as the teen culture becomes inescapable. It might well develop that the real socialization for power will take place in the trenches of the dormitories and in the struggle to survive in the competitive student culture. The collective identity the schools hope to create by compelling students to share their lives may have the consequence of creating a collective identity that has very little to do with shared discipline, and a lot to do with shared indulgence.

8

The Student Underlife and the Loss of Innocence

IT IS a clear New England morning when Chip, a student guide at a select 16 school, shepherds us from chapel to gym to dorm. Bright and articulate, the tall, thin, redheaded junior is bubbly in his praise of his school. "This is a great school," he says several times. "My father went here, this is a great school." A public relations natural, Chip knows everything about his school. He rattles off figures with ease; he is particularly proud of the new science wing and the Gothic chapel with "real" stained glass windows. "Hey, I'll bet you'd be interested in this," Chip says, pointing to a bluff behind the library.

The path up the bluff is narrow and rocky. As we struggle along, Chip glides ahead—and patiently waits for us at the top.

"Isn't the view incredible!" he says, sweeping the horizon with his arms.

The view is magnificent. The sloping green hills run down to the blue water for miles up and down the Atlantic coast. Sailboats, their colorful spinnakers at full wind, dart among the whitecaps. Chip suddenly becomes quiet, his youthful face less poised and more innocent. His eyes follow the boats for several seconds. "And this," he says simply, "is where I come to cry. Everybody's got to have a place to cry."

Pain and loneliness are as much a part of the boarding school experience as empowerment and entitlement; in fact, pain and empowerment are often inextricably linked together. Without a rite of passage, empowerment is psychologically empty; "proving one's worth" is what gives it value. As we shall discuss in this chapter, for some students, particularly those at the top, life at boarding school can be like an extended family, supportive and caring; for others, particularly those in the middle, it can be oddly depersonalizing, in much the same way that David Riesman described how individuals become alienated from themselves and each other in *The Lonely Crowd* (1960).

As James McLachlan (1970) points out, the invention of adolescence and the invention of boarding school occurred during the nineteenth century. Through the work of such early psychologists as Stanley G. Hall, adolescence was defined as a kind of demilitarized zone between childhood and adulthood where growth was rapid and the possibilities of fulfillment and despair extreme. Part of the answer to "Who am I?" can be found in gaining academic competence. But the question of "Who am I?" is also more personal and profound. The question implies a longing to know how to be and how to act at an intimate, often sexual, level, as well as finding a code for living. The hedonistic elements of teen culture often conceal the anguish young people experience in struggling to find a set of values by which to live.

From this perspective, adolescent deviance in the form of rule breaking may be seen as a normal behavior, the developmental object of which is to define standards of conduct by experimenting with different moral stances. In some ways adolescence is the most moral stage in an individual's life; the yearning of young people to answer the question of "Who am I?" is often morally intense and for some overpowering.

In some ways society recognizes that adolescents should not be held fully accountable for their behavior, although an inner-city adolescent is probably much less likely to get a second or third chance than a middle-class or upper-class adolescent if he or she breaks a law. We expect adolescents to stop playing and learn the rules of the game. The adolescent discovery that they, like their parents, are born into a world they did not create, and that they are constrained by the limitations of language, custom, and law can be a rude awakening for young people who have grown accustomed to the freedom of childhood.

It is in adolescence that the academic and social sorting and selection process begins in earnest. At the same time that adolescents are disengaging from their parents' emotional embraces they are also required to accept the facts of life which include, for middle- and upper-middle-class youngsters, the prospect of a lifetime of competition. Schools and society seem intent on separating the winners from the losers, and for many youngsters the discovery that they must prove their worth can be a rude awakening. The scramble for success leaves many adolescents in the middle of the pack as the dreams of childhood become tempered by the realities of adulthood.

In the prep crucible there is little sympathy for mediocrity or failure, and students who cannot excel are caught between the external expectations of school and family and their inner need to find self-worth. Squeezed by adults and peers alike, students caught in the middle at boarding school must give up hope of being stars and settle for second or third place, a scenario that belies the call to greatness. To be in the middle at a boarding school is a lonely and difficult position, making students ripe for the lure of the student underlife.

Authenticity and Relative Deprivation

How does stress affect students in boarding schools? While students wrote many comments on our questionnaires, we also asked them to respond to a series of seventeen statements about their school.[1] Through the technique of factor analysis, we found that answers to seven of these statements were statistically clustered, suggesting they were indicators of a common underlying factor. After reviewing the content of these questions (see exhibit 8–1), it seemed to us that they all tap the students' perception of the authenticity of their prep school experience.

We call this measure of seven items the authenticity index. Insofar as students believed their school had effective and fair discipline, that classes were not boring, that teachers and other students encouraged learning for its own sake, and that a few students did not shut everyone else out, the authenticity of the school was perceived as high. Otherwise, its authenticity was considered low. Although most students' responses fell somewhere in the middle, and not at either extreme, there was some variation. What explains variations in perceived authenticity? Responses did not vary significantly in different types of schools, but they did vary according to student characteristics.

Girls admitted to former all-boys schools are less likely to perceive the schools as authentic than are the boys at those schools or the girls at other

1. Fourteen of these statements were developed by McDill and Rigsby 1973, 177–85 and three were modified from the National Opinion Research Center.

EXHIBIT 8–1

Items Used to Measure Authenticity Factor

True	False	
—	—	Teachers here are very interested in their students.
—	—	Many classes here are boring.
—	—	The discipline here is effective.
—	—	There is a lot of interest here in learning for its own sake, rather than just for grades or for graduation credits.
—	—	Teachers here encourage students to value knowledge for its own sake, rather than just for grades.
—	—	The discipline here is not fair.
—	—	There are a few students who control things in this school, and the rest of us are out in the cold.

NOTE: Four of these items were developed by McDill and Rigsby (1973) to measure educational climates and three were from NORC (1980).

schools. Some of these schools seem to have admitted girls to partake of the rigors of their life. If the girls can be as tough as the boys, they can be members. If they can deal with the loneliness, the assault on privacy, and the pressure to perform with no place to hide, they are welcome to join the club. This experience may affect their perception of the school's authenticity.

Other former boys schools have spent considerable time and thought focusing on how adolescent girls and boys may have different needs. One indication of a school's commitment to coeducation may be the presence of high-level women administrators and faculty, as well as women on the board of directors. These results are more likely when boys and girls schools merge, although some administrators told us that the girls school tends to get submerged when this happens. While that may be true to some degree, the resulting school tends to be more attuned to the needs of both boys and girls than are the former boys schools that seem to have simply decided to admit girls. Girls at schools that went coeducational by merger generally have higher perceptions of their school's authenticity than the girls at schools that became coeducational by enrollment.

Family background and academic prowess are also related to how students perceive the authenticity of their schools. Students from high socioeconomic backgrounds[2] have higher authenticity perceptions than middle

2. Socioeconomic background (SES) was measured by combining father's education, father's occupation, mother's education and family income into a composite SES score. Mother's occupation was not included in the measure because many of the mothers do not work outside the home. Education was measured by the following categories: some grade school, finished grade school, some high school, finished high school, some college, finished college, and attended graduate school or professional school after college; occupation was scored on the Duncan.

or low socioeconomic status students, and students with high SAT scores are more likely to perceive their schools as authentic than students who do not score as well. One reason students with high family status and high college board scores are more likely to find boarding school authentic may be that they sense the schools will deliver academic and social status to them.

Black students perceive their schools as less authentic than do whites or Asian students. The case of black students is especially poignant, because they are the only group whose authenticity score is below the average, indicating that many do not perceive prep school life the same way that other students do, despite the school's best efforts and claims. When we visited prep schools we often saw black students eating separately. The sense of estrangement experienced by blacks is all the more apparent when compared to Asian students, who appear to adjust relatively well to boarding school life. Other minorities, such as Jewish students, also appear able to integrate into the total institution—only the blacks appear substantially isolated.

While this finding may be more an indictment of racism in America than the inability of prep schools to manage racial differences more adroitly, it does leave one with an uneasy impression that racism in the prep school is not unknown. One senior said, "I have become able to handle racial slurs and deal with very sticky questions about being black." For black students, then, a certain feeling of alienation may explain their lower perceptions of authenticity in the schools they attend.

Day students, perhaps because they can escape the confines of the total institution, find the schools a bit more authentic than do boarding students, and noncitizens find life in an American total institution less authentic than American citizens.[3] Students' religious backgrounds do not appear to be related to perceptions of authenticity. The "preppiness" of students' families is related to authenticity; students who come from families with no prep school background and those with two or more relatives who attended prep school are happier than the middle group, with only one prep relative.

Socioeconomic Index (SEI) scale (Duncan 1961), and income was measured with the following categories: under $15,000, $15,000 to $25,000, $25,001 to $75,000, $75,001 to $100,000, and more than $100,000. A factor analysis was done on these items. The factor loadings of each item were then used as weights to form an SES score. These SES scores were then standardized for this population, and each student received a single standardized SES score. On the basis of that score, the sample was divided into thirds. The scores within each third were as follows: bottom third (−6.187 to −0.182), middle third (−0.178 to 0.528), top third (0.540 to 1.353).

3. We might hypothesize that a school that admits, for financial purposes, a great number of foreign students may suffer in the long term with a drop in perceived authenticity.

Taken separately, each of these findings is difficult to decode. Whether we are examining SAT scores, socioeconomic status, or preppiness of family, students in the middle range are less likely to perceive their schools as authentic than students at either the high or the low end of the measures. Students in the middle socioeconomic range consider their schools to be less authentic than other students, no matter how academically competitive the school. This pattern is maintained for white and Asian students, but not for black students. Black students with middle-range socioeconomic scores are, surprisingly, the black students with the highest authenticity scores. Except for black students, then, the findings are consistent—it is not fun to be a middle-range student in prep school.

Why is this? Intuitively one would expect the students at the bottom of the socioeconomic or SAT range to be the least happy, as they are at the bottom of the social and academic heap. The sociological theory of relative deprivation offers one possible explanation. It suggests that deprivation is not an absolute phenomenon, especially in the daily lives of individuals, but is experienced in reference to others. If individuals have few material possessions but live among others similarly deprived, they are less likely to feel deprived than individuals who have more but live among those who have a great deal. Those at the very bottom of the status, wealth, and power hierarchy are less likely to rebel or demand reform than those in the middle, who are close enough to the top to see it, but too far away to reach it.

Whether or not the theory of relative deprivation captures all the possible varieties of the deprivation experience, it illuminates the finding that middle-range prep school students are the least likely to see their schools as authentic. A student, for example, who has middle-range SAT scores may aspire to acceptance at the best colleges, but will probably have to accept his or her second choice, while a student in the low SAT range knows that unless he or she is a star athlete or a "development" case there is little hope of getting into a top-ranked college.

Similarly, a relatively less affluent student cannot compete with a wealthy student in terms of status and possessions, whereas a middle-range student is affluent enough to get into the status race, but not affluent enough to win. A middle-range student, like the middle class generally, is caught between the anxiety of downward mobility and the frustration of blocked upward mobility. This structural dilemma underscores many admissions officers' comments that "You've got to have someplace to hang your hat in this school."

Middle-range students may sense that the sacrifices of privacy and effort that they are being called upon to make will not pay off as handsomely for them as they may for more advantaged students, or even as well as they will for less advantaged students whose attendance at prep school promises relatively greater rewards compared to their alternatives.

The theory of relative deprivation might also explain the anomalous finding that the least happy blacks at boarding school are of relatively high socioeconomic status. Again, we might expect the wealthy black students to be more comfortable in the prep environment than poor or middle-class blacks, but they are not. If, however, their reference group is the wealthy white students rather than the other black students, then the theory leads us to conclude that wealthy black students might feel relatively deprived or less happy than other black students.

From a larger perspective, all of these findings and conclusions point out something important about prep school life—that it is very, very competitive. No matter how much schools stress community and cooperation, students feel the competitiveness and act accordingly. A number of students indicated that what they like least about boarding school is "the competitive—at all costs—attitude" and the way "competition separates us." The anxiety and stress involved can be acute and, for those in the middle, chronic.

Joining the Group for Survival

The lonely search of adolescents, especially those removed from home, family, and old friends and those for whom the payoff of boarding school seems uncertain, heightens the importance of the peers they encounter. These same peers are important both during school and in later life. They contribute in a major way to the forging of a collective rather than simply an individual identity.

Many of the novels about boarding schools, such as *A Separate Peace* by John Knowles, reveal how intense, even overpowering, student cliques are and how those who are not granted full membership by the other students often suffer feelings of isolation, rejection, and inferiority.

"There are walls around the groups," the first new boy said. "For security. Everybody has to be secure. In a boarding school, where you have no other security than friends, you *must* form a clique. Or else you're lost, you don't have anybody to turn to. If you're having a feud with somebody, who can you go to?

It's sort of a basic necessity at a boarding school to form a clique." (Quoted in Prescott 1970, 157)

Joining a clique is a matter of survival, because without friends a student is vulnerable to the antisocial, sometimes cruel, behavior of other students.

When alumni reflect on their boarding school experiences they almost never talk of a specific course or teacher, and even the head may only be dimly remembered. What alumni do remember, vividly in many cases, are the other students: the bullies, the saints, the good guys, and the nice girls. They remember the time they were caught smoking outside the dorm with good old Jack, who put out his cigarette in his French book and almost burned the school down. They remember the water balloon fights, panty raids, fist fights, love affairs, scandals, and triumphs. They recall how they smuggled girls into their rooms, and they remember all the times they broke the rules and beat the system. They remember the time they poured gin in the chaplain's water glass, and crazy old Lance, who claimed to be having a love affair with the dean's wife and had a set of stockings to prove it. Bull sessions, rank sessions, blow-outs, and crap-outs are what makes boarding life exciting, scary, rewarding—and alienating.

In boarding schools a smug or disloyal student may be given a cold shower, thrown in the pond, stripped, or ignored. Cover-ups are commonplace. After all, what are friends for? An alumni told us, "We covered for each other pretty well. Once I was off campus at a party and the headmaster came to my locked door and banged and banged. Finally he left a note saying that I was to see him at whatever time I got back. My buddies called me at the party and my pals there drove me back in 45 minutes, a new and still-standing record as far as I know. I went to see the headmaster and he said that he was very disappointed in me. I denied the whole thing and said that I hadn't felt well and had gone for a walk. We got over that one, but it was close."

To help a friend in need is the essence of the relationship, and prep school students learn this through experience. Students and alumni tell of helping their best friends through an unwanted pregnancy, family break-up, or attempted suicide. Loyalty and grace under pressure are intrinsic to the prep posture, and these social skills are learned at boarding school. One wrote that boarding school has "helped me control my temper around people who get on my nerves." Another said, "I have learned grace under pressure in our competitive little society."

Loyalty to one's school is loyalty to one's friends, therefore friendship networks are important in determining a school's personality and tone. The schools are also pleased to see students form close ties because they help bring them back for reunions. The friendships are also part of the prep rite of passage. Numerous students wrote about the "strong, wonderful friends" they made at school. When offered the opportunity to indicate what boarding school's best feature was, 32 percent chose the "other students," 23 percent chose the "academics," and 5 percent chose "the teachers."

Boys and girls bring different elements to the peer culture. Girls verbalize and act out their social rituals more than boys. At girls schools there is considerable stress on friends, including leaving notes and little gifts for special friends. At some schools girls whose mother or other relatives attended are called a special name, such as "Its." Often the daughters will belong to the same school team that their relative did. Traditions such as these tend to enhance the family tradition aspects of certain boarding schools. Birthdays receive special recognition, with friends providing gifts and parties in place of the absent family, although the family may provide abundant gifts as well. At one school, friends unfurled a banner down the side of a classroom building to celebrate the birthday of one of their number.

There are few tender mercies among boys, who establish finely graded pecking orders. Big, strong, and aggressive boys often demand deference from smaller boys and, as a group, seniors tend to band together and lord it over the rest. Violations of the pecking order may be punished physically and verbally and woe be it to a younger boy who challenges the wrong older boy. In one case a freshman who "gave lip" to a senior was treated to a long, icy cold shower before being tossed out of the dorm nude, in which state he was required to run about until he agreed to "apologize."

The threat of this kind of humiliation has a sobering effect on potential mavericks or troublemakers, and "punishments" serve as graphic reminders that the collective identity of the group must take precedence over individual identities. Nobody wants to be at the bottom of the pecking order because that sorry individual is usually scapegoated and routinely victimized even by the weaker boys. What one boy described as the "dog-eat-dog" elements in the boy culture provide ample opportunities to learn that survival and success do not go to the weak but to the strong, a philosophy of life well suited to managing power relations in the financial and business world.

Girls like the other students more than boys do, and at girls schools 47 percent choose the other students as the school's best feature. Boys are less fond of each other, perhaps even snarly, and they rank academics only slightly behind other students as the school's best feature. Boys at boys schools like sports more than other boys or girls do, and girls at girls schools may barely know who their teachers are—less than one percent indicated that the teachers were boarding school's best feature, and less than one percent indicated that teachers were the worst feature of their school.

Students at coed schools tend to be less extreme in their likes and dislikes than students at single-sex schools, substantiating the oft-repeated phrase that girls humanize a school, but raising the issue of whether boys might not also humanize girls as well. Girls are more likely than boys to feel that when they look back ten years from now the most valuable part of their school experience will be the experience of "relating to people." This is especially true of girls at coed schools, where 70 percent said that this aspect of school would be most valuable for them. Boys at boys schools feel that they have not learned as many social skills as students at other types of schools.

Girls are less likely than boys to agree strongly that "I take a positive attitude toward myself," and that "I am able to do things as well as most other people." While the differences are fairly small, there is a consistent pattern that girls at girls schools are more likely to agree strongly with these statements and the statement, "On the whole, I am satisfied with myself," than girls at coed schools. Girls in general and boys at coed schools are less likely than boys at all-boys schools to disagree strongly with the statement "I feel I do not have much to be proud of" (see table 8–1).

One might argue that boarding school students are little different than other teenagers in their fascination with relationships and friends; after all,

TABLE 8–1

Indicators of Self-Confidence by Sex and School Sex Composition

	Girls at Girls Schools (%)	Girls at Coed Schools (%)	Boys at Coed Schools (%)	Boys at Boys Schools (%)
I take a positive attitude toward myself (Agree strongly)	37	33	45	46
I am able to do things as well as most other people (Agree strongly)	37	33	43	42
On the whole, I am satisfied with myself (Agree strongly)	34	27	31	34
I feel I do not have much to be proud of (Disagree strongly)	56	54	56	61

NOTE: Based on 2,475 student questionnaires at twenty schools.

the suburban teen culture is built around dating, cruising, and hanging out. Few suburban or urban adolescents, however, have to live with their friends, and this intimacy creates an opportunity for more intense and lasting relations than at day schools. Students themselves often commented on the differences in the intensity of friendships. One noted, "friends that are boarders hang closer than a boarder and a day student."

Prep friendships may be created by proximity, balance, status, and exchange. Because of the closeness of boarding school life, proximity is seldom a problem in establishing friendships. Neither is balance, known by most students and adults as "give and take." Despite the fact that there are some status differences among boarding school students, compared to most high schools and colleges the populations of boarding schools are relatively homogeneous. As one alumna said, "I had much more in common socially with my boarding school classmates than my college classmates, who were much more diverse." And, lastly, the opportunities for exchange, as underground food exchanges illuminate, are ample. A boarding school, in other words, is an environment where friendships can flourish, although, as we have seen, students who are unable to find their own special place within the student status hierarchy are less happy than students who can establish a clear identity.

We should also point out that "Intimacy," as one teacher expressed it, "can breed contempt." One student wrote that attending boarding school made him "realize that rich WASPs are stupid, ignorant bastards." Other students wrote about the "cynicism and the rich homogeneity" of the student body. A few expressed anger at the "elitist attitude of the students and faculty."

The eternal adolescent dilemma between individual identity and membership in the group is heightened in the prep school atmosphere. Friendship networks can tighten to become cliques from which there is little escape, or into which there is virtually no entry. Students who are "different" can be left out in the cold, isolated and vulnerable to psychological and occasionally physical attacks by adolescent predators who pick on the weak in order to feel strong. A day student at a predominantly boarding school wrote he felt "ostracized as a day student," and that the experience "has destroyed me." A senior girl wrote that boarding school "taught me about unhappiness, took away my cherished freedom, and made me hate people."

A "cliquey" school can be very hard on a student who cannot or will not play the game as the dominant students define it. Several students wrote that the worst feature of boarding school was the cliques. Students in the same clique will eat together, study together, play together, party together, and perhaps sleep together. One of the strongest arguments in favor of a central, regulated feed is that it allows the school to mix students and presumably weaken the power of cliques. Yet friendship networks and cliques form the basis of everyday living for prep students. The true loner is difficult to find in the total institution; the pressure to conform from the school and the students is too powerful. As one student wrote, "I've learned how hard it is to stand up against a crowd." Another student wrote, "By living close to people you discover things about yourself you can't hide."

Drugs, Alcohol, and Crime

In *The Magic Mountain,* Thomas Mann retells the tale of Hans Castorp's dream. Hans has been transported to a magical place where "beautiful young human creatures" live and play together. "So blithe, so good and gay," they seem to Hans to be "wise and gentle through and through." But one boy, "his full hair drawn sideways across his brow and falling on his temples," suddenly becomes "inexpressive, unfathomable," withdrawn into a "deathlike reserve." Behind the boy are towering columns, and Hans reluctantly climbs the high steps that lead to a sanctuary door which he opens with dread and anguish. What he sees fills him with an "icy coldness"—two gray witches are destroying and dismembering a young and beautiful child—"cracking the tender bones between their jaws." They see Hans and shake their "reeking" fists uttering curses "soundlessly, most vilely and with the last obscenity . . ."(Mann 1960, 491–94).

To borrow from Mann's dark vision, there is an underside to boarding school life. Behind the ivy walls of the cloistered elite there is at times sadness, despair, even tragedy. There are more than a few prep school students who lead lives of quiet desperation. Depression, withdrawal, and suicide attempts hint that not all is always well within the status seminary. Boarding school "has made me more cynical as I watch all the people I care about slowly disintegrate into the pits of depression," wrote one student. Someone else noted that boarding school "has created a deep cynical streak which will carry me into the darker side of life."

An unbalanced student can be pushed to extremes in an atmosphere where there is little or no escape from public exposure. In one case, a lonely tenth-grade boy at a western school kept a loaded pistol at the bottom of his clothes chest. Often this boy was the object of ridicule because he was awkward and withdrawn. Occasionally, he would remove his pistol from its hiding place and slowly wave it about, silently threatening his roommates and their friends. This strange behavior was not reported by the other boys because that would be considered a violation of the code of silence students impose on each other. This code was not broken even after he placed the barrel of his pistol against another boy's temple and threatened to pull the trigger. After a horrified moment of frozen panic, the boy with the gun was persuaded that murder was not "cool," and he reluctantly replaced his pistol in his belt. He seemed indifferent to his own strange behavior, and the other boys treated him with the respect a dangerous lone wolf deserves. To the day he graduated the boy kept a pistol at the bottom of his clothes chest, and was never detected by the school authorities.

Adaptation to the total institution is difficult and, for some students, virtually impossible without the aid of alcohol and drugs. Kevin McEneaney, the director of drug prevention at Phoenix House Foundation in New York, has been quoted as saying, "At some leading prep schools, at least one-quarter of the students smoke marijuana regularly, and if alcohol is thrown in, our estimate climbs to 40% to 50%" (Malabre 1983, 34). Not everyone would agree with this appraisal, however. One dean of students says that "Student estimates that one-third of his school's 500-odd boarders use alcohol or illicit drugs regularly are 'too high.' He believes drug use at the school is declining, though he adds, 'Who really knows?' " (Malabre 1983, 34). It is true that no one really does know how many prep school students get stoned, drunk, "bummed out," or "wasted" in the course of the school week. We know a lot do. As one senior wrote, "This place has greatly added to my consumption of drugs. I seldom take them at home and yet they are part of my daily life here."

One recent alumna of a rural New England school said: "There was a lot of pot, booze, psychedelics, mescaline, a little coke, but it was pretty awful. It had been cut, and cut, and cut some more. I don't know about heroin. Some hash, easy to get. Lots of speed. On the day a shipment would arrive on campus everyone was so wired you'd think the place was going to explode. At college the fascination diminished a little with people from boarding schools, but got uglier for some because it was based on need, not kicks."

Drugs may be brought in either by day students or by boarding students who go off campus.

It's 3 P.M. . . . and Theodore W. boards a bus for the nearby University. . . . It's a winter Wednesday, and he doesn't have to check back until 8 P.M.; he has no sports and the 6 P.M. school dinner is optional. So he has lots of time to pick up marijuana from a freshman at a university dormitory. He pays with $400 collected from 20 other . . . students with whom he will share the purchase. (Malabre 1983, 34)

One prep student returning from Venezuela was arrested at Kennedy Airport in New York with three-quarters of a pound of cocaine in May 1984, estimated street value: $300,000. The drugs had been bought with a $5,000 investment raised by fourteen students; all were expelled. A student from another school was quoted in the *New York Times* as saying he and his friends had had to postpone their trip to Venezuela because "those idiots . . . got caught." Virtually no prep school is free of drugs. A staff member of the Freedom from Chemical Dependency Foundation is quoted as saying that cocaine is "on 99 percent of the campuses" (*New York Times,* 27 May 1984, 1, 50).

"Cocaine is more of a preppie drug," a 17-year-old boy says. "It's the radical thing, the new cool thing. I never met anybody who was really messed up by cocaine." (*New York Times,* 27 May 1984, 1.)

Preppies are a perfect market for drug dealers because they have the money and the need. The generous allowances many boarding school students receive make it relatively easy for them to buy drugs. If they do not have money, others often share their drugs. At some schools stealing, perhaps to support a drug habit, can be a problem.

Alcoholism is also prevalent at boarding schools. A psychological counselor at one select 16 school was quoted in the *New York Times* as saying, "Once they've learned that all you have to do to cope is swallow, it's awfully hard to circumvent that." A select 16 senior explains his "heavy bouts" with cheap gin and vodka as follows: "We want to follow the pattern set for us. We go to [prep school]. We go to an Ivy League college. We get a nice job. We live in New Canaan, Connecticut, have a Volvo and a golden retriever and send our kids to [the same prep school]. Then we go back and have tailgate parties and drink Bloody Marys" (*New York Times,* 27 May 1984, 50).

Drinking, of course, is a time-honored prep tradition, and one has to be careful not to overreact to or exaggerate the importance of teenage experimentation with alcohol and drugs. After all, reliance on drugs is part of adult society, and some students are, as the student said, just following in Mom and Dad's footsteps. But because boarding schools stand *in loco parentis,* they cannot afford to ignore the problems of addiction.

The schools cope with the problem in one of two ways, both of which place the responsibility for the problem firmly on the student. Students who engage in drugs or drinking either have a "moral" problem or a "psychological" problem. While the personal qualities of students do, no doubt, explain some of the reasons why some students use drugs and liquor while others do not, such personal explanations do have the ring of "blaming the victim" or sometimes even "blaming the family." The use of alcohol and drugs is too widespread to make the moral and psychological explanations totally convincing.

Another favorite adult explanation for adolescent addiction is the "world-is-going-to-hell-in-a-handbasket" point of view. This is a variant of the impending fall of western civilization theme that some heads and teachers are fond of elaborating. From this perspective adolescents are similar to barbarians—hedonistic, selfish, and wild. Because prep school students are adolescents, they too must be hedonistic, selfish, and wild unless disciplined and, to use that favorite adult phrase, "straightened out."

Virtually no prep school heads offered us an organizational theory as to why preps spend so much time getting numbed, buzzed, and blotted. Surely there is something in the prep school culture that gives rise to the student underlife; after all, is not the immorality of the student underlife almost a perfect inversion of the morality of the dominant school culture?

In his work on total institutions Erving Goffman noted that in order to survive, inmates develop strategies for avoiding the restraints placed on them by the authorities—he called this "working the system." Like the hero in James Clavell's *King Rat*, some of the most clever students in prep schools are those who know how to work the system. Unfortunately, the nobility of working the system is almost always tarnished by corruption. The fact that there are elements of the student culture that are outright corrupt is one of the nastier elements of the underlife at boarding schools. Some prep school students are not into drugs for fun or escape—some are into it for the money. Drug deals in prep schools require extensive subterranean webs of affiliation among students, and, like prison, stoolies will be treated harshly. The very solidarity and loyalty developed in the prep crucible can serve to support the student underlife, which in turn strengthens peer solidarity. The guerrilla leaders of the prep underlife are usually capable of engineering little cons—on the spot hustles—as well as big cons, which require long-range planning and careful coordination. Basically, there are three categories of lawlessness in the total institution: petty larceny, white-collar crime, and "major deals."

Stealing, or "expropriating," school and student property is quite common. Some theft is relatively benign, such as taking an extra milk or blanket. Often a student will "relieve" the student co-op of a candy bar or two. Other larceny is not so benign, as when a student steals another's books, or an article of clothing, and occasionally the legal line between petty and grand larceny is crossed when students steal another's money or a record collection.

White-collar crimes include buying homework, leasing notes for an upcoming exam, forging late notes and weekend passes, or obtaining a copy of an upcoming examination. Not all prep school students engage in these activities, but during the course of a school year these acts are likely to occur at schools. Given the academic pressure most boarding school students are placed under, some white-collar crime is undertaken in the spirit of Robin Hood and student solidarity. Certain white-collar crimes, such as sharing homework, are essentially considered misdemeanors, punishable by lecture, restriction of privileges, and enforced study hall. Theft of an exam is more likely to be branded a felony offense, punishable by possible expulsion.

Major deals occur less often than petty larceny or white-collar crime because they require planning, daring, and a level of corruption beyond the capacities of most adolescents. The creation of a major deal has all the earmarks of organized crime, complete with vows of silence, secret codes, and major earnings. A major deal would certainly include a large drug transaction, the importation of large amounts of liquor on campus, and, for a boarder, having a car on or near campus. When the bosses of prep crime are caught, they are invariably dismissed. To break the prep connection in the drug trade, prosecution may also be necessary.

In the course of a prep school career, most students will learn to work the system, if not by breaking the rules then by learning to bend them. "I've learned to escape almost any consequences of my actions," wrote one senior. To many students, getting "wasted" on liquor or high on drugs is a kind of game, the object of which is not to get caught. It is a game school authorities sometimes play as well.

> A former school Head says that "school administrators often feel pressure to go easy on drug users whose parents are influential. . . . One parent may be on the board of trustees, another is giving a lot of money to the school," she says. "What comes out is uneven justice; some heads succumb to the pressure while others don't." (Malabre 1983, 34)

Covering up is especially likely if a school has an enrollment problem. The effects are not lost on students. As one senior wrote, boarding school has "taught me how politics work, and to cover my own ass in life." Another learned, "When in trouble lying is the best way to save yourself."

The student underlife is, in effect, a private adolescent society forced on students by the demands of the organization. Unfortunately, it is not particularly supportive, and sometimes can be predatory. Much of prep socialization occurs beyond the view of adults; students, to survive, must be tough and resourceful. A prep student is caught between a rock and a hard place where his or her identity is in danger of being crushed.

Many prep school adolescents become apathetic, cynical, and self-destructive. "I've grown old before my time," wrote one senior, and another wrote, "At boarding school you are forced to grow up faster than at day school." For some, the preservation of the private self in such an environment is nearly impossible. A few retreat inwardly into a private world induced, in some cases, by alcohol and drugs, where the safety of oblivion is preferable to the vulnerability of exposure. Thus the dilemma of development that faces many prep school students goes unresolved or denied, creating an inner anguish only barely masked by the jaunty air associated with preppiness.

Entitlement, Illusion, and the Perils of Preppiness

In part, character development was and is seen as an antidote against the insidious effects of wealth on a child's sense of duty. Moral issues and personal ethics are central to the prep school ethos:

> You are important to Lawrenceville, for you help set the tone of the School, help establish its character, help make it a good place to be—or its opposite. Therefore, it is important that you meet your responsibilities, be considerate of others, face up to challenges, discipline yourself, and grow intellectually and socially. (*The Lawrenceville Experience* 1982–83, 8)

But the ethical rite of passage that prep school students are supposed to undergo has a number of unintended consequences. Because of the extraordinary stress on morality, the distance between ideal and reality becomes quite obvious to most students. Idealism gone sour is cynicism; a point of view more prevalent among prep school students than is admitted by pious heads and earnest teachers. As one head said, "I can accept the idea of a school for the unusually talented; that's okay, but I would fight the idea of a school simply for the privileged." Or as another put it, "I have no use for schools that are enclaves for the privileged." A typical student comment was, boarding school "might have fed teen-age cynicism."

The student culture at boarding school may represent a kind of rebellion against the hypocrisy of the adult world. Already pushed by their parents to be successful, assaulted by an official morality that can ring hollow, and surrounded by a student culture that generally celebrates gratification rather than service, prep school students may find that rather than having their values clarified, all their beliefs have been muddied, or shattered.

The official ideology of the schools conveniently overlooks the obvious: prep school students are in an enormously competitive environment. Success, not service, is what the families of the students are likely to expect from their children. The student cultures of many schools reflect parental values, not school values; money, success, and power are life's objectives, not delayed gratification and aesthetic contemplation. What you own, where you go on vacation, who you know, are all important in the student status system. As one student wrote, boarding school has "made me realize how many jerks are going to be successful and how I'm going to deal with those people in my own business life." Students must try to conform to the demands of two cultures which have little in common. Not only are they expected to be good students, they are also expected to drink, socialize, speak, and dress in the culturally approved manner. The pressure this double bind places on students is a recipe for psychic stress.

Thus admission into the members only club of the prep school status system requires students to balance contradictory imperatives without losing their "cool." Idealism and cynicism, generosity and self-interest, denial and narcissism, must all be kept in the correct balance if full membership is to be granted.

The most potent psychic product of the prep crucible is the loss of innocence; the recognition that goodness unadorned by power is impotent in the struggle for privilege. Greatness implies the sacrifice of innocence; the cost of leadership is the acceptance of the world the way it is, not the way it ought to be. This is not easy for students to accept. One wrote, "Sometimes I wonder whether education is the way to happiness and whether going to college will make me more or less happy—Certainly I've been miserable since I've lost all values and beliefs. I wonder if it's temporary. I wonder whether I should sink into the homogeneous masses or continue the questioning that has made me dour and unhappy. What am I looking for—just happiness (is there such a thing?)."

The prep rite of passage is endured by most students because, as one student put it, "present pain for future gain." Another noted, "I have become more confident than my friends who do not go to boarding school about myself and my future." In effect, prep school students come to believe that they are entitled to privilege because they are true aristocrats. As one student candidly phrased it, "Boarding school has made me quite arrogant. I cannot reasonably believe that I am not better than most people."

The service mission of the schools, so cherished by generations of heads and teachers, fails to change many students. As one head said, "My goals for the school involve working with the value issue, so that people will use their lives in constructive ways, and have a sense of service." Indeed, the official high morals of the schools appear to have little impact on students' social conscience: 17 percent of ninth graders believe it is "very important" to be a community leader, as do 17 percent of the seniors; 25 percent of ninth graders believe that correcting inequalities is very important as do 25 percent of the seniors.

Far from being ideal, there is much in boarding school life, especially in the student culture, that is squalid. The sense of being among the best is in fact a kind of socially created and culturally cultivated illusion, a necessary perpetual blind spot that allows preps to maintain the illusion of earned status. The underside to upper-class socialization is that it is terribly constricting, even suffocating. The arrogance of being the best can distort, even warp, perception. As one alumna told us, when she graduated she felt she knew everyone she needed to know, either through her family or from boarding school connections, a feeling that made her uninterested in meeting new people.

The structured, almost prison-like quality of boarding school life socializes some students for lives as prisoners of their class. After prep school they will go to the right college, marry the right man or woman, get the right job, join the right clubs, travel to the right places, and grow weary in the right style. Thus the cycle of socialization recreates generations of individuals whose potentials are often crippled, not freed, by privilege.

PART

III

THE WORLD
BEYOND

9

The Vital Link: Prep Schools
and Higher Education

LIKE YOUTHS undergoing a tribal rite of passage in which the badge of manhood is killing their first lion, prep youths have historically sought to bag an Ivy League college acceptance. But, like lions, Ivy League acceptances have become more difficult to obtain. Their growing scarcity means that prep schools need to convince many students and parents that X, Y, and Z colleges are as good as Harvard, Yale, and Princeton, and therefore as worthy a prize for undergoing the grueling period of preparation.

The students whose families are seeking their socialization for power, however, are skeptical. Virtually everyone in prep school is going to college, so whether or not one goes is not the critical question; *where* one goes is what matters. Going to the right college is "part of the formula for their lives," as a select 16 college advisor phrased it. As we shall discuss in this chapter, the students' collective identity functions in their collective aspiration for similar colleges, including those with relatively modest academic or social backgrounds.

Many students come to boarding school with the hope that it will enable them to get into a better college. The prep schools know that this promise poses certain problems for them, given the changes that have occurred in college admissions during the last twenty-five years. In the past most of their graduates could easily get into the college of their choice, but today it is not so easy. Prep schools have responded by honing their very professional college advisory operation and by exercising what political clout they can in relation to the colleges. The result is a higher—though not perfect—payoff for elite prep school graduates, compared to other applicants.

Collective Aspiration

Prep school parents are undoubtedly the first source of pressure urging prep school students to attend the "right" college. Among freshmen, 51 percent said that they thought that ten years from now the most valuable part of their boarding school experience would be "where it helped you get into college." Many students enter boarding school with high expectations about how it will help them get into a prestigious college.

Parents and students are not totally divorced from reality. Where one goes to college is related to occupational and financial success. Researchers have found significant relationships between the particular colleges people attend and career success in a variety of fields. For example, the social prestige and selectivity of one's college is related to the prestige of the graduate or professional school one attends (Crane 1969; Brint 1980), to a person's professional occupational attainment (Brint 1980; Tinto 1980), to attaining a high rank in business (Pierson 1969; Useem and Karabel 1984), and to becoming an editor with a major publishing house (Coser, Kadushin, and Powell 1982). Half of Ronald Reagan's "sagebrush" cabinet have an Ivy League connection.

The opinions of parents and preps alike help to forge a collective sense of what is an appropriate prep college. The parental and student "vision of what constitutes a 'good' college is very narrow," said a college advisor at a select 16 school, and "acceptance at lesser known colleges is equivalent to failure." "Parents keep resuscitating dreams, which die hard," says another advisor. "The worst parents are those who didn't go to the top colleges themselves." And part of the problem originates with "the admissions office [of the boarding school] which keeps admitting kids from high-achieving families."

One college advisor said a student told him that he thought he would "make better contacts" at the major university in the state than at a nationally respected liberal arts college in a neighboring state. While the student may be right, what is notable is that a seventeen-year-old was articulating the importance of making the right contacts.

If students have not focused on where they want to go to college, the other students in a boarding school will readily offer opinions about the prestige of various colleges, and peer opinions play an important role in shaping the collective view of what is an acceptable college. This helps to explain why a student would tell his college advisor, "I'd be happy at any of the Ivy League colleges," despite the fact that the advisor knows they are such very different places.

One of the most visible indicators that prep school students share a collective identity is the similarity in their aspirations for college, despite the range of competence among them. With a third having combined SAT scores of 1,050 or below, and some with *combined* scores in the 500s (a perfect combined score is 1,600), they apply in overwhelming numbers to the most selective private colleges in the United States. They have what one college advisor in a select 16 school called, "a strong sense of entitlement about them."

While nationally 78 percent of college students attend public institutions, only 58 percent of boarding school students even apply to public institutions. Similarly, while 2 percent of the national college population attends the most highly selective colleges and universities, fully 84 percent of boarding school students apply to such colleges. Finally, while less than one percent of college students attend the Ivy League colleges, 46 percent of boarding school students apply to one or more of the eight Ivy League colleges.

A handful of colleges receive a significant share of their applications from prep school students. Five colleges received a total of 647 applications (or 13 percent of those filed), and ten schools received 1,110 applications (or 22 percent of all the applications these seniors filed). This convergence of taste suggests that certain colleges are much more likely than others to be perceived as appropriate by prep school students. Exhibit 9–1 lists the fifty colleges receiving the most applications, grouped in terms of whether they received more than 100, 51 to 99, or 26 to 50 applications from prep school students. These colleges are almost all private.

This convergence of aspirations contributes to the pressures felt by prep school students over the issue of college acceptance. They feel that their collective membership is at stake, not just their individual egos. How else can we explain the otherwise mystifying statement that students "feel like

EXHIBIT 9–1

Colleges Receiving the Most Prep Applications
(1982–83)

More than 100 Applications	26–50 Applications
*Princeton	*U. of Pennsylvania
*Brown	Skidmore College
*Harvard	Trinity College
*Yale	Wesleyan University
	St. Lawrence
	Bates College
	Wellesley
51–99 Applications	Bucknell
	Pomona College
*Dartmouth	U. of New Hampshire
Tufts	Ohio Wesleyan University
Georgetown	U. of Richmond
Duke	Holy Cross
*Cornell	Tulane
Stanford	Kenyon
U. of Michigan	Hobart & William Smith College
U. of Virginia	Dickinson College
Middlebury College	Michigan State
Williams College	Lewis and Clark College
U. of Vermont	Johns Hopkins
Amherst	U. of Rochester
U. of North Carolina (Chapel Hill)	
U. of California (Berkeley)	
Denison	
Connecticut College	
Colgate	
Vanderbilt	
Boston College	
Northwestern	
Boston University	
Colby College	
Bowdoin College	
Hamilton College	
*Columbia	

*Ivy league colleges
NOTE: Based on the college destinations of 1,035 seniors in our sample; data provided by the boarding schools. Colleges are listed within groups by the number of applications received.

failures when they get accepted at Brown, Bowdoin, or Amherst, instead of Harvard, Yale, or Princeton," as one select 16 college advisor noted. The pain of rejection is intensified by its immediate public nature in boarding school. Unlike public high-school and day school students, boarding school students must undergo acceptance or rejection in full public view at their adjacent mail boxes. There is precious little physical or psychic space in the total institution for face saving; everybody knows the score, and the body count as well.

Part of the promise of the prep rite of passage is that it will help students traverse this last trial successfully. But the potency of the prep magic has been weakened in the last few decades, leaving the schools with the problem of being less effective than in the past, although they are still more effective than most other secondary schools.

The Increasingly Competitive Admissions Environment

Historically, a small group of boarding schools, including the select 16, have had very close relationships with the Ivy League colleges, and with Harvard, Yale, and Princeton in particular. In the 1930s and 1940s, two-thirds of all graduates of twelve of the select 16 boarding schools attended Harvard, Yale, or Princeton (Karabel 1984). But by 1973, the average had noticeably slipped to 21 percent, although attendance rates between schools ranged from 51 percent to 8 percent (Cookson and Persell 1978, table 4). In the last half century, then, the proportion of select 16 school graduates who attended Harvard, Yale, or Princeton dropped from two out of three to one in five, on average.

This drop was paralleled by an increase in the level of competition for admission to Ivy League colleges. In 1940, 90 percent of all applicants to Harvard were accepted, and in the early 1950s, about half of all applicants to Ivy League colleges were accepted, according to several colleges advisors at select 16 boarding schools. In 1982 the national rate for all eight Ivy League schools was 26 percent (National College Databank 1984).

There was yet another shift in the pattern of Ivy League college admissions during this time. Before World War II, about 80 percent of the entering freshmen at Princeton, for example, came from private secondary schools (Blumberg and Paul 1975, 70). Perhaps reflecting the decline of the northeastern Protestant Establishment and the increasing power and wealth of other ethnic and geographical groups, the Ivy League colleges began to admit more public school graduates. In 1982, 34 percent of the freshman class at Harvard, 40 percent of Yale freshmen, and 40 percent of Princeton freshmen were from nonpublic high schools. While this still leaves private secondary schools disproportionately represented (less than 10 percent of all secondary school students attend private schools), it does represent a historic shift.

Federal and other forms of financial aid for needy students, and an educational inflationary trend that put emphasis on which college one attends, contributed to the increased numbers of applications to certain colleges. Thus, while the number of college-age students has declined in the past decade, the number of students applying to one group of colleges, namely Ivy League colleges, has increased in recent years (Maeroff 1984). In the spring of 1984, six of the eight Ivy League colleges set all-time records for numbers of applicants (Winerip 1984, 71).

A key reason for the large number of prep school students who apply to private rather than public colleges may be the greater flexibility in the admissions process at private colleges. Admission to state institutions is usually based on a formula which includes grades, SAT or other test scores, and rank in class. Among two-year public institutions, for example, 69 percent said they did not consider the college counselor's letter of recommendation in their admissions decision, and 30 percent of public four-year institutions said the same. Among four-year private colleges, however, 75 percent said the counselor's recommendation was either a "very important" factor or "one of several" factors considered (Fitzsimmons and Reed 1982, 7).

There is often less room at public institutions for interpretation about whether or not someone is admissable. Such flexibility, which includes giving preference to the children of alumni, may enhance the admissions chances of boarding school students at private colleges. Moreover, the flexible nature of private college admissions may leave room for personal relationships between boarding school college advisors and college admissions officers to play a role and influence the admissions decision.

How Elite Colleges Make Admissions Decisions

In the early 1920s, admission to Harvard, Yale, and Princeton was by examination. Virtually all of those who passed the exam were admitted, those who failed were not. While the exam tested mastery of a traditional curriculum, including Latin, and therefore favored graduates of private preparatory schools, increasing numbers of public schools, especially in the

Northeast, began offering such a curriculum. But in a 1926 letter sent to four thousand secondary schools, Harvard announced that it would consider "character, personality and promise as well as scholarly attainments" (Karabel 1984, 6–7). Since that time the Ivy League colleges, as well as other highly selective private colleges, have weighed both academic and personal factors in their decision to admit candidates.

Every college is not as explicit as Princeton, which says that "our current admission policy gives equal weight to the candidate's academic and nonacademic strengths,"[1] but they all consider both sets of factors. At Princeton, candidates are ranked from one to five (one being the highest) on academic and personal qualities. Harvard readers assign numerical ratings to several important elements, including academic potential, personal promise, and demonstrated character, extracurricular activities, athletics, staff-alumni interview(s), teacher recommendations, and the counselor report (Fitzsimmons and Reed 1982, 8).[2] Journalist Evan Thomas sat in on the Brown admissions committee:

> The committee passes around a thick application from "Mary." "Whoops!" says Rogers. "A 'Pinocchio'!" In Brown admissions jargon, that means her guidance counselor has checked off boxes rating her excellent for academic ability but only good or average for humor, imagination and character. On the printed recommendation form, the low checks stick out from the high ones like a long, thin nose. "A rating of average usually means the guidance counselor thinks there is something seriously wrong." explains Admissions Officer Paulo de Oliveira. Mary's interview with a Brown alumnus was also lukewarm, and worse, she has written a "jock essay," i.e., a very short one. Rogers scrawls a Z, the code for rejection, on her folder. (Thomas 1979, 73)

Personal qualities are "a function of *both* the level of achievement and the evaluations of an applicant's contributions that are received from counselors, teachers, and Alumni Schools Committee volunteers" (Wickenden 1979). Not only do applicants need to have a variety of interesting activities, but their schools need to describe their applicants in convincing detail to the colleges and demonstrate their support for the candidate. Thus, a student's personal and social qualities are filtered through the statements of college counselors. In the words of Harvard's director of admissions:

1. Letter to all Princeton alumni from James W. Wickenden, Jr., '61, Director of Admissions, October 1979.
2. Brown uses a 1–6 rating for personal qualities and academic promise (Thomas 1979, 73), and Dartmouth uses a scale of 1–9 for academic and personal attributes, with 18 being a perfect rating (National Public Radio 1981, 9).

The more explicit and descriptive the report, the easier it is for the reader to judge its intent at any level. But the amount and quality of anecdotal detail and supporting evidence in a positive report is ordinarily taken as a measure of its strength: evidence that the writer is "going to the wall" for the candidate. (Fitzsimmons and Reed 1982, 8)

Obviously such a process favors candidates whose schools write detailed recommendations, such as the one to Dartmouth which said:

In English, he has a sensitive understanding for poetry and a superb vocabulary. In math, there is precious little room for further improvement. His history teacher last year reported that F's writing is a skillful mix of analysis, interpretation, and factual support, while he was described simply as "the best student in the class" in chemistry.

Deeply committed to learning, F will make his mark as a scholar. His talents in a variety of academic areas are truly remarkable. He has earned a very strong college recommendation. (National Public Radio, 20 April 1981, 10)

Being a legacy—having one or more parents or other relatives who attended the college to which one applies—is a decided bonus for admission. Seventeen percent of the Princeton class of 1983 were alumni children. The applications from all Princeton children are personally reviewed by the director of admissions, as well as by one of six regional admissions directors. Thus, they are considered more thoroughly than other candidates, and are more likely to be accepted. Several college advisors said that legacies were two to two-and-one-half times as likely to be admitted to Ivy League colleges as nonlegacies.

The legacy advantage seems to increase substantially in the middle ground, where most applicants fall.

In a process where very fine lines must be drawn, the advantage Princeton children receive can perhaps be best appreciated when one analyzes the admission ratios of candidates with certain ratings. For instance, of all candidates with 3/2 ratings, only 21 percent were admitted. However, 100 percent of the Princeton children with this combination of ratings gained admission. Similarly, 29 percent of all candidates with 2/3 ratings were admitted, as compared to 89 percent of all Princeton children in this category. Finally, only 6.7 percent of all applicants with 3/3 ratings were offered admission, as compared to 28.8 percent of the alumni children. (Wickenden 1979, 3)

At Yale during the 1960s about one-quarter of the entering class were legacies, a figure that dropped to 13 percent in the 1970s, but returned to between 20 and 24 percent in 1984 (Winerip 1984, 173). Similarly, at Brown:

> "Peter" is a "double leg"—both his mother and father went to Brown. He is unexciting but unobjectionable, and his grades and scores are good. "We're trapped," sighs a committee member. There is laughter around the table, but no one doubts that keeping the alumni happy is worth it. (Thomas 1979, 73)

Parents who had the opportunity and money to attend an elite college are able to increase their child's chances for admission to that college. Strong athletes also possess desired personal qualities that increase their chances for admission. Ivy League coaches may obtain information on a candidate's athletic prowess by observing players when they have scrimmages with certain prep schools. A number of colleges make depth charts, "listing athletes by sport, the position they play and ranking by Brown coaches, usually on a scale of 1 to 6" (Thomas, 1979, 73).

Students lacking athletic ability may stand out because they are "B for B," meaning "Burning for Brown." One way a school raises its "yield" figures is by accepting students who will definitely enroll. In 1982, Harvard's yield was 70 percent, Yale's was 60 percent, and Princeton's was 55 percent (National College Databank 1984). Brown's was 51 percent that year, so reliable evidence that a student really wants to attend a college may tip the balance in a candidate's favor. Prep school college advisors can generally provide reliable information on this subject to college admissions officers.

Personal sparks of other kinds are sought in applicants. Harvard says it reads folders looking for:

> The relative personal promise of the candidate. "Personality," "character," "pizzazz," "inner strength," are all phrases to describe this variable. Pulling together the impressions conveyed by the reports in the folder, only sometimes with direct personal contact, the admissions officer tries to assess whether a candidate who has been personally outstanding in the high school context will continue to be so in college and beyond. (Fitzsimmons and Reed 1982, 8)

Comments by schools or counselors may help to highlight a candidate's "pizzazz." Interviews are another avenue through which candidates may impress college admissions officers. Out of 11,122 applicants for the Princeton class of 1983,

> 3,500 candidates were interviewed here at Princeton and 6,000 candidates were interviewed by Alumni Schools Committee volunteers. For the past few years, we have not been able to accommodate all those who requested an on-campus interview. (Wickenden 1979, 2)

Who gets interviews? Historically the selective colleges and Ivy League colleges in particular have found prep schools good hunting grounds for students. Select 16 schools in particular attract droves of recruiters each year. Some Ivy League colleges will send recruiters directly to the campus twice a year. Selective college recruiters are far less likely to visit public high schools in a systematic way, and many public high-school students have to settle for a "college night" when colleges retail themselves as a group (Cookson 1981). Compared to their prep school peers, many public high-school students must do their college shopping in a supermarket atmosphere, whereas prep school students are often treated as preferred specialty shop customers.

Even the academic ratings of candidates benefit from prep school attendance. Princeton states that it considers "Grades, test results, rank-in-class, teachers' recommendations, and quality of the secondary school program" in its academic rating of a candidate. To be rated a "1," an applicant must have excellent grades and high class standing in a difficult program and score above 725 on each SAT exam (Wickenden 1979, 1).

In addition to grades and test scores, Harvard considers "projects or activities of an academic nature beyond formal course requirements, special academic recognition, the quality of the application essay, and any other evidence that might be available" (Fitzsimmons and Reed 1982, 8). Dartmouth asks applicants to "describe in writing their primary interests, their goals, the books that have most influenced their lives, and the famous persons under whom they would choose to serve as an apprentice" (National Public Radio 1981, 9). Prep schools that offer a demanding curriculum with many chances for independent projects and writing assignments are providing students with opportunities to shine in this dimension.

Professionalism and Private Politics

The college advisors at most elite boarding schools are well attuned to the world of private college admissions. They organize the process so as to smooth as many kinks as possible out of it and to present their students in the most favorable light. They have responded to the increasingly competitive college admissions scene with two major strategies—professionalizing their operation and using their political networks.

The resources most leading boarding schools devote to college advisement are considerable, and they enable advisors to manage the process in a competent and effective manner. Advisors at most of the leading schools are savvy and highly organized. Most do not teach because of their travel schedules, frequent visits by college admissions officers, and numerous phone calls. Especially at the select 16 schools, they have been doing the job for a number of years, and learned the ropes by assisting an experienced college advisor for several years. Many have visited sixty, seventy, or more colleges.

Each advisor is responsible for from 65 to 140 students, a contrast to many public high schools in which college advisors may have as many as 400 to 500 students in their care, although the average is 323 (Coleman, Hoffer, and Kilgore 1982, 179). Most boarding schools have substantial clerical and, increasingly, computerized support services. All college advisors seem to have unlimited long-distance telephone access. With fewer facilities, big public high schools often limit students to a fixed number of college aplications, say six or seven. Boarding school students may file as many as fifteen or twenty applications, although the average number is 4.8.

The contrast between the professional operations of the elite schools which are socializing their students for power and the more relaxed attitude of, for example, a progressive school is dramatic. For example, in one of the latter schools, the college advisor was new, and had not visited any colleges, and had himself attended a minor state college. His office was located in a remote building a good distance from the center of campus. The office was a single room, with one counselor, a secretary who came in two half days per week, a typewriter that was shared with several other departments, and a filing system that reposed in a single desk drawer.

The difference in the focus of the college advisory program in a girls school was also apparent. The advisor said, "There is almost more anxiety about the process of applying to college than the result." At a boys or coed school, no one would suggest that there was no anxiety about the result.

The highly professional operations of the prep schools engaged in socializing their students for power is evident in three activities: the organization of the timetable, written materials, and letters of recommendation. College advisors at these schools have rationalized the admissions process through time and can readily rattle off the timetable of events in the process. A typical timetable is presented in exhibit 9–2. It is designed to assuage the worries of students and parents about the process. Don't worry, the message is, everything is under control; there is a time and a place for all the necessary steps, and we will guide you through the process.

Many college advisors prepare voluminous materials to help students and their families through the process. Many have questionnaires for students and parents to obtain information about what they want in a

EXHIBIT 9–2

Advisors' College Preparation Timetable for Prep School Students

Ninth Grade	Students choose the right curriculum. Build reading and vocabulary skills.
Tenth Grade	Students take PSAT (a two-hour version of the SAT) for practice. Talk with students after the test results are in. Speak to students and parents about the college application process. Encourage the development of good homework and study habits, reminding them that sophomore year counts equally.
Eleventh Grade	Schedule panel on colleges for parents and students. Students take PSAT. Encourage students to keep studying. January, take SAT. Start building a preliminary list of colleges, including some that are not certain, some with about a fifty/fifty chance for admission, and some with more than a 75% chance for admission. Give copies of this list to student, mail one to parents, keep one for school file. Encourage student to read college catalogues and decide which colleges they want to visit that summer.
Twelfth Grade	Meet individually again with each senior once or twice before Christmas. Perhaps schedule a college night with parents or have a college day during Parents' Weekend in the fall. Early admissions decision applications are due in November, National Merit Scholarship Applications are due, collect faculty comments on students for that term. Regular applications need to be in by January, including school letters of recommendation.
Between April 15 and May 1	After acceptances, students decide which colleges they will attend.

college; particular colleges they are considering; where relatives attended college (to know what legacy factors they have); whether or not they need financial aid; and what summer work, travel, volunteer, athletic, student government, club, publications, or debate activities they have been involved in. Other questionnaires ask what books they have read in the last six months, what musical, artistic, or theatrical involvement they have had, and ask about independent study and research. Often advisors ask students to prepare a written autobiography or self-evaluation. They might ask students to say how they are unique, what they do best, or how particular experiences have affected them.

Some advisors at elite schools prepare guidebooks for students to help them make their college selections. Aside from providing the timetable for tests, early admissions, application deadlines, and so forth, they may suggest factors to consider about colleges—such as their size, location, program, quality of undergraduate life, facilities, instruction, or financial factors. The guidebook will explain how to arrange visits and interviews, what might be asked in an interview and ways to respond, how to dress, how to prepare questions to ask the interviewer, and how to complete an application, including checking the spelling. The guidebook is an effective way of sharing the advisor's experience and wisdom.

College advisors also use their knowledge when writing letters of recommendation. All secondary schools are asked to write letters of recommendation for their applicants, but differences exist in the effort and backup support that various schools are able to provide. Given the small number of students boarding school advisors have to supervise, they are able to write a well-reasoned letter for each student.

At one boarding school, where about half the graduating class goes to Harvard, Yale, or Princeton, the advisor interviews the entire faculty on each member of the senior class. He tapes all their comments and has them transcribed. This produces a "huge confidential dossier which gives a very good sense of where each student is." In addition, housemasters and coaches write reports. Then the advisor interviews each senior. After each interview, he makes verbal notes on a dictaphone. After assimilating all these impressions of each student, the college advisor writes his letter of recommendation, which he is able to pack with corroborative details illustrating a candidate's strengths. The thoroughness, thought, and care that goes into this process insures that anything and everything positive that could be said about a student is included, thereby maximizing his or her chances for a favorable reception.

Some advisors include their assessment of the difficulty of the academic course load a student is taking in their letters of recommendation. Where possible, they may try to compare the applicant with others from the school who have attended the college and been successful there.[3]

We saw some of the letters of recommendation, without the students' names on them. They were beautifully crafted, one-page presentations. One advisor said his goal in the letter was "to present the student as accurately and fully as possible to the college." He was relatively new to the job and wanted to be seen as "trustworthy and holding nothing back," to establish credibility for future dealings with the colleges. College admissions officers had told him that "the quotes from the teachers are the things they respected most" in his letters.

The importance of well-designed letters of recommendation is under-

---

3. This assumes they know how their graduates do once they get to college. The Ivy League colleges used to send transcripts back to the prep schools so they could see how they did, but recent concerns about privacy have stopped that practice. Several college advisors said they had sent a questionnaire to their graduates, or would like to do one, to see how they were faring. In general, this is an area where many feel they could do more than they are doing.

scored by James W. Wickenden, Jr., director of admissions at Princeton University, in his letter to Princeton alumni:

> In evaluating each applicant the admission staff also takes into account the supporting documents from college counselors and teachers. These materials can vary greatly in quality: while most are good, and some exceptional, about 25 percent do little to help the applicants. For example, the entire secondary school report on one applicant was: "Real fine candidate." Another teacher prepared the same report for *all* applicants, made a xerox copy of the report with blank spaces left for the names of students who might ask for recommendations, and simply filled in the blanks before sending these statements off to the various colleges. Obviously, candidates with this type of counseling and support are at a real disadvantage in the admission race. (Wickenden 1979, 1)

Such a policy indeed favors schools with the resources and personnel to write good letters.

The help the elite prep schools give their students extends beyond the curriculum and teaching they offer and the highly professional formal procedures they follow in getting them into college. Their help reaches into the informal, interpersonal world of "horsetrading" that exists in friendly phone calls, beers, and dinner with college admissions officers.

The close social relationships between college advisors, especially those in select 16 schools, and admissions officers, particularly those in Ivy League colleges, rest on social similarities, frequent contact over an extended time, a sense of trust, shared information, and mutual cooperation. The existence and operation of these ties may well improve a boarding school student's chances for admission to a highly desired college. College advisors at select 16 prep schools are much more likely to be Harvard, Yale, or Princeton graduates than other schools' advisors. Among the eleven select 16 school college advisors on whom data were available, ten were Harvard, Yale, or Princeton graduates, while among the twenty-three other schools' advisors on whom data were available, only three were Ivy League graduates, and none were from Harvard, Yale, or Princeton, suggesting that the select 16 prep schools consider such a connection to be important.

The close personal relationships between select 16 college advisors and college admissions officers have been built up over a considerable number of years. College advisors at select 16 schools tend to have longer tenures (ten, fifteen, or even more years is not unusual) than college advisors at other schools (who are more likely to have recently assumed the job). Given the "importance of continuity on both sides of the relationship" that was stressed by an advisor at one select 16 school, the greater continuity at select 16 schools is one of several factors in their favor.

Often prep school college advisors are invited to sit in on admissions committee decisions, to see how a college puts its class together. By doing this, they can see the makeup of the applicant pool. Such information helps them to see the competition their students face and may suggest strategies they can use in putting their candidates forward. They learn other useful information from personal contacts as well, such as which colleges are having an "admissions pinch," and hence might be receptive to somewhat weaker candidates, and that it is important for a student who has taken a year off between high school and college to document what was done during that year.

One advisor knew of a student who had enhanced his chances for admission to an elite college by writing a journal of a trip to Mozambique. Another knew that a borderline student could try for admission in February rather than September at an elite college, and might have a better chance then. This kind of inside lore about the admissions process helps boarding school college advisors sell their students more effectively than advisors without such knowledge can.

The close relationship between elite schools and colleges is reflected in another indicator. At least one Ivy League college (Harvard) puts the applications from certain boarding schools into different colored folders (Karen 1985). Hence, the admissions committee knows immediately which applicants are from certain boarding schools. Moreover, sociologist David Karen found that being from one of those select boarding schools was positively related to admission to Harvard, even when academic and personal factors were comparable.

College advisors cooperate with the colleges in several ways. They try to screen out hopeless prospects, or as one advisor tactfully put it, "I try to discourage unproductive leads." They also "try to shape up different applicant pools for different colleges." They push students to choose which of the Ivy League colleges they want, rather than applying to all of them. A student's first choice is information they often use in their bartering sessions with colleges to clinch the promise of an acceptance. In these ways, college advisors anticipate the colleges' reactions and do some of the pre-screening of applicants for them.

In addition to cooperating with the colleges, a group of select 16 school college advisors cooperate among themselves, sharing information and developing common strategies for dealing with colleges. They meet together regularly and share college admissions statistics within their group.

This organization began as an informal group of friends that played poker together. As they were comparing statistics and discussing common problems, they agreed that the practice of class ranking hurt their students, since most of them were in the top quarter of their class before coming to boarding school, but invariably half of the students ended up in the bottom half of their prep school class.[4]

Colleges had indicated to them that "it didn't look good on their profiles to have students who ranked low in their class." The group of select 16 school advisors agreed to stop providing an absolute class rank to colleges, but instead to indicate the decile or quintile rank of each student. Colleges can put such students in a "not ranked" category or can report the decile or quintile rank. No entering student from such a secondary school is labeled as the bottom person in the class. No other eight schools in the country would have had the political clout to modify admissions rules like this.

College advisors, especially those at the select 16 schools, use their close personal relationships with college admissions officers to lobby for their students. "We want to be sure they are reading the applications of our students fairly, and we lobby for our students," said one select 16 school college advisor. "The colleges make their best decisions on our students and those from [another select 16 school], because they have the most information on these students." "When I drive to the [Ivy League] colleges, I give them a reading on our applicants. I let them know if I think they are making a mistake." Another select 16 school college advisor reported, "I try to make the case for a particular student if I think the college is making a mistake." Another said, "I don't very often tell a college they are making a mistake, but when I do, that case is often reconsidered."

Select 16 school advisors do not stop with simply asking elite college admissions officers to reconsider a decision, however. They try to barter, and the colleges leave this possibility open when they say, "Let's talk about your group." One select 16 school college advisor stresses that if his school recommends someone and he or she is accepted, that student will come. While not all colleges heed this warranty, some do and it may help the process.

Another select 16 school advisor said, "It is getting harder than it used to be to say to an admissions officer, 'take a chance on this one,' especially at Harvard which now has so many more applications." But it is significant that he did not say that it was impossible to make such a statement. If all

4. Seniors at some of the elite schools suggested their awareness of this situation when they said, in effect, "If only I'd stayed home in my public school, I would have gotten into Harvard easily."

else fails in a negotiation, a select 16 advisor said, "We lobby for the college to make him your absolute first choice on the waiting list." Such a compromise represents a chance for both parties to save face.

Most public high-school counselors do not know elite college admissions officers, nor do they have the resources to call them up or drive over to talk with them. One counselor from the Midwest, however, did come to an eastern Ivy League college to sit in on the admissions committee decision for his truly outstanding candidate—SATs in the 700s, top in his class, class president, star athlete, and nevertheless a friendly, modest person. An advisor from an elite eastern prep school was also there, lobbying on behalf of his candidate—a nice, undistinguished fellow with SATs in the 600s, middle of his class, average athlete, and no strong signs of leadership. After hearing both the counselors, the Ivy League college chose the latter candidate. The public school counselor walked out in disgust. Afterwards, the Ivy League admissions officer said to the prep school advisor, "We may not be able to have these open meetings anymore." Even in the unusual case where a public school counselor did everything that a select 16 boarding school college advisor did, it was not enough to help the applicant to gain admittance. Despite today's competitive admissions environment, the elite prep school advisors are still listened to more closely by college admissions officers than public school counselors, suggesting that the prep school advisor is known to consistently offer the colleges a steady supply of socially elite and academically prepared students.

"You have to go to one of those prep schools. . . ."

The collegiate destinations of prep school students are very different from those of high-school students in the United States. Nationally, only seven out of ten eighteen-year-olds graduate from high school (Plisko 1984, 13). Of those seven, less than three have taken a strong academic curriculum (Fiske 1983, C8) and are prepared for four-year liberal arts colleges in the country. So by the time they reach the starting block for college, three-quarters of American young people are already considerably behind prep school students.

Even among American young people who go to college, vast differences exist; 78 percent go to public institutions and 38 percent attend two-year colleges or universities (U.S. Bureau of the Census 1984, 161). Nationally, only 2 percent of all college students attend the most highly selective colleges in the United States (that is, those whose entering freshmen have an average combined verbal and mathematics SAT score of 1,175 or better, as determined by Astin, King, and Richardson 1981), and much less than one percent nationally attend one of the eight eastern Ivy League colleges.

Almost all boarding school students attend four-year colleges immediately after graduation. Three-quarters of them attend private colleges or universities, half attend the most highly selective colleges in the United States, and one in five attends an Ivy League college. The colleges they attend are heavily concentrated on the East Coast and in California.[5]

Prep school students are also likely to attend colleges that have large numbers of their graduates from the upper class or who have otherwise achieved high status. A college's social prestige and social achievement were measured by Gene R. Hawes in his *Comprehensive Guide to Colleges* (1978); the more graduates a college has listed in the *Social Register,* the higher its social prestige, and the more graduates it has listed in *Who's Who,* the higher its social achievement. Thirty-seven percent of the seniors in our sample were bound for colleges in the top two social prestige categories established by Hawes, and 59 percent of the seniors were bound for colleges in the top two categories for social achievement.

Public high-school students do not fare so well, even when they have similar aspirations. An article in the *New York Times* captured the poignant case of a very strong public school applicant (eleventh in his class, 790/800 on his SATs) who was rejected by Harvard. After hearing the news his father said, "To get into Harvard . . . you have to go to one of those prep schools" (Winerip, 20 April, 1984, B4).

The father's perceptions are not completely off the mark. When four sets of application pools to Ivy League colleges are compared (see table 9–1), the acceptance rate is highest for select 16 boarding school applicants, followed by other leading boarding school applicants, then by students who graduate from an academically selective public high school,[6] and finally by the entire national application pool.

Is this higher rate of acceptance due to the superior academic credentials or the higher social family backgrounds of prep school students compared to public school students? Cookson (1981) addressed this question when he compared the college destinations of prep school students with those

5. The top six states, in order, where more than 50 preps attended college are: Massachusetts (129), New York (127), California (93), North Carolina (61), Connecticut (58), and Pennsylvania (55).
6. To be admitted to this particular science high school, which is in large northeastern city, students must be recommended by their junior high school and score high on math and verbal admissions tests.

TABLE 9–1

Acceptance Rates of Ivy League Colleges from Four Application Pools

College	Select 16 Boarding Schools (1982–83)[a]	Other Leading Boarding Schools (1982–83)[a]	Selective Public High School (1984)[b]	National Group of Applicants (1982)[c]
Brown University				
% accepted	35	20	28	22
Number of applications	95	45	114	11,854
Columbia University				
% accepted	66	29	32	41
Number of applications	35	7	170	3,650
Cornell University				
% accepted	57	36	55	31
Number of applications	65	25	112	17,927
Dartmouth				
% accepted	41	21	41	22
Number of applications	79	33	37	8,313
Harvard University				
% accepted	38	28	20	17
Number of applications	104	29	127	13,341
Princeton University				
% accepted	40	28	18	18
Number of applications	103	40	109	11,804
University of Pennsylvania				
% accepted	45	32	33	36
Number of applications	40	19	167	11,000
Yale University				
% accepted	40	32	15	20
Number of applications	92	25	124	11,023
Overall % accepted	42	27	30	26
Total Number of applications	613	223	960	88,912

[a]These 836 applications from prep school seniors were made by the 1,035 seniors in our sample who applied to one or more Ivy League colleges.
[b]Based on data supplied by college advisor at the school.
[c]Figures available as of November 1984, *National College Databank*.

of suburban high-school students. He found that public school students who were similar to prep school students in terms of their SAT scores and family backgrounds were accepted at less selective colleges and generally planned to attend less prestigious colleges than their prep school peers. He also found that in the transition from secondary school to college, public schools had much less organizational clout than did prep schools. This was indicated by the fact that the personal qualities (for example, SAT scores and family backgrounds) of public school students play a larger role in where they go to college than do the personal qualities of prep school students, who apparently benefit from the reputations of their schools when college admissions officers select freshmen. In effect, prep schools themselves are able to place "floors" under their less able students and thus insure that in the transition from school to college there are fewer casualties.

We explored this issue further by comparing students from select 16 and other leading prep schools, while holding their SAT scores constant. In table 9–2, SAT scores are related to being accepted at both Ivy League and other very highly selective colleges, for both select 16 and other boarding school students who applied to those colleges. Select 16 school students, however, are more likely to be accepted than students from other leading boarding schools with similar scores, for every category of scores except one (low SATs at Ivy League colleges). This exception may be due to the large numbers of high-scoring select 16 school students who apply to Ivy League colleges. But in general, select 16 school students do very well in their quest for admission to elite colleges. Among those with high SATs (1,220–1,580 combined verbal and math scores), 90 percent of those who applied to the most highly selective colleges were accepted, and 66 percent of those who applied to Ivy League colleges were accepted.

The vital link between prep schools and elite colleges results in one of three discernible outcomes for students. Some, specifically those with good academic credentials and SAT scores, appear to be "turbocharged" by the prep rite of passage, especially if it occurs in a select 16 school. These students are easy for college advisors to place because the colleges are delighted to admit highly qualified students who have flourished in a prep school. They are strong students who would, undoubtedly, have gone to elite colleges in good numbers anyway, but attending a select 16 prep school magnifies their chance for success.

A second group of students benefit from what might be called the "knighting effect" of attending an elite prep school. As table 9–3 indicates, 89 percent of students who scored between 1,220 and 1,580 on their SAT exams, and who came from families in the bottom third of the socioeconomic status range in our sample, were accepted by a highly selective college. For the academically talented but less affluent student, prep schools provide a route for upward mobility. A similar trend is evident for minorities and girls. Ralph Turner's belief (1966) that private schools offer no special mobility opportunities to students is not supported by these findings. In fact, for a few outstanding individuals, attending a prep school may be a critical first step in upward mobility. These findings give credence

TABLE 9–2

Acceptances at Ivy League and Highly Selective* Colleges by Boarding School Status and SAT Scores

	High SATs (1,220–1,580)		Medium SATs (1,060–1,216)		Low SATs (540–1,050)	
	Select 16 Schools	Other Leading Prep Schools	Select 16 Schools	Other Leading Prep Schools	Select 16 Schools	Other Leading Prep Schools
Accepted at Ivy League College (%)	66	45	39	27	19	27
Number of students applying (Total: 471)	(217)	(64)	(99)	(37)	(31)	(26)
Accepted at most highly selective colleges (%)	90	71	81	70	57	39
Number of students applying (Total: 870)	(265)	(86)	(190)	(114)	(85)	(130)

*Highly selective colleges are classified in Alexander W. Astin, Margo R. King, and Gerald T. Richardson, *The American Freshman: National Norms for Fall 1981* (Los Angeles: University of California, Laboratory for Research in Higher Education, 1981).
NOTE: Based on our sample of 1,035 prep school seniors.

to Digby Baltzell's claim (1964) that prep schools integrate new brains with old wealth to revitalize the upper classes.

Table 9–3 also indicates that a high percentage of those with weak SATs (540 to 1,050 combined scores), do manage to gain admission to the highly selective colleges. Fifty-nine percent of the high socioeconomic status–low SATs group gain acceptance to a selective college, an indicator that the schools not only serve mobility functions, but maintenance functions as well. These are the students who have had floors placed under them by attending prep school.

TABLE 9-3

Acceptances at Most Highly Selective Colleges by Socioeconomic Status and SAT Scores

Socioeconomic Status	SATs (Combined Scores)		
	1,220–1,580	1,060–1,216	540–1,050
Top Third (%)	83	74	57
N	(126)	(109)	(64)
Middle Third (%)	85	81	38
N	(128)	(112)	(69)
Bottom Third (%)	89	75	42
N	(97)	(83)	(82)

When we view the college admissions process in general, it becomes clear that prep schools, especially the select 16 schools, offer strong and relatively weak students alike a tremendous boost in gaining acceptance to the colleges of their choice. For girls, minorities, and students from modest family backgrounds, the schools provide educational mobility, and for upper- and upper-middle-class students with good academic records, the schools help with their connections to prestigious colleges.

The organizational support that the schools offer to students is matched by few, if any, public schools, or, for that matter, matched by few private day schools. From the moment prep school students enter their schools, they know they are expected to enter a selective college, and they have been given the tools to gain acceptance. They also know that the college admissions environment is highly competitive. To fail to go to a selective college is considered by most prep school students a serious detour on the road to social and economic success. Where you go to college defines in good measure who you are, and the days when preps could automatically expect to go to an Ivy League or other highly selective college are over. They have to earn their way—or at least part of their way. Prep schools open doors for students, but then they must know how to walk through the doors themselves. Yet compared to their public school peers, prep school students start the race for college with substantial advantages. The safety net of organizational support is wide and strong, and should a student fall from academic grace there is somebody to help them get up.

In a college admissions system that stresses merit, the advantages prep school students enjoy raise some complex and disturbing issues. How fair is it to public school students to allow prep school students to be consistently given the competitive edge so that they win a disproportionately high number of coveted acceptances? What is really being rewarded when students are accepted at the best private colleges—personal achievement or institutional affiliation? For the prep school student, the first major dividend that he or she collects from surviving the prep rite of passage is acceptance to a suitable college, and the feeling that the acceptance is a deserved one.

10

Preps at Play and in the Power Structure

IF the sociologist Randall Collins is correct in his assertion that class position is best defined by shared behaviors and "repetitive encounters" (1975, 53), then prep school graduates may not all be upper class, but they are in a class by themselves. For public high-school or even private day school graduates the amount of time prep school graduates devote to "staying in touch"—swapping life histories, attending alumni parties and gatherings, and writing checks for their school would seem extraordinary. Loyalty, most heads and development officers believe, is most clearly expressed in contributions, and while hard work and moral support are appreciated, the bottom line is the large contributions that are expected of former students.

In a real sense prep school graduates own their schools. It is not unusual, for example, for the alumni and wealthy friends of an elite school to give annual gifts in excess of $1 million (Cookson 1982). Schools keep close tabs on who's giving what and name names in their financial reports. Classes compete as to how much they give and what percentage of the graduates contributed. Endowments can be impressive; as of 1982, Andover's endowment was over $82 million, St. Paul's was over $61 million, and Hotchkiss's over $30 million. The endowment per student at St. Paul's in 1981 was over $123,000; Milton Academy seems relatively poor with "only" $20,000 per student.

Most schools have a development office, which at the more successful schools is a busy place. Trustees, development officers, alumni, and "giving" chairpersons can be extremely inventive in devising strategies to encourage alumni and friends to part with their money. They put together any number of financial packages, including life income trusts, insurance policies, and other bequests. Elite boarding schools invest heavily and their cash reserves attract brokers and other money market managers. Exeter's Third Century Fund was worth $20,453,000 as of September 1981. The girls school Santa Catalina, which has a relatively small endowment and no wealthy male alumni to tap, still managed to raise over $300,000 in 1981–82.

The collective portfolio of America's most elite prep schools is impressive, but then they got a good start. Morgan money helped to finance Groton, Taft was founded by Horace D. Taft, brother of President Taft, Hotchkiss was founded by Maria Hotchkiss, whose deceased husband perfected the machine gun, and St. George's School was helped by John Nicholas Brown, the Rhode Island industrialist whose family helped establish Brown University. Choate can count Mellons as benefactors, and a Lowell and a Forbes funded Middlesex School in Massachusetts. The Kent School was given an early boost by several DuPonts.

High society may seem something of an anachronism to some people. To those, however, who have a large psychic and business investment in their social pedigree, bloodlines are no laughing matter. After all, upper-class marriages are often as much about business as love. When two upper-class families merge there can be a considerable amount of money involved. Thus it is the hope of patricians and some parvenus who send their children to elite prep schools that they will begin to meet suitable partners. Many dances, balls, cotillions, trips, and charity activities are expressly designed for the purpose of bringing together upper-class boys and girls. Sociologists Paul Blumberg and P.W. Paul (1975) found that in the period between 1962–72, 70 percent of the grooms whose wedding announcements appeared in the *New York Times* were from private schools. Of those grooms that were listed in the Social Register, 20 percent were from St. Paul's alone; 8 percent were from Exeter, and 6 percent were old Grotonians. A private school, and particularly a prep school, education appear to be still important in establishing social pedigrees.

Boarding schools are only part of the upper-class enclosure movement. A survey of, for instance, the home addresses of students and alumni makes it clear that one of the benefits of having the right family and the right education is the right address. In some exclusive neighborhoods in New York, Boston, and Washington, preps could be said to have achieved a critical mass, insulating themselves against outsiders through high prices and high taxes. Preps are particularly fond of Connecticut suburban areas such as Darien, Greenwich, and New Canaan. In fact, Connecticut is probably *the* prep state.

From alumni interviews it is apparent that what prep school students expect in terms of work, marriage, and leisure they find in the affluent suburbs where life revolves around marriage, work, the kids, and the club. Sports are still an important part of life; tennis, squash, and golf, in particular, continue to be prep sports. As a former head of Exeter said, "Most of us are upper- or upper-middle class, country-club-coming-out-party, stockbroker-Tudor-French-Provincial-suburban."

Prep school graduates can also be found in other areas such as Grosse Pointe, Michigan, and Middleburg, Virginia, and some have migrated westward to California, although alumni directories show that most live on the East Coast, especially in New England and New York City. Many preps have more than one home and it is not unusual for preps to belong to a private development, often situated around a cove or a lake. Their communities are hard to find and almost impossible to be admitted to without the proper credentials. Discretion is key; there are no advertisements, no road signs, and often no mailboxes. If you have to ask, you don't belong.

Preps often name their houses; Treetops is still popular, as is The Chimneys, Green Trees, and The Old Farm. Gentlemanly and gentlewomanly farming is popular, and alumni bulletins are peppered with news flashes about how so-and-so is raising organic vegetables or runs a model dairy farm. Many preps also own houses in Europe and the Caribbean, making some of them part of a truly international class. Not all preps, of course, have the money or the inclination to live the affluent life. Progressive school graduates, in particular, are likely to live in Greenwich Village or the Upper West Side in Manhattan. A few preps go Hollywood and a handful live truly rural lives, but in the main, prep school graduates are suburban and urban creatures.

The Tie That Binds or the Noose That Strangles?

Part of the pleasure and the pain of going to a prep school is that one joins a club, from which escape is difficult. Each graduating class has a class agent or correspondent who tries to keep track of who's where, who's with whom, who got what job, and who's who. Graduates often write to the correspondents to tell of marriages, job changes, the arrival of new children, and to shoot the breeze. Often alumni will include an address where they can be reached and invitations are extended to all classmates to "drop by" or "spend an evening." A number of alumni said that one of the good things about being a graduate is that they had friends in every major American city as well as some overseas. The tone of most alumni bulletins is friendly, as though the good old days had never really ended. Most graduates tend to correspond with their schools during big reunion years such as the fifth, tenth, and twenty-fifth reunions.

Alumni gatherings and reunions can be extravagant affairs where old boys and old girls can rekindle past glory and bask in reflected prominence. These are times for hijinks, a good deal of drinking, and nostalgia. Often there is a dance in memorial to dances past, sometimes called the Senior Sock-hop. Heads almost always attend the class dinner to congratulate the graduates on their excellence and plead for more contributions. To some extent, reunion fun is a natural extension of the dorm fun which the alumni shared; the secret drinking parties of the past are carried on into the present, although no longer in secret. It is not just by chance that it was a prep school graduate who wrote *The Silver Bullet: The Martini in American Civilization.*

Some graduates serve the school's regional associations where they act as recruiters and talent scouts for the school. Regional and local associations also host the head when he or she passes through on a fund-raising drive. Often these regional associations will organize "phonothons" and try to reach the entire bevy of graduates. Private, small reunions are also arranged at graduates' clubs or at exclusive hotels, and, of course, individual friendships can last a lifetime. Wealthy or otherwise outstanding alumni are often asked to serve on special committees, some receive awards, and a few become trustees.

Errant or missing members are often tracked down and most alu[mni] bulletins will include a list of those for whom the school has no ad[dress]. Alumni magazines cover obituaries as well as marriages and birth[s]. is no part of an individual's life that is not grist for the alumni recent graduates, relieved perhaps to have escaped from the total institution, are less likely to be intensely interested in their old school than their new life. As they develop and acquire good jobs and families, they become somewhat more receptive to requests for gifts and begin to attend alumni functions. As they grow into middle age, a good number of them become strong school supporters and some of them are, by then, placed well enough in the power structure to do the school a few favors. Loyalty indeed seems to increase with age, and almost no alumni magazine will be without a picture of the oldest alumni back to celebrate their reunions. The positive relationship between increasing age and increasing loyalty is intriguing because one might expect the total institution's greatest effect to be on recent inmates rather than those who have been in "civilian" life longer.

Many graduates may begin to think more about their prep school when they have children of their own. Time may have mellowed graduates' memories concerning some of the more difficult aspects of living in a total institution, and legacy children get special attention in the admissions process. Children of graduates who have financially and otherwise contributed to the school have an inside track in the admissions process.

At a deeper level, boarding school graduates may look back on their cloistered adolescence as a golden period in their lives. The idyllic settings of the schools can easily provoke a sentimental attitude where the battered ego can find safety. For some alumni their attachment to their school may be regressive; there is something sad about graduates who return to all the alumni functions seeking a camaraderie that they can find nowhere else, and may never have really existed at the school either. Much like the military veteran, whose war experiences take on a romantic hue as the years pass, the actual hardships and deprivations of living in the total institution may seem unimportant or even laudable to the prep school graduate. Adults as well as adolescents ask "Who am I?" and it may be that for the prep school graduate a positive part of "Who am I?" is that "I went to a great prep school."

Not all boarding school graduates look back fondly; in fact, many look ⌐nger, holding their schools in contempt. One well-known actor, ⌐ prep school at a young age, described his former school has left him with many bitter memories. He described e total institution as "awful" and the life of a student ing." In general, individualistic and creative gradu- mories about the time they spent in prep school, hool graduates are often exceptions to this general ecause progressive school students are required to give up less of their identity because they are not being socialized for power.

Thus there is a variety of alumni response to the prep rite of passage, ranging from the totally loyal "superschoolies" to the disloyal rebels. Most graduates fall in between. For them, their schools are useful tools with which to pick their way through the world. But because the schools are not their only tools, their attitude resembles the kind of loyalty one feels toward members of an extended family, a devotion that is real but nonetheless should not be tested too often.

Graduates seem to cluster in five types. The most loyal group are the superschoolies, who often become annual campaign organizers, alumni representatives, and class correspondents. The "true preps" follow the superschoolies in intensity of loyalty. They are the suburban country club group who support the schools and can usually be counted on to send their children to the schools. Below the true preps in loyalty are the "neutrals" who did not hate boarding school, but did not love it either. They contribute now and then to the annual fund and some will send their children to boarding school. Next in order are the "ambivalent," whose loyalty is torn by the love/hate relationship they feel for the school. Their feelings about the schools are not very positive, but there is a part of them that holds on to their prep background. Finally there are the "anti-preps" who really do not like the schools.

Generally, it is the superschoolies, true preps, and neutrals who lead upper- and upper-middle-class life-styles. They are essentially a business class, and for them the old school tie is often important because it advances their economic and political interests as well as cements their social bonds. We may wonder, however, whether their social bonds affect the larger society. Do the interpersonal relationships of preppies become interorganizational and interinstitutional, linking corporate boards, banks, industries, government cabinets, and philanthropic organizations? If so, then they have the potential to shape issues and events on a national canvas.

From Boarding School to Corporate Board

A substantial minority of prep school graduates are headed for careers in business. Among the students surveyed, 23 percent said that their career goal was to become a business manager; 40 percent of the parents who send their children to boarding school are business managers. In his study of

Hotchkiss graduates between 1940 and 1950, Christopher Armstrong found that 39 percent had become businessmen (1974, 46). Similarly, a study of more than 7,000 Exeter alumni revealed that 30 percent of the graduates were business executives or owners, though the proportion declined from 37 percent of the graduates prior to 1933 to 14 percent of the graduates from 1954–1966 (Eckland and Peterson 1969, 144), and even though business organizations are hierarchical, few preps got trapped at the lower or middle levels.

Michael Useem's more recent study (1984, 67) found that thirteen elite boarding schools[1] educated 10 percent of the members of the board of directors of large American business organizations. Considering that these thirteen schools enroll fewer than one percent of the population, 10 percent is striking. Even more so is the fact that 17 percent of those who become directors of two large companies (rather than just one) attended one of the thirteen elite boarding schools, as did 15 percent of those who are directors of three or more large companies (Useem 1984, 68). Similarly, Armstrong found that the Hotchkiss alumni who were businessmen and were listed in *Who's Who* all held multiple directorships and served as trustees on many boards (1974, 78).

As boarding schools help their graduates gain admission to the most prestigious colleges in the United States, this credential might be what helped their careers in business, particularly their ascent into the inner circle. To analyze the relative importance of educational credentials and social background (as measured by attending one of fourteen elite boarding schools[2] or having one's family listed in the *Social Register*), Michael Useem and Jerome Karabel (1984) compared business people with different educational and social backgrounds.

A number of interesting results are seen in table 10–1 from their data. For everyone in all categories of educational background, having high social origins was positively related to attaining high corporate positions. Having a B.A. from a top university was strongly related to becoming a chief executive officer and somewhat related to being a director of more than one firm regardless of social origins. What is most striking, however, is the way the combination of a B.A. from a top university and high social origins catapults individuals into multiple directorships and into positions

1. The schools designated as elite were: Andover, Choate, Deerfield, Exeter, Groton, Hill, Hotchkiss, Lawrenceville, Milton, St. George's, St. Mark's, St. Paul's, and Taft. This list is similar to the select 16 list used for this study.
2. The schools in this instance were: Choate, Deerfield, Groton, Hill, Hotchkiss, Kent, Lawrenceville, Middlesex, Milton, Portsmouth Abbey, St. George's, St. Mark's, St. Paul's, and Taft.

TABLE 10-1

Senior Corporate Managers Achieving High Corporate Position, by Social Origin and Educational Background

University background	Chief Executive		Multiple Directorships		Business Associations		N of Managers	
	Other Origin (%)	Upper-class Origin (%)	Other Origin (%)	Upper-class Origin (%)	Other Origin (%)	Upper-class Origin (%)	Other Origin	Upper-class Origin
No university	26.4	26.7	6.9	33.3	3.8	10.0	(261)	(30)
B.A., lesser univ.	34.6	55.4	18.0	46.2	13.7	27.7	(688)	(65)
B.A., top univ.	51.9	51.3	32.6	46.2	14.4	35.3	(187)	(119)
M.B.A., top program	44.9	45.0	25.9	43.8	22.0	38.8	(305)	(80)
All educational backgrounds	37.3	47.3	22.2	44.8	15.7	32.4	(2,287)	(422)
Significance*								
Education	<.001	.053	<.001	.003	<.001	.056		
Social origin		<.001		<.001		<.001		

*The social origin significance level compares the two origin groups for managers of all educational backgrounds.

NOTE: Michael Useem and Jerome Karabel, "Educational Pathways Through Top Corporate Management: Patterns of Stratification Within Companies and Differences Among Companies," paper presented at the American Sociological Association annual meeting, San Antonio, Texas, August 1984 (revised November 1984). Copyright © Michael Useem and Jerome Karabel, 1985. Used with permission.

in business associations, such as the Committee for Economic Development, Business Council, Council on Foreign Relations, and the Business Roundtable.

Select 16 boarding schools provide a "booster shot" for success. Nearly half of the senior corporate managers who achieved the high corporate positions in Useem and Karabel's study had prep school or social register backgrounds. While their background does not guarantee success, it greatly increases the probabilities of attaining a high position.

A similar phenomena seems to occur in banking. Armstrong found that 16 percent of Hotchkiss graduates from 1940–1950 became bankers or brokers, and about a third of them became president, vice-president, or a partner in their company, firm, or brokerage house (1974, 46). While not quite as likely to enter banking as Hotchkiss graduates, 8.2 percent of Exeter alumni become bankers or financiers (Eckland and Peterson 1969, 144).

While to our knowledge no systematic sociological studies have been made of bankers and their social and educational backgrounds, there is considerable impressionistic evidence to suggest that substantial numbers of boarding school graduates enter banking. Historically, many Groton, St. Paul's, St. Mark's, and Middlesex fathers were bankers and financiers (see Levine 1980, 74, for data on Groton and St. Mark's). The alumni directories of elite boarding schools today list many who are bankers or brokers. A report on the twenty-fifth reunion class of one elite girls' school indicates that one-third of those who are married and provided information on their husbands are married to someone in banking or finance.

LINEAGE, ABILITY, AND PERSONALITY IN LAW

Ten percent of the fathers of boarding school students are lawyers, and slightly more (15 percent) of the students we surveyed want to become lawyers. Among Hotchkiss alumni from 1940 to 1950, Armstrong found that 13 percent earned law degrees (1974, 39a), compared to 6 percent of Putney graduates. Among Exeter graduates, 10.6 percent are lawyers, although the number increased from 8.9 percent of the pre-1933 graduates to 13.7 percent of the 1954–1966 graduates (Eckland and Peterson 1969, 144). Nationally, only half of one percent of the labor force are lawyers (U.S. Bureau of the Census 1984, 416).

Paralleling business, preps who become lawyers tend to rise to partnerships in major Wall Street law firms. When they hire new lawyers, "the big firms prefer the man with all three attributes: lineage, ability, and personality," noted Erwin O. Smigel in *The Wall Street Lawyer* (1964, 72). Historically, prep school graduates tend to be judged favorably, at least on the first and third traits. "As many as 55% of the partners in one admittedly atypical firm had gone to prep schools, mainly the very social Groton, St. Paul's, St. Mark's, and Kent" (Smigel 1964, 37). Colleges and law schools are also used to judge a lawyer's lineage and ability. In 1962, 42 percent of all partners from the large New York City law firms listed in the *Martindale-Hubbell Law Directory* had attended Harvard, Yale, or Princeton as undergraduates (Smigel 1964, 73).

The historical importance of attending socially prestigious prep schools, colleges, and law schools was underscored by Smigel's rating of each of these three educational institutions on a scale of one to five, with one being highest. Among preparatory schools, Groton, St. Paul's, and St. Mark's were rated one and public schools were rated five (Smigel 1964, 120). Smigel found that 54 percent of the partners in Cravath, Swain & Moore from 1906 to 1948 ranked in the top (most social) five educational positions (out of a possible thirteen); 50 percent of the partners at another major law firm held such a rank; and 63 percent of the partners in a third major firm also did (1964, 120–21).

While the importance placed upon attending an elite boarding school may have waned somewhat in the 1970s,[3] it is still not unusual for a candidate being interviewed for a job as an associate at a major firm to be asked where he or she prepped. "As one eastern-born St. Paul's graduate put it when talking about some fellow lawyers from the less socially acceptable mid-west: 'If they had just gone to St. Paul's they would not be so naive about human relations in a law firm' " (Smigel 1964, 72–73). Firms still recruit heavily from Harvard, Yale, and Columbia law schools, as well as from other schools. Admission to these law schools, as well as to very selective colleges, has become increasingly competitive, so that the cultural capital acquired in a demanding boarding school may be as useful as the social imprimatur it provided in an earlier era.

Not only do prep and Ivy League graduates tend to rise to partnerships in major firms, but their connections extend beyond the firm. Some lawyers are corporate directors of major companies, serve in state or federal legislatures, lobby, or are judges or other high public officials. They are active in major bar associations which often screen candidates for judgeships, they help negotiate international treaties and contracts, and they

---

3. In 1961, twenty-six of the thirty-eight partners at Davis, Polk & Wardwell were listed in the *Social Register,* but "as the legal profession has become increasingly business conscious," Davis, Polk has moved to shake its "white shoe" image. The forty new lawyers hired by the firm in 1983 "come from a variety of backgrounds, locales and law schools—representing, as one partner put it, the firm's belief that 'the cream is the cream no matter where you skim it.' " (Margolick, 30 November 1983, B1, B7).

serve on important philanthropic, arts, and welfare organizations (Smigel 1964, 4–11). A recent study of the Chicago Bar Association found that the leadership cadre in the center of the association consisted of a "group of local aristocrats, well connected to major corporate and civic organizations" (Cappell and Halliday 1983, 291). Similarly, the top law firms link business elites to government elites (Salzman and Domhoff 1980, 121–135).

POLITICAL INFLUENCE

Ties in the financial and corporate world are not confined to economic institutions alone. They also connect to political individuals and institutions through political action committees, personal political contributions, service on government advisory boards, and influence over the appointment of cabinet members, for example. The business elite also influences American government policy formulation through numerous advisory panels. These panel members advise government agencies on virtually all major questions of public policy.

Participants on such boards are much more likely to be members of the inner circle of American business, which in turn includes a considerable number of prep school graduates. When openings occur on government advisory boards or when a new administration is appointing cabinet members, government officials turn to the inner circle of business leaders. This process of inner-circle action not only occurs, but is strongly related to the results. Nearly 90 percent of all U.S. cabinet officers between 1897 and 1973 were members of either the business or the social elite; two-thirds were members of the social elite, more than three-quarters were members of the business elite, and more than half (55 percent) were members of both elites (Mintz 1975, 135).

Interpersonal and institutional ties exist at the highest levels of business, finance, and government. The evidence of such interconnections makes the claim made by John Lupton, director of development at Choate, seem reasonable: "There is no door in this entire country that cannot be opened by a Choate graduate. I can go anywhere in this country and anywhere there's a man I want to see . . . I can find a Choate man to open that door for me" (Prescott 1970, 67).

The web of affiliations among the inner group in business, government, and the nonprofit sector, has important social implications. Such connections provide information about the world, including economic and political events, as well as purely social ones. Michael Useem (1984) found that one of the benefits multiple directors felt they received from being on various boards was what he called a "business scan" of economic climates and conditions in various industries or regions. Similarly, serving on government boards provided a "government scan." While board membership provides an intensified scanning of relevant trends, having friends who are well situated in a variety of realms—from banking, to law, to business, to the arts, to education, to religion—provides useful background information.

Managing Symbolic Control

Elite domination of the arts parallels elite domination of other major American institutions. Elites dominate the governing boards of arts organizations, and they compose the major audience for art events. The arts help reaffirm and perpetuate class identity (DiMaggio and Useem 1978, 358). This linkage between elites and the arts is part of why the arts are such an important part of the curriculum of boarding schools.

Being on the board of directors of the Philadelphia Orchestra, for example, has been "from its inception a leading index of upper-class membership, social recognition, and exclusivity" (Arian, quoted in DiMaggio and Useem 1978, 360).

Another observer noted, museum boards are "frequently closed groups of wealthy and civic-minded people" (Meader, quoted in DiMaggio and Useem 1978, 361). Virtually no members of the middle class, working class, or the poor serve on arts-organization boards (DiMaggio and Useem 1978, 361).

Elite groups are also heavily represented as consumers of art events. A review of more than 200, mainly unpublished, studies of American arts audiences found that arts audiences are predominantly upper and upper-middle class (DiMaggio, Useem, and Brown 1978). Dominance of the arts helps to preserve the cultural capital that identifies status group membership and often accompanies class membership.

The efforts of preps and other members of the business elite to exercise influence in public affairs and the arts extends to efforts to influence the media. Useem reports a widespread desire "within the American business community to control the power of the media." Managers "perceive the media to be the single most influential institution in America" (1984, 89). Their perception that journalists are more liberal on such issues as income redistribution and the welfare state and more critical of the legal system and other institutions than they are is largely correct (Rothman and Lichter

1982, quoted in Useem 1984, 89). As a result, inner-circle business leaders go out of their way to be available to the press, to communicate "the private enterprise perspective on a variety of critical issues."[4]

The willingness of business leaders to serve as spokesmen for American capitalism is evident in the frequency with which they appear in the *New York Times*. Useem's analysis revealed that 62 percent of multiple directors appeared in the *Times* between 1975–77 (with an average of 4.11 appearances each), compared to only 27 percent of single directors, who appeared only 1.14 times each, on average (1984, 90). Thus, "the inner circle seeks out, and is accorded, greater access than other business leaders to those broad publics served by the print media" (Useem 1984, 90). This contact provides the opportunity for influencing the media.

"Maintaining Private Institutions"

Upper-class and prep influence in the public realm is continued by many of the wives of elite men. Although traditionally they have not been socialized for power the way men have been, upper-class women often serve on the boards of welfare agencies or educational institutions. This is in keeping with their prescribed life scripts, which called for a woman to manage her family's social life. Women orchestrated who was in and who was out socially, keeping an eye out for what would be in the family's best interests. Social activities, including charity balls, arts events, and other galas, as well as "good works" of various kinds, affirmed and helped to solidify their family's social status, and might even benefit the family's class interests. Upper-middle-class women modeled themselves on the roles played by patrician and parvenu wives alike, in a perhaps less extravagant way.

One class of an exclusive New England girls school, for example, did a survey of its members on the occasion of their twenty-fifth reunion, revealing that two-thirds were doing volunteer work, including serving on the boards of health, welfare, educational, arts, preservationist, land trust, conservationist, and church groups.

Susan Ostrander's study of upper-class women shows that they had an awareness of their own class interest, a sense of solidarity with others

---

4. Willard C. Butcher, successor to David Rockefeller as president and chief executive of Chase Manhattan Bank, quoted in Useem 1984, 89.

similar to themselves, an awareness of underlying conflict with other classes, and a willingness to work to maintain or advance their class interests (Ostrander 1980, 42). Class solidarity was revealed in the way participation in certain forms of volunteer work was not open to everyone. As one respondent said:

> The members [of the Junior League] do have a certain caliber. I would hate to see just anybody get in. Manners are still important and a little breeding, a little polish. It's in one's carriage, a way of speaking, well-bred. (Ostrander 1980, 42)

Women socialized in socially elite boarding schools are taught many of these cultural subtleties. Ostrander's respondents described "acceptable" persons as "congenial" or "compatible," indicating a clear sense of "we-ness," a sense of belonging together (Ostrander 1980, 42). Newcomers to the community were screened, and needed to be sponsored if they were to be considered acceptable for membership.

The upper-class women volunteers Ostrander studied were quite aware of how their efforts were serving their class interests. When she asked what their personal reasons were for doing volunteer work, they stressed the importance of their family tradition of volunteerism and the opportunities volunteer work offered to be involved in policymaking. *Noblesse oblige* was expressed in such statements as, "When you have more than your share, you should return what you can to the community," and "If you're privileged, you have a certain responsibility" (Ostrander 1980, 45).

The ideology of *noblesse oblige* is part of the curriculum of a number of boarding schools, especially girls schools, which require community service for graduation. The pursuit of power and its implications for maintaining an ascendant position were indicated by the comments that "You can get higher in volunteerism than you would be able to as a paid employee. You can direct procedures and policy and get involved in the power structure," and "The board level is where the decisions are made. I don't want the little jobs" (Ostrander 1980, 45). Or, as one highly placed volunteer said, "If I went into paid work, I would have to put up with a job too menial for me. I'm not really trained for anything" (Ostrander 1979–80, 7).

Although the women volunteered their time, they saw their primary contribution as a financial one, through direct contributions as well as through fund-raising. Charitable donations provided the economic basis for influencing how those funds could be used and for preventing the expansion of public funds and public decision making (Ostrander 1979–80, 46).

Without that help, said one woman, "You'd have to go into government funds. That's Socialism. The more we can keep under private control, the better it is." Another one said, "It's our job to keep things from going too far to the left politically—to keep private institutions alive" (Ostrander 1979–80, 46).

As Ostrander observed," 'Maintaining private institutions' is the upper class catchword . . . for elite control (or dominance) and upper class opposition to leftist ideologies" (1979–80, 46). The ideal upper-class woman is a society lady or a lady bountiful, rather than a career-minded achiever, but these activities further the family's class and status interests far more than would a paid job. Class and status interests mutually enhance each other in these volunteer activities, as they do for the men who serve on multiple boards of corporations and nonprofit organizations.

The Legacies of Elite Education

This brief review of preps at play and in the power structure shows that the "resonating relationships" that many preps develop in the total institution can and do carry over into adulthood. There is not a perfect fit, however, between boarding school attendance and admission to elite circles. The fathers of Exeter alumni, for instance, are much more likely to be listed in *Who's Who* than their adult sons. Nineteen percent of the fathers, compared to only 7 percent of their adult sons, were listed (Eckland and Peterson 1969, 123). Some preps, of course, do drop out of the status race, and some are simply not swift enough to win no matter how many early advantages they have been given. Kennedy's and Peabody's call to prep greatness, in fact, falls on many deaf ears; many preps are more concerned about maintaining their life-styles than they are about pushing themselves to greatness.

The original intention of the prep school founders, that American boarding schools would forge a collective identity in the children of the privileged classes has succeeded, but not exactly in the way the founders imagined. The students tend to learn their social rules from other students, not from pious heads or even hardworking teachers. The values of the teen culture emphasize fulfillment rather than denial. Only a few prep students are really prepared to pay the price of privilege. When told we were doing a book about prep schools, one alumna asked, "Is it titled 'Playboys and Powerbrokers'?" Certainly prep schools produce some playboys, which may be an indication of how much the culture of narcissism has eroded the traditional values of the Protestant Establishment.

As Daniel Bell has pointed out, the exercise of power requires a degree of asceticism, discipline, and collective identity that seems to be disappearing from all levels of American life (Bell 1976, chap. 1).

> In the hedonistic life, there is a loss of will and fortitude. More importantly, men become competitive with one another for luxuries, and they lose the ability to share and sacrifice. . . . They also lose the sense of solidarity which makes men feel as brothers to one another . . . [and] some moral purpose, a *telos* which provides the moral justifications for the society. (Bell 1976, 83)

Hedonism and narcissism, rather than asceticism, appear to be on the ascendancy in the social landscape today. Status and its badges, rather than work and the election of God, have become the mark of success in our society (Bell 1976, 74). Many young people today are less interested in power and pain than in creature comforts and consumer goods. From their inception, boarding schools have been designed to provide a moral antidote to the potential decadence of privilege. They remove young people from the temptations of pizza parlors, video games, shopping malls, discos, and soap operas. But young people bring the teen culture with them. So, while the physical temptations may be lessened, the values do not disappear. Instead, they may be intensified by more concentrated contact among other young people.

Today, prep schools are still trying to put some fiber into the children who need to keep their edge if they are to retain control, as well as to sharpen the wits of the children of upper- middle-class professionals and managers who are not insulated from the vagaries of life by substantial wealth. As Bell noted:

> Asceticism emphasizes non-material values, renunciation of physical pleasures, simplicity and self-denial, and arduous, purposeful discipline. That discipline is necessary for the mobilization of psychic and physical energies for tasks outside the self, for the conquest and subordination of the self in order to conquer others. (Bell 1976, 82)

But asceticism is increasingly difficult to sell to young people today. "Why should I work so hard?" a young man asks the resident psychologist at one of America's most elite New England prep schools. "Am I doing it for myself or for my parents?" A moral or religious justification is almost entirely unconvincing, and a personal or family reason is difficult to support. Hence it is increasingly difficult for schools, parents, or society to provide a compelling answer. For young people without family wealth, the absence of effort does portend high personal costs—their enjoyment cannot be sustained through life. But for those with substantial family wealth, the means for consumption and display are available.

The psychic costs of the prep crucible are high by today's standards, the outcomes uncertain. Increasing numbers of parents and children may feel the costs and risks are not worth it. More children may say they do not want to go away to school, as happened in the 1960s, and more parents may listen. The schools made considerable concessions to youth culture in the late 1960s and early 1970s—coeducation, intervisitation, relaxed dress rules, greater freedom in room decoration, allowing stereos, increasing weekend leaves, eliminating mandatory chapel, allowing more choice of food and seating arrangements at meals, and so forth. The result has been an enormous transfusion of teen culture into the schools, reflected in the content of the student underlife—which no doubt always existed, but took different forms in earlier eras.

Nevertheless, in its totality, the prep rite of passage is still tougher than a suburban high school or day school, not only with its demanding curriculum and teaching, but also because of the experience of being away from home, and dealing constantly with school rules, authorities, and ubiquitous peers twenty-four hours a day. Some students get their minds trained, their social skills sharpened; they lose their innocent illusions, and are prepared to exercise power. But others are lost rather than empowered by their experience. Some leave or are expelled, others try to commit suicide. Some withdraw, others contribute actively to the flourishing student underlife.

And virtually no one is unaffected by their experience. In the life script of a prep school student, the social and psychic rewards and scars of having endured the prep rite of passage are a lasting legacy. For those who survive the prep ordeal, there is a sense that they are entitled to the privileges and positions that they attain. Their "specialness" has been confirmed by their experience. They feel an affinity with others of their group who have shared the prep ordeal with them and their nerve for action has been hardened. And some of their number will have the will to exercise power.

Are boarding schools a remnant of the past or is the socialization for power relevant in America today? As power and wealth in America shift from the Northeast to the Southwest, does the largely eastern phenomenon of the elite boarding school provide the best preparation for exercising class power? By forging a sense of collective consciousness among a relatively narrow economic, religious, ethnic, and regional subset of people, do individuals attending these schools run the risk of shutting themselves off from many of the sources of vitality in the United States and the world? Are their social radii long enough to touch the expanding circumference of a changing society? Does their preoccupation with old forms impede their receptivity to new ones?

For what kind of a life is the prep rite of passage the best preparation? It may prepare some well for a life and world governed by traditional, established, conservative ways of doing things. But, does it help prepare venture capitalists, for instance, to choose the "most likely to succeed" computer companies? Does it develop successful entrepreneurs and risk takers? Does it encourage innovative scientists or inventors?

Some people have attributed the stagnation of the British economy to its rigid class structure and the support provided to that class structure by its public schools. Can similar criticisms be leveled against boarding schools in the United States, not so much because of the official program of the school but because of the stranglehold the peer culture exercises over creative individual behaviors?

In a period of economic scarcity and contraction, we might expect the prep experience to become relatively more important, as those already holding power try to cling to what they have. Yet if we are entering an era of unprecedented growth and prosperity, as some project, then those who are less shackled by conventional ways of doing things and less socialized for a common collective identity will probably benefit more than those who are prisoners of their class.

Appendix

Schools Visited
(Total: 65)

School Name	Location	Program
Admiral Farragut Academy	Pine Beach, New Jersey	College Prep/Military
The Barlow School* (1)	Amenia, New York	College Prep
Berkshire School* (3)	Sheffield, Massachusetts	College Prep
The Bishop's School (2)	La Jolla, California	College Prep
Broughton Tower Special School	Broughton-in-Furness, England	Special Mission
Canterbury School	New Milford, Connecticut	College Prep
The Cate School	Carpenteria, California	College Prep
Choate-Rosemary Hall	Wallingford, Connecticut	College Prep
The Choir School of St. Thomas Church*	New York, New York	Pre-prep
The Church Farm School	Paoli, Pennsylvania	Special Mission
Colorado Rocky Mountain School	Carbondale, Colorado	College Prep
Cranbrook School	Bloomfield Hills, Michigan	College Prep
Darrow School*	New Lebanon, New York	College Prep
Dartington Hall School	Totnes, England	English Boarding School
Deerfield Academy	Deerfield, Massachusetts	College Prep
Eaglebrook School	Deerfield, Massachusetts	Pre-prep
The Episcopal High School	Alexandria, Virginia	College Prep
The Ethel Walker School	Simsbury, Connecticut	College Prep
Eton College	Windsor, England	English Public School
Fountain Valley School	Colorado Springs, Colorado	College Prep
Foxcroft School	Middleburg, Virginia	College Prep
Groton School	Groton, Massachusetts	College Prep
Harrow School	Harrow-on-the-Hill, England	English Public School
The Hill School	Pottstown, Pennsylvania	College Prep
The Hockaday School	Dallas, Texas	College Prep
The Hotchkiss School* (3)	Lakeville, Connecticut	College Prep
Kingswood School	Bloomfield Hills, Michigan	College Prep
The Lawrenceville School	Lawrenceville, New Jersey	College Prep
The MacDuffie School for Girls*	Springfield, Massachusetts	College Prep
The Madeira School	Greenway, Virginia	College Prep
Midland School	Los Olivos, California	College Prep
Milton Academy	Milton, Massachusetts	College Prep
Miss Porter's School	Farmington, Connecticut	College Prep

EXHIBIT A–1 *(continued)*

School Name	Location	Program
New York Military Academy*	Cornwall-on-Hudson, New York	College Prep/Military
North Carolina School of Science and Mathematics	Durham, North Carolina	Public College Prep
Northfield Mount Hermon School*	Northfield, Massachusetts	College Prep
Ojai Valley School	Ojai, California	College Prep
The Orme School	Mayer, Arizona	College Prep
Overbrook School for the Blind	Philadelphia, Pennsylvania	Special Mission
The Pennsylvania School for the Deaf	Philadelphia, Pennsylvania	Special Mission
Phillips Academy	Andover, Massachusetts	College Prep
Phillips Exeter Academy	Exeter, New Hampshire	College Prep
Pomfret School*	Pomfret, Connecticut	College Prep
Portsmouth Abbey School	Portsmouth, Rhode Island	College Prep
The Putney School	Putney, Vermont	College Prep
Robert Louis Stevenson School	Pebble Beach, California	College Prep
Rodean School	Brighton, England	English Girls Boarding School
Rugby School	Rugby, England	English Public School
St. George's School	Middletown, Rhode Island	College Prep
St. Mary's Convent	Ascot, England	English Girls Boarding School
St. Paul's School	Concord, New Hampshire	College Prep
St. Stephen's Episcopal School	Austin, Texas	College Prep
Salisbury School*	Salisbury, Connecticut	College Prep
Santa Catalina School	Monterey, California	College Prep
Solebury School	New Hope, Pennsylvania	College Prep
Summerhill School	Leiston, England	English Boarding School
The Taft School	Watertown, Connecticut	College Prep
The Thacher School	Ojai, California	College Prep
Trinity-Pawling School*	Pawling, New York	College Prep
Verde Valley School	Sedona, Arizona	College Prep
Webb School of California	Claremont, California	College Prep
Wellington School	Crowthorne, England	English Public School
Westtown School	Westtown, Pennsylvania	College Prep
Winchester College	Winchester, England	English Public School
Wooster School	Danbury, Connecticut	College Prep

NOTE: *Visited as part of the teacher evaluation study in 1978–79.
(1) No longer open
(2) No longer residential
(3) Participated in both the teacher evaluation and the later study

Appendix

TABLE A–1

Leading Private Secondary Boarding Schools and Three Subsamples: A Comparison of Selected Characteristics

	Total Population N 289 (%)	Field Sample N 48 (%)	Questionnaire Sample N 19 (%)	Select 16 Sample N 16 (%)
Schools with no religious affiliation	65	73	84	63
Schools by Region				
New England, Mid-Atlantic	53	60	53	88
South Atlantic	16	6	11	13
Middle West	12	8	11	0
Plains, Mountain, Pacific	19	25	26	0
Size				
1–400 students	77	60	53	36
401–1,630 students	23	40	47	63
Sex Composition				
Boys	28	23	26	31
Girls	17	19	21	0
Coeducational	55	58	53	69

SOURCE: Adapted from data in *The Handbook of Private Schools* (1981). Data on the field and questionnaire samples exclude one public boarding school not listed in the *Handbook*, and data on the field sample excludes one school which closed in 1981.

EXHIBIT A–2

Freshman Questionnaire *

This questionnaire is part of a study being carried out in selected boarding schools to learn more about the educational attitudes and educational careers of boarding school students. We think you will find the questions interesting and easy to answer. Please answer exactly the way you feel; no one in this school will ever see the answers. This questionnaire is anonymous. You have a right to refuse to participate, although your contribution is very important if the results are to be meaningful. You may also choose not to answer any item within this questionnaire. Remember that this is an attitude and educational career plan survey; therefore, there are no right or wrong answers. Please do not spend too much time on any single question. When finished, hand your questionnaire to the researcher who will take it, with the other completed questionnaires, directly to the university for statistical tabulation.

If you have a problem, please raise your hand and the researcher, who has given you the questionnaire, will come to your desk and answer your question. Thank you for your cooperation.

Because this is an educational survey there are no right and wrong answers. Please check the answers that seem most appropriate to you.

1. What is your age?
    12 or younger   ( )
    13   ( )
    14   ( )
    15 or older   ( )
2. Please indicate your sex.
    Female   ( )
    Male   ( )
3. What is your religious background? (Please Check One)
    Baptist   ( )
    Methodist   ( )
    Lutheran   ( )
    Presbyterian   ( )
    Episcopalian   ( )
    Other Protestant denomination   ( )
    Catholic   ( )
    Other Christian   ( )
    Jewish   ( )
    Other religion   ( )
    None   ( )
4. Please indicate your racial background.
    White   ( )
    Black   ( )
    Oriental   ( )
    Other (Please indicate)_____   ( )

*Completed by 1,130 freshmen in twenty boarding schools.

5. Are you a citizen of the United States?
   Yes   ( )
   No   ( )
   If no, what is your nationality? _____

6. In what grade are you?
   9th   ( )
   10th   ( )
   11th   ( )
   12th   ( )
   Post Graduate   ( )

7. Are you a boarding or a day student at this school? (Please Check One)
   Boarding   ( )
       (PLEASE SKIP TO QUESTION 13)
   Day   ( )
       (PLEASE GO ON TO QUESTION 8)

8. Do you see any advantages to being a day student at a boarding school?
   Yes   ( )
   No   ( )
   If YES, what advantages do you see? _____

   _____

9. Do you see any disadvantages to being a day student at a boarding school?
   Yes   ( )
   No   ( )

   If YES, what disadvantages do you see? _____

   _____

10. Why did you come to this school? (Please check all that apply and circle the reason that was most important.)
    All my friends were going   ( )
    My parents wanted me to   ( )
    I thought I would get a better education   ( )
    I wanted the sports and other facilities they had   ( )
    Other   ( )
    (Please specify) _____

11. What do you like *best* about this school? (Please Check One)
    The other students   ( )
    The teachers   ( )
    The academic program   ( )
    The sports program   ( )
    Other (Please Specify)   ( )

    _____

12. What do you like *least* about this school? (Please Check One)
    The other students   ( )
    The teachers   ( )
    The academic program   ( )

The sports program	( )
Other (Please specify what)	( )

_____

There is nothing I like least	( )

(PLEASE SKIP TO QUESTION 16 ON THIS QUESTIONNAIRE)

13. Was it your personal choice to come to boarding school?

Yes	( )
No	( )

13A. Why did you come to boarding school? (Please check all that apply and circle the reason that was most important.)

I wanted to get away from home	( )
All my friends were going	( )
My parents wanted me to	( )
I thought I would get a better education	( )
I wanted the sports and other facilities they had	( )
Other (Please specify)	( )

_____

14. What do you like *best* about boarding school? (Please Check One)

The other students	( )
The teachers	( )
The academic program	( )
The sports program	( )
Other programs (Please specify what)	( )

_____

Dorm life	( )
Being away from home	( )
Other (Please specify)_____	( )

15. What do you like *least* about boarding school? (Please Check One)

The other students	( )
The teachers	( )
The academic program	( )
The sports program	( )
Dorm life	( )
Being away from home	( )
The food	( )
The location of the school	( )
Other (Please specify what)	( )

_____

There is nothing I like least	( )

16. Ten years from now, as you look back on your high school experience, what do you think will have been the most valuable part about it for you? (Please check all that apply and circle the one that you think will be *most* important.)

The people you met	( )
The education you received	( )
Where it helped you get into college	( )

Study skills that you learned   ( )
Religious education   ( )
Experience in relating to people   ( )
Other (Please specify what)   ( )

_____

17. Did one or more of your relatives attend this or another boarding school?
    Yes   ( )
    No   ( )

    If YES, did they attend this boarding school?
      Yes   ( )
      No   ( )

    If YES, which relatives of yours attended this
    school? (Please list them here, for example, your
    brother)_____

_____

18. Have you participated in any of the following types of activities this year? (Please make one check on each line)

	Have not participated	Have participated actively (but not as a leader or officer)	Have participated as a leader or officer
Varsity athletic teams	( )	( )	( )
Other athletic teams	( )	( )	( )
Cheer leaders, pep club	( )	( )	( )
Debating or drama	( )	( )	( )
Band or orchestra	( )	( )	( )
Chorus or dance	( )	( )	( )
Hobby clubs such as photography, model building, electronics, crafts	( )	( )	( )
Honorary clubs, such as Beta Club or National Honor Society	( )	( )	( )
School newspaper, magazine, yearbook, annual	( )	( )	( )
School subject-matter clubs, such as science, history, language, business, art	( )	( )	( )

Student council,
student
government,
political club ....( ) ....( ) ....( )

19. During weekdays at school about how many hours per day do you watch TV?
(Please Check One)

Don't watch TV during week	( )
Less than 1 hour	( )
1 hour or more, less than 2	( )
2 hours or more, less than 3	( )
3 hours or more, less than 4	( )
4 hours or more, less than 5	( )
5 or more	( )

20. How often has each of the following been used in the courses you are taking
this year? (Please make one check on each line.)

	Never	Seldom	Fairly Often	Frequently
Listening to the teacher's lecture	( )	( )	( )	( )
Participating in student-centered discussions	( )	( )	( )	( )
Working on a project or in a laboratory	( )	( )	( )	( )
Writing essays, themes, poetry, or stories	( )	( )	( )	( )
Having individualized instruction (small groups or one-to-one with a teacher)	( )	( )	( )	( )
Using computers	( )	( )	( )	( )

21. Approximately what is the average amount of time you spend on homework
a week? (Please Check One)

No homework is ever assigned	( )
I have homework, but I don't do it	( )
Less than 1 hour a week	( )
Between 1 and 3 hours a week	( )
More than 3 hours, less than 5 hours a week	( )
Between 5 and 10 hours a week	( )
More than 10 hours, less than 20 hours a week	( )
More than 20 hours a week	( )

Following is a list of true-false statements about high school: the characteristics of teachers and courses, activities of students, etc. The statements

may or may not be characteristic of your school because high schools differ from one another in many ways. You are to decide which statements are characteristic of your school and which are not, and your answers should tell us how things really are here rather than what you would like them to be. Circle "T" when the statement is generally or mostly true as a description of this school and circle "F" when it is generally or mostly false. Please give only one response to each item.

22.	The teachers here encourage the students to take as many science courses as possible.	T	F
23.	Many students here are planning careers in science.	T	F
24.	Most students here dress and act pretty much alike.	T	F
25.	Very few students here would be interested in a field trip to an art museum.	T	F
26.	Teachers here are very interested in their students.	T	F
27.	This school doesn't offer many opportunities to get to know important works of art, music, drama.	T	F
28.	Many teachers here are more interested in practical applications of what they are teaching than in the underlying theory.	T	F
29.	Many classes here are boring.	T	F
30.	Students having difficulty with their courses find it difficult to get help from teachers.	T	F
31.	The discipline here is effective.	T	F
32.	In this school, teachers do not adjust assignments and projects to the individual student's interests.	T	F
33.	There is a lot of interest here in learning for its own sake, rather than just for grades or for graduation credits.	T	F
34.	Few students try hard to get on the honor roll.	T	F
35.	Teachers here encourage students to value knowledge for its own sake, rather than just for grades.	T	F
36.	The discipline here is not fair.	T	F
37.	It takes more than memorizing what's in the textbook to get an "A" in courses here.	T	F
38.	There are a few students who control things in this school, and the rest of us are out in the cold.	T	F

39. How much formal education did your parents have? (Please check one for each parent)

	Father	Mother
Some grade school	( )	( )
Finished grade school	( )	( )
Some high school	( )	( )
Finished high school	( )	( )
Some college	( )	( )
Finished college	( )	( )
Attended graduate school or professional school after college	( )	( )
I don't know	( )	( )

40. On the lines provided below, please indicate the occupation and the job title (if you know it) of your parents. (If your mother or father have more than one job, write down the one on which they spend the most time. If either are retired, out of work or not living, write down the one they did last.) PLEASE BE SPECIFIC

OCCUPATION   JOB TITLE

Father_____   _____

Mother_____   _____

41. Does your father own his own business? (Please Check One)

    Yes   ( )
    No   ( )
    I don't know   ( )

42. Does your mother own her own business? (Please Check One)

    Yes   ( )
    No   ( )
    I don't know   ( )

43. Are your mother and father married, separated, divorced, or widowed? (Please check one)

    Married   ( )
    Separated   ( )
    Divorced   ( )
    Widowed   ( )
    Other (Please specify)   ( )

    _____

44. Which areas of the world have you visited? (Please check all that apply.)

    North America outside of the U.S.A.   ( )
    Europe   ( )
    Africa   ( )
    South America   ( )
    Asia   ( )
    Australia   ( )
    None   ( )

45. Please estimate the number of books in your home. (Please check one)

    None or few (1–25)   ( )
    One bookcase full (26–100)   ( )
    Two bookcases full (101–250)   ( )
    Three or four bookcases full (251–500)   ( )
    A room full—a library (501 or more)   ( )

46. My family's total yearly income is approximately: (Please Check One)

    Under $15,000   ( )
    15,000–25,000   ( )
    25,001–75,000   ( )
    75,001–100,000   ( )
    More than 100,000   ( )
    I don't know   ( )

47. Does your family have a home computer? (Please check one)

Yes	( )
No	( )
I don't know	( )

48. How do you feel about each of the following statements? (Please make one check on each line)

	Agree strongly	Agree	Disagree	Disagree strongly	No opinion
I take a positive attitude toward myself	( )	( )	( )	( )	( )
Good luck is more important than hard work for success	( )	( )	( )	( )	( )
I feel I am a person of worth, on an equal plane with others	( )	( )	( )	( )	( )
I am able to do things as well as most other people	( )	( )	( )	( )	( )
Every time I try to get ahead, something or somebody stops me	( )	( )	( )	( )	( )
Planning only makes a person unhappy, since plans hardly ever work out anyway	( )	( )	( )	( )	( )
People who accept their condition in life are happier than those who try to change things	( )	( )	( )	( )	( )
On the whole, I am satisfied with myself	( )	( )	( )	( )	( )
What happens to me is my own doing	( )	( )	( )	( )	( )
At times I think I am no good at all	( )	( )	( )	( )	( )

When I make plans,
  I am almost
  certain I can make
  them work ....( ) ....( ) ....( ) ....( ) ....( )
I feel I do not have
  much to be proud
  of ....( ) ....( ) ....( ) ....( ) ....( )

49. How important is each of the following to you in your life? (Please make one check on each line)

	Not important	Somewhat important	Very important
Being successful in my line of work	( )	( )	( )
Finding the right person to marry and having a happy family life	( )	( )	( )
Having lots of money	( )	( )	( )
Having strong friendships	( )	( )	( )
Being able to find steady work	( )	( )	( )
Being a leader in my community	( )	( )	( )
Being able to give my children better opportunities than I've had	( )	( )	( )
Living close to parents and relatives	( )	( )	( )
Getting away from this area of the country	( )	( )	( )
Working to correct social and economic inequalities	( )	( )	( )
Having children	( )	( )	( )
Having leisure time to enjoy my own interests	( )	( )	( )

50. When you think about the future, how do you feel and what can you do about it?

Thank you very much for your cooperation.

EXHIBIT A–3

Senior Questionnaire *

This questionnaire is part of a study being carried out in selected boarding schools to learn more about the educational attitudes and educational careers of boarding school students. We think you will find the questions interesting and easy to answer. Please answer exactly the way you feel; no one in this school will ever see the answers. The questionnaire is anonymous. You have a right to refuse to participate, although your contribution is very important if the results are to be meaningful. You may also choose not to answer any item within this questionnaire. Remember that this is an attitude and educational career plan survey; therefore, there are no right or wrong answers. Please do not spend too much time on any single question. When finished, hand your questionnaire to the researcher who will take it, with the other completed questionnaires, directly to the university for statistical tabulation.

If you have a problem, please raise your hand and the researcher, who has given you the questionnaire, will come to your desk and answer your question. Thank you for your cooperation.

In order to complete this study we need to know your grade point average, class rank, Scholastic Aptitude Test scores, the names of the colleges you applied to, the names of the colleges at which you were accepted, the name of the college you will attend and any special honors or awards you received in high school. Because some of you may not know all this information, it will be obtained from your school records. The following procedure has been developed to protect your identity.

On the top right hand corner of this questionnaire you will find a number; this is your I.D. number for this research. Accompanying the questionnaire are two cards: on Card A you will find your research I.D. number and a space for your name; on Card B you will find your research I.D. number and the spaces needed to fill in the information required from your school record.

When you have completed the questionnaire, return it and the cards to the researcher. No one at this school will see the questionnaires. The two cards will be submitted to the school office. Somebody there will use Card A to look up the needed information and transfer this information onto Card B. Card A will then be destroyed. Card B will be returned to the researcher. In this way the researcher will be able to complete the study without knowing your name.

Now, place your name on Card A. Once you have finished this, you may start the questionnaire immediately. Thank you again for your cooperation.

*Completed by 1,345 seniors in twenty boarding schools.

CARD A

Research I.D. Number_____

Name _____
    Last   First   Middle

CARD B

Research I.D. Number_____

Grade Point Average_____   Class Rank_____

S.A.T. Scores: verbal_____   quantitative_____

College Applications_____

_____

_____

College Acceptances_____

_____

College Attending_____

Other Special Honors & Awards (Athletic, Scholastic & Leadership): _____

_____

_____

Because this is an educational survey there are no right and wrong answers. Please check the answers that seem most appropriate to you.

1. What is your age?
   16 or younger ( )
   17 ( )
   18 ( )
   19 or older ( )

2. Please indicate your sex.
   Female ( )
   Male ( )

3. What is your religious background? (Please Check One)
   Baptist ( )
   Methodist ( )
   Lutheran ( )
   Presbyterian ( )
   Episcopalian ( )
   Other Protestant denomination ( )
   Catholic ( )
   Other Christian ( )
   Jewish ( )
   Other religion ( )
   None ( )

4. Please indicate your racial background.
   White ( )
   Black ( )
   Oriental ( )
   Other (Please indicate)_____ ( )

5. Are you a citizen of the United States?
   Yes ( )
   No ( )
   If no, what is your nationality?_____

6. In what grade are you?
   9th ( )
   10th ( )
   11th ( )
   12th ( )
   Post Graduate ( )
   In what grade did you enter this school?_____

7. Are you a boarding or a day student at this school? (Please Check One)
   Boarding ( )
   (PLEASE SKIP TO QUESTION 13)
   Day ( )
   (PLEASE GO ON TO QUESTION 8)

8. Do you see any advantages to being a day student at a boarding school?
   Yes ( )
   No ( )
   If YES, what advantages do you see?_____

   _____

9. Do you see any disadvantages to being a day student at a boarding school?
   Yes   ( )
   No   ( )

   If YES, what disadvantages do you see? _____

   _____

10. Why did you come to this school? (Please check all that apply and circle the reason that was most important.)
    All my friends were going   ( )
    My parents wanted me to   ( )
    I thought I would get a better education   ( )
    I wanted the sports and other facilities they had   ( )
    Other   ( )
    (Please specify) _____

11. What do you like *best* about this school? (Please Check One)
    The other students   ( )
    The teachers   ( )
    The academic program   ( )
    The sports program   ( )
    Other (Please specify)   ( )

    _____

12. What do you like *least* about this school? (Please Check One)
    The other students   ( )
    The teachers   ( )
    The academic program   ( )
    The sports program   ( )
    Other (Please specify what)   ( )

    _____

    There is nothing I like least   ( )

    (PLEASE SKIP TO QUESTION 16 ON THIS QUESTIONNAIRE)

13. Was it your personal choice to come to boarding school?
    Yes   ( )
    No   ( )

13A. Why did you come to boarding school? (Please check all that apply and circle the reason that was most important.)
    I wanted to get away from home   ( )
    All my friends were going   ( )
    My parents wanted me to   ( )
    I thought I would get a better education   ( )
    I wanted the sports and other facilities they had   ( )
    Other (Please specify)   ( )

    _____

14. What do you like *best* about boarding school? (Please Check One)
    The other students   ( )
    The teachers   ( )

The academic program ( )
The sports program ( )
Other programs (Please specify what) ( )

_____

Dorm life ( )
Being away from home ( )
Other (Please specify) ( )

_____

15. What do you like *least* about boarding school? (Please Check One)
    The other students ( )
    The teachers ( )
    The academic program ( )
    The sports program ( )
    Dorm life ( )
    Being away from home ( )
    The food ( )
    The location of the school ( )
    Other (Please specify what) ( )

_____

    There is nothing I like least ( )

16. Ten years from now, as you look back on your high school experience, what do you think will have been the most valuable part about it for you? (Please check all that apply and circle the one that you think will be *most* important.)
    The people you met ( )
    The education you received ( )
    Where it helped you get into college ( )
    Study skills that you learned ( )
    Religious education ( )
    Experience in relating to people ( )
    Other (Please specify what) ( )

_____

17. Did one or more of your relatives attend this or another boarding school?
    Yes ( )
    No ( )
    If YES, did they attend this boarding school?
    Yes ( )
    No ( )
    If YES, which relatives of yours attended this school? (Please list them here, for example, your brother)_____

_____

18. Have you participated in any of the following types of activities this year? (Please make one check on each line)

	Have not participated	Have participated actively (but not as a leader or officer)	Have participated as a leader or officer
Varsity athletic teams	( )	( )	( )
Other athletic teams	( )	( )	( )
Cheer leaders, pep club	( )	( )	( )
Debating or drama	( )	( )	( )
Band or orchestra	( )	( )	( )
Chorus or dance	( )	( )	( )
Hobby clubs such as photography, model building, electronics, crafts	( )	( )	( )
Honorary clubs, such as Beta Club or National Honor Society	( )	( )	( )
School newspaper, magazine, yearbook, annual	( )	( )	( )
School subject-matter clubs, such as science, history, language, business, art	( )	( )	( )
Student council, student government, political club	( )	( )	( )

19. During weekdays at school about how many hours per day do you watch TV? (Please Check One)

Don't watch TV during week	( )
Less than 1 hour	( )
1 hour or more, less than 2	( )
2 hours or more, less than 3	( )
3 hours or more, less than 4	( )
4 hours or more, less than 5	( )
5 or more	( )

20. How often has each of the following been used in the courses you are taking this year? (Please make one check on each line.)

	Never	Seldom	Fairly Often	Frequently
Listening to the teacher's lecture	( )	( )	( )	( )

Participating in
student-centered
discussions..........................( ) ....( ) ....( ) ....( )
Working on a
project or in a
laboratory ....( ) ....( ) ....( ) ....( )
Writing essays,
themes, poetry, or
stories.................................( ) ....( ) ....( ) ....( )
Having
individualized
instruction (small
groups or
one-to-one with a
teacher) ....( ) ....( ) ....( ) ....( )
Using computers ....( ) ....( ) ....( ) ....( )

21. Approximately what is the average amount of time you spend on homework
a week? (Please Check One)

No homework is ever assigned   ( )
I have homework, but I don't do it   ( )
Less than 1 hour a week   ( )
Between 1 and 3 hours a week   ( )
More than 3 hours, less than 5 hours a week   ( )
Between 5 and 10 hours a week   ( )
More than 10 hours, less than 20 hours a week   ( )
More than 20 hours a week   ( )

Following is a list of true-false statements about high school: the characteristics
of teachers and courses, activities of students, etc. The statements may or may
not be characteristic of your school because high schools differ from one another
in many ways. You are to decide which statements are characteristic of your
school and which are not, and your answers should tell us how things really
are here rather than what you would like them to be. Circle "T" when the
statement is generally or mostly true as a description of this school and circle
"F" when it is generally or mostly false. Please give only one response to each
item.

22. The teachers here encourage the students to take as many science
courses as possible.   T   F
23. Many students here are planning careers in science.   T   F
24. Most students here dress and act pretty much alike.   T   F
25. Very few students here would be interested in a field trip to an art
museum.   T   F
26. Teachers here are very interested in their students.   T   F
27. This school doesn't offer many opportunities to get to know important
works of art, music, drama.   T   F

28. Many teachers here are more interested in practical applications of what they are teaching than in the underlying theory. T F
29. Many classes here are boring. T F
30. Students having difficulty with their courses find it difficult to get help from teachers. T F
31. The discipline here is effective. T F
32. In this school, teachers do not adjust assignments and projects to the individual student's interests. T F
33. There is a lot of interest here in learning for its own sake, rather than just for grades or for graduation credits. T F
34. Few students try hard to get on the honor roll. T F
35. Teachers here encourage students to value knowledge for its own sake, rather than just for grades. T F
36. The discipline here is not fair. T F
37. It takes more than memorizing what's in the textbook to get an "A" in courses here. T F
38. There are a few students who control things in this school, and the rest of us are out in the cold. T F

39. How much formal education did your parents have? (Please check one for each parent)

	Father	Mother
Some grade school	( )	( )
Finished grade school	( )	( )
Some high school	( )	( )
Finished high school	( )	( )
Some college	( )	( )
Finished college	( )	( )
Attended graduate school or professional school after college	( )	( )
I don't know	( )	( )

40. On the lines provided below, please indicate the occupation and the job title (if you know it) of your parents. (If your mother or father have more than one job, write down the one on which they spend the most time. If either are retired, out of work or not living, write down the one they did last.) PLEASE BE SPECIFIC

OCCUPATION   JOB TITLE

Father_____   _____

Mother_____   _____

41. Does your father own his own business? (Please Check One)
    Yes ( )
    No ( )
    I don't know ( )
42. Does your mother own her own business? (Please Check One)
    Yes ( )
    No ( )
    I don't know ( )

43. Are your mother and father married, separated, divorced, or widowed? (Please check one)

Married	( )
Separated	( )
Divorced	( )
Widowed	( )
Other (Please specify)	( )

_____

44. Which areas of the world have you visited? (Please check all that apply.)

North America outside of the U.S.A.	( )
Europe	( )
Africa	( )
South America	( )
Asia	( )
Australia	( )
None	( )

45. Please estimate the number of books in your home. (Please check one)

None or few (1–25)	( )
One bookcase full (26–100)	( )
Two bookcases full (101–250)	( )
Three or four bookcases full (251–500)	( )
A room full—a library (501 or more)	( )

46. My family's total yearly income is approximately: (Please Check One)

Under $15,000	( )
15,000–25,000	( )
25,001–75,000	( )
75,001–100,000	( )
More than 100,000	( )
I don't know	( )

47. Does your family have a home computer? (Please check one)

Yes	( )
No	( )
I don't know	( )

48. How do you feel about each of the following statements? (Please make one check on each line)

	Agree strongly	Agree	Disagree	Disagree strongly	No opinion
I take a positive attitude toward myself	( )	( )	( )	( )	( )
Good luck is more important than hard work for success	( )	( )	( )	( )	( )

I feel I am a person of worth, on an equal plane with others ....( ) ....( ) ....( ) ....( ) ....( )

I am able to do things as well as most other people ....( ) ....( ) ....( ) ....( ) ....( )

Every time I try to get ahead, something or somebody stops me ....( ) ....( ) ....( ) ....( ) ....( )

Planning only makes a person unhappy, since plans hardly ever work out anyway ....( ) ....( ) ....( ) ....( ) ....( )

People who accept their condition in life are happier than those who try to change things................................( ) ....( ) ....( ) ....( ) ....( )

On the whole, I am satisfied with myself ....( ) ....( ) ....( ) ....( ) ....( )

What happens to me is my own doing ....( ) ....( ) ....( ) ....( ) ....( )

At times I think I am no good at all ....( ) ....( ) ....( ) ....( ) ....( )

When I make plans, I am almost certain I can make them work ....( ) ....( ) ....( ) ....( ) ....( )

I feel I do not have much to be proud of ......( ) ....( ) ....( ) ....( ) ....( )

49. How important is each of the following to you in your life? (Please make one check on each line)

	Not important	Somewhat important	Very important
Being successful in my line of work	( )	( )	( )
Finding the right person to marry and having a happy family life	( )	( )	( )
Having lots of money	( )	( )	( )
Having strong friendships	( )	( )	( )

Being able to find
steady work ....( ) ....( ) ....( )
Being a leader in my
community ....( ) ....( ) ....( )
Being able to give
my children better
opportunities than
I've had ....( ) ....( ) ....( )
Living close to
parents and
relatives ....( ) ....( ) ....( )
Getting away from
this area of the
country ....( ) ....( ) ....( )
Working to correct
social and
economic
inequalities.............................( ) ....( ) ....( )
Having children ....( ) ....( ) ....( )
Having leisure time
to enjoy my own
interests ....( ) ....( ) ....( )

50. Please check the highest level of education you expect to complete.
High school graduation   ( )
(If this is the highest level of education you expect
to complete, please skip to question 52.)
Plan to get an Associate's degree at a two year col-
lege   ( )
Plan to get a Bachelor's degree (4 years)   ( )
Plan to do one year of graduate study (Master's de-
gree)   ( )
Plan to obtain a professional degree (medicine, den-
tistry, business, law, etc.)   ( )
Plan to obtain a Doctorate degree (Ph.D.) (for exam-
ple, in physics, math, English)   ( )
I have not made a decision about my plans   ( )

51. What will you study in college? (Please check one)
Undecided   ( )
A liberal arts program   ( )
Performing Arts   ( )
A business program   ( )
Engineering   ( )
Architecture   ( )
Education   ( )
Other (Please specify)   ( )

_____

(PLEASE SKIP TO QUESTION 53)

52. Please check the important reasons why you are not going to college. (Please check as many as apply)

I can't afford it	( )
I decided to get married	( )
I don't need a college education for my intended occupation	( )
I decided to enter a non-college training course	( )
My grades aren't high enough	( )
I couldn't get admitted to the college I wanted to attend	( )
My high school wouldn't give me a high recommendation	( )
I prefer to work rather than take time out for college	( )
I decided to go into military service	( )
Most of my friends are not going to college	( )
My parents haven't encouraged me to go	( )
Other	( )

_____

(PLEASE GO ON TO THE NEXT QUESTION)

53. What occupation do you expect to enter when you finish your education?

_____

54. Do you feel that being in boarding school has changed you in any significant ways?

Yes	( )
No	( )

If YES, how has it changed you?

_____

_____

_____

55. When you think about the future, how do you feel and what can you do about it?

Thank you very much for your cooperation.

EXHIBIT A-4

Teacher Questionnaire *

NEW YORK UNIVERSITY
Teacher Evaluation and Professional Growth in Independent Schools

Dear Teacher:

You have been selected to participate in a research project which is investigating the methods by which teacher effectiveness and professional growth is evaluated in a variety of independent schools. This questionnaire will remain anonymous and all information gathered during the course of the research will be confidential. Individuals will not be identifiable and schools will not be identified in the text of the report. The results of this research will be sent to your school in the summer of 1978.

Your participation in this project is vital if our findings are to be of maximum value and utility. This brief questionnaire should not take more than twenty minutes to complete. After completing the questionnaire, please return it to us in the attached self-addressed stamped envelope. This form is in the process of development, and any comments you may have would be most appreciated.

Thank you for your cooperation.

Kind regards,

Peter W. Cookson, Jr.
Project Director

PART ONE

-PLEASE ANSWER BRIEFLY THE QUESTIONS BELOW ON TEACHER EVALUATION IN YOUR SCHOOL-

1. Which of the following techniques for assessing professional growth and teacher effectiveness are used in your school? (Please check the appropriate items.)

  _____ Observations by other faculty members.
  _____ Observations by members of the administration.
  _____ Use of formalized evaluation instruments.
  _____ Student evaluation.
  _____ Self evaluation.
  _____ Other. (Please specify) _____

_____

*Completed by 382 teachers in twenty private schools, eleven of which were boarding schools.

2. What part of the present evaluation process in your school is most helpful to your professional growth?

3. What part of the present evaluation process in your school is least helpful to your professional growth?

4. What changes in teacher evaluation, if any, would you like to see instituted at your school?

PART TWO

-BELOW ARE A SERIES OF QUESTIONS DESIGNED TO ASSESS YOUR ATTITUDES ABOUT TEACHING AND EDUCATION IN GENERAL-

1. How would you rate the following background characteristics or personal qualities as they apply to your profession? Please circle the number next to each statement which you feel is most appropriate.	Essential	Very Important	Important	Somewhat Important	Unimportant
A. General Educational Background	1	2	3	4	5
B. Education Courses	1	2	3	4	5
C. Professional Experience (Academic)	1	2	3	4	5
D. Professional Experience (Non-academic)	1	2	3	4	5
E. Personal Style, Manners	1	2	3	4	5
F. Verbal Facility	1	2	3	4	5
G. Knowledge and Ability	1	2	3	4	5
H. Dedication to Children	1	2	3	4	5
I. Independence of Thought	1	2	3	4	5
J. Kindness	1	2	3	4	5

2. Please RANK ORDER the groups below in terms of the importance of their opinions if you were to evaluate the professional growth of a colleague. (1 = most important, 2 = second most important, etc. up to 7.)

_____ Tenured or senior faculty members

_____ Administrators

_____ Alumni

_____ Students

_____ Junior faculty members
_____ Trustees
_____ Parents
_____ Other (Please specify)_____

---

3. Please RANK ORDER the qualities listed below in terms of their importance for the development of an outstanding teacher. (1 = most important, 2 = second most important, etc. up to 7.)

_____ Moral character
_____ Efficiency
_____ Ability to deal effectively with students
_____ Ability to deal effectively with parents
_____ Tolerance and consideration
_____ Resourcefulness
_____ Intellectual acuity
_____ Other (Please specify)_____

---

4. Please RANK ORDER the qualities listed below in terms of their importance for the development of an outstanding headmaster. (1 = most important, 2 = second most important, etc. up to 7.)

_____ Moral character
_____ Efficiency
_____ Ability to deal effectively with students
_____ Ability to deal effectively with parents
_____ Tolerance and consideration
_____ Resourcefulness
_____ Intellectual acuity
_____ Other (Please specify)_____

---

5. If you had a chance to evaluate your fellow faculty members how would you rate the importance of the qualities or achievements listed below? Please circle the number next to each statement which you feel is most appropriate.

	Essential	Very Important	Important	Somewhat Important	Unimportant
A. Maintains classroom order	1	2	3	4	5
B. Has rapport with students	1	2	3	4	5
C. Enhances student's academic performance	1	2	3	4	5
D. Establishes cooperative relationships with other faculty members	1	2	3	4	5

E.	Adheres to school policy	1	2	3	4	5
F.	Maintains friendly relations with parents	1	2	3	4	5
G.	Develops innovative teaching techniques	1	2	3	4	5
H.	Is willing to participate in extracurricular activities	1	2	3	4	5
I.	Is personally stable	1	2	3	4	5
J.	Has strong leadership qualities	1	2	3	4	5
K.	Grasps subject matter	1	2	3	4	5
L.	If there are qualities which you feel are important but not mentioned, please list below:						

_____

_____

_____

6. **The following series of statements relate to school life and teachers in particular. Please circle the number next to each statement which you feel is most appropriate.**

		Agree Strongly	Agree Somewhat	Undecided	Disagree Somewhat	Disagree Strongly
A.	Generally, teachers do not work best when closely supervised.	1	2	3	4	5
B.	A teacher should not be expected to be a "pal" with his or her students.	1	2	3	4	5
C.	A good teacher has to be entertaining.	1	2	3	4	5
D.	It's very important for teachers to have well organized daily lesson plans.	1	2	3	4	5
E.	Teachers should be free to speak publicly on important social issues.	1	2	3	4	5
F.	Teachers should play an important part in helping the administration run the school.	1	2	3	4	5
G.	Teachers are very important in shaping the moral character of their students.	1	2	3	4	5
H.	Teachers should be very careful about expressing their personal opinions in the classroom.	1	2	3	4	5

7. Do you plan to remain in teaching in the forseeable future?
   Yes_____ No_____ Undecided_____
8. What is your ultimate career goal?

9. What do you like best about teaching?

10. What do you like least about teaching?

IN THE SPACE BELOW WE WOULD APPRECIATE ANY COMMENT YOU MIGHT HAVE ON TEACHER EVALUATION AND PROFESSIONAL GROWTH IN INDEPENDENT SCHOOLS AND/OR ANY COMMENTS YOU MAY HAVE ABOUT THIS QUESTIONNAIRE.

PART THREE

TEACHER BACKGROUND INFORMATION

Please Circle the Appropriate Answer

1. SEX   FEMALE   MALE
2. AGE
20–25	46–55
26–35	56–65
36–45	66 and over
3. LEVEL OF EDUCATION

High School	Master's Degree
Some College	Doctoral Degree
Bachelor's Degree	Other (Please Specify)

   _____

4. EMPLOYMENT STATUS at your present position.

   Part-Time   Full-Time

Please Answer the Following Questions in the Space Provided

5. NAME OF THE COLLEGES, both undergraduate and graduate, you have attended or are attending._____

   _____

6. How many years have you been teaching?_____
7. How many years have you been teaching at this school?_____

   _____

8. Do you have tenure in your present position? _____
9. What subject(s) do you teach?_____

   _____

10. What grade level(s) do you teach? _____

_____

11. Name of the school in which you are presently teaching.

_____

Thank you very much for your cooperation.

References

Abramowitz, Susan. "Private High Schools: A Descriptive Profile and Comparison with Public High Schools." Paper presented at the American Educational Research Association annual meeting, San Francisco, April 1979.

Adelman, Clifford. "Devaluation, Diffusion and the College Connection: A Study of High School Transcripts, 1964–1981." Washington, D.C.: National Commission on Excellence in Education, 1983.

Alba, Richard, and Moore, Gwen. "Ethnicity in the American Elite." *American Sociological Review* 47 (June 1982): 373–83.

Aldrich, Nelson W., Jr. "Preppies—The Last Upper Class?" *Atlantic Monthly,* January 1979, 56–66.

Alexander, David. "A Himalayan Eton for India's Elite." *Asia Magazine,* May/June 1982, 36–41.

Alexander, Karl, and Eckland, Bruce K. "Contextual Effects in the High School Attainment Process." *American Sociological Review* 40 (June 1975): 402–16.

———. "High School Context and College Selectivity: Institutional Constraints in Educational Stratification." *Social Forces* 56 (September 1977): 166–88.

Anderson, Pauline. "A Selected Bibliography of Literature on the Independent School." Milton, Mass.: Independent Schools Education Board, 1959.

Apple, Michael. *Ideology and Curriculum.* Boston: Routledge & Kegan Paul, 1979.

Arian, Edward. *Bach, Beethoven, and Bureaucracy: The Case of the Philadelphia Orchestra.* University, Ala.: University of Alabama Press, 1971.

Arieli, Mordecai; Kashti, Yitzhak; and Shlasky, Simcha. *Living at School: Israeli Residential Schools as People Processing Organizations.* Tel Aviv: Ramot Publishing, 1983.

Ariès, Philippe. *Centuries of Childhood: A Social History of Family Life.* New York: Vintage Books, 1962.

Armor, David J. *The American School Counselor.* New York: Russell Sage Foundation, 1969.

Armstrong, Christopher F. "Privilege and Productivity: The Cases of Two Private Schools and Their Graduates." Ph.D. diss., Department of Sociology, University of Pennsylvania, 1974.

———. "Boarding Schools: Sequestered Isolation and Elite Preparation." Paper presented at the Eastern Sociological Society annual meeting, New York, March 1979.

References

Astin, Alexander W.; King, Margo R.; and Richardson, Gerald T. *The American Freshman: National Norms for Fall 1981.* Los Angeles: University of California, Laboratory for Research in Higher Education, 1981.

Baird, Leonard L. *The Elite Schools.* Lexington, Mass.: Lexington Books, 1977.

Baltzell, E. Digby. *Philadelphia Gentlemen—The Making of a National Upper Class.* Chicago: Quadrangle Books, 1958.

——. *The Protestant Establishment.* New York: Random House, 1964.

——. *Puritan Boston and Quaker Philadelphia.* New York: Free Press, 1979.

Bamford, T. W. *The Rise of the Public Schools.* London: Nelson, 1967.

Barrett, Joan, and Goldfarb, Sally F. *The Insider's Guide to Prep Schools.* New York: E. P. Dutton, 1979.

Bell, Daniel. *The Cultural Contradictions of Capitalism.* New York: Basic Books, 1976.

Bernstein, Basil. *Class, Codes and Control.* Vol. 3, *Towards a Theory of Educational Transmissions.* Rev. ed. London: Routledge & Kegan Paul, 1977.

——. *Class, Codes and Control.* Vol. 2, *Applied Studies Towards a Sociology of Language.* London and Boston: Routledge & Kegan Paul, 1973.

——. *Class, Codes and Control: Theoretical Studies Towards a Sociology of Language.* 2d rev. ed. London: Routledge & Kegan Paul, 1974.

Birmingham, Stephen. *The Right People: A Portrait of the American Social Establishment.* Boston, Mass.: Little, Brown, 1968.

Birnbach, Lisa, ed., *The Official Preppy Handbook.* New York: Workman Publishing, 1980.

Blumberg, Paul M., and Paul, P. W. "Continuities and Discontinuities in Upper-Class Marriages." *Journal of Marriage and the Family* 37 (February 1975): 63–77.

Bourdieu, Pierre. "Systems of Education and Systems of Thought." In *Knowledge and Control,* edited by Michael F. D. Young. London: Collier-Macmillan, 1971.

Bourdieu, Pierre, and Passeron, Jean-Claude. *Reproduction: In Education, Society, and Culture.* Beverly Hills, Calif.: Sage, 1977.

Bowen, James. *Soviet Education: Anton Makarenko and the Years of Experiment.* Madison and Milwaukee, Wis.: University of Wisconsin Press, 1965.

Bowles, Samuel, and Gintis, Herbert. *Schooling in Capitalist America.* New York: Basic Books, 1976.

Boyd, David. *Elites and Their Education.* Slough, England: NFER Publishing, 1973.

Bray, Mark. "The Re-emergence of Private Education in China." *International Review of Education* 28 (1982): 95–97.

Brint, Steven G. "The Occupational Class Identifications of Professionals." Paper presented at the American Sociological Association annual meeting, San Antonio, Texas, August 1984.

——. "Intra-occupational Stratification in Six High Status Occupations: An Analysis of Status and Status Attainment in Academe, Science, Law, Corporate Management, Engineering and Medicine." Photocopy. Yale University, New Haven, 1980.

Cappell, C. L., and Halliday, T. C. "Professional Projects of Elite Chicago Lawyers, 1950–1974." *American Bar Foundation Research Journal* (1983): 291–340.

Charters, W. W., Jr. "Social Class Analysis and the Control of Public Education." *Harvard Educational Review* 23 (Fall 1953): 268–79, 283.

Clavell, James. *King Rat.* Boston, Mass.: Little, Brown, 1962.

Coleman, James S. *The Adolescent Society: The Social Life of the Teenager and Its Impact on Education.* New York: Free Press, 1961.

Coleman, James S., et al. *Equality of Educational Opportunity.* Washington, D.C.: U.S. Government Printing Office, 1966.

Coleman, James S.; Hoffer, Thomas; and Kilgore, Sally. *High School Achievement.* New York: Basic Books, 1982.

Coles, Robert. *Children of Privilege.* Boston: Little, Brown, 1977.

Collins, Randall. "Functional and Conflict Theories of Educational Stratification." *American Sociological Review* 36 (December 1971): 1002–19.

——. "Where are Educational Requirements for Employment Highest?" *Sociology of Education* 47 (Fall 1974): 419–42.

——. *Conflict Sociology: Toward an Explanatory Science.* New York: Academic Press, 1975.

——. "Some Comparative Principles of Educational Stratification." *Harvard Educational Review* 47 (February 1977): 1–27.

——. *The Credential Society.* New York: Academic Press, 1979.

Cookson, Peter Willis, Jr. "Teacher Evaluation and Professional Growth in Independent Schools." Report to the Spencer Foundation, New York University, 1978.

——. "Teacher Evaluation in Independent Schools: An Empirical Investigation." *Independent School* 39 (May 1980): 47–54.

——. "The Educational Attitudes of Private School Educators." Paper presented at the American Sociological Association annual meeting, New York, August 1980.

——. "Private Secondary Boarding School and Public Suburban High School Graduation: An Analysis of College Attendance Plans." Ph.D. diss., New York University, 1981.

——. "Boarding Schools and the Moral Community." *Journal of Educational Thought* 16 (August 1982): 89–97.

Cookson, Peter Willis, Jr., and Persell, Caroline Hodges. "Social Structure and Educational Programs: A Comparison of Elite Boarding Schools and Public Education in the United States." Paper presented at the American Sociological Association annual meeting, San Francisco, September 1978.

——. "A Typology of American Boarding Schools Today." Paper presented at the American Educational Research Association annual meeting, New York, April 1981.

——. "The Men's Club: Gender Stratification in Elite School Leadership." Paper presented at the Eastern Sociological Society annual meeting, Philadelphia, March 1985a.

——. "English and American Residential Secondary Schools: A Comparative Study of the Reproduction of Social Elites." *Comparative Education Review,* 29 (August 1985b): 283–98.

Conover, James Potter. *Memories of a Great Schoolmaster (Dr. Henry A. Coit).* Boston: Houghton, Mifflin and Company, 1906.

Coser, Lewis A. *Masters of Sociological Thought.* New York: Harcourt Brace Jovanovich, 1971.

Coser, Lewis A.; Kadushin, Charles; and Powell, Walter W. *Books: The Culture & Commerce of Publishing.* New York: Basic Books, 1982.

Coser, Lewis A., and Rosenberg, Bernard, eds. *Sociological Theory: A Book of Readings.* 4th ed. New York: Macmillan, 1976.

Crane, Diana. "Scientists at Major and Minor Universities: A Study of Productivity and Recognition." *American Sociological Review* 30 (October 1965): 699–714.

Cremin, Lawrence A. *Traditions of American Education.* New York: Basic Books, 1977.

Csikszentmihalyi, Mihaly, and Larson, Reed. *Being Adolescent: Conflict and Growth in the Teenage Years.* New York: Basic Books, 1984.

Curran, J. "Exams that Keep the Elite on Top." *London Times,* 29 June 1983, 10.

DiMaggio, Paul. "Cultural Capital and School Success: The Impact of Status Culture Participation on the Grades of U.S. High School Students." *American Sociological Review* 47 (April 1982): 189–201.

DiMaggio, Paul, and Brown, Paula. *The American Arts Audience: Its Study and Its Character.* Washington, D.C.: National Endowment for the Arts, 1978.

DiMaggio, Paul, and Useem, Michael. "Coming to Our Senses—Significance of Arts for American Education." *Harvard Educational Review* 48 (February 1978): 103–6.

——. "Social Class and Arts Consumption: The Origins and Consequences of Class Differences in Exposure to the Arts in America." *Theory and Society* 5 (Spring 1978), 141–216.

——. "Cultural Property and Public-Policy—Emerging Tensions in Government Support for Arts." *Social Research* 45 (1978): 356–89.

Domhoff, G. William. *Who Rules America?* Englewood Cliffs, N.J.: Prentice-Hall, 1967.

——. *The Bohemian Grove and Other Retreats.* New York: Harper & Row, 1970.

——. *The Higher Circles.* New York: Vintage, 1974.

——. *Who Really Rules? New Haven and Community Power Reexamined.* New Brunswick, N.J.: Transaction Books, 1978.

——. *Who Rules America Now?* Englewood Cliffs, N. J.: Prentice-Hall, 1983.

Dornbush, Sanford M. "The Military Academy as an Assimilating Institution." *Social Forces* 33 (1955): 316–21.

Dreeben, Robert. *On What is Learned in School.* Reading, Mass.: Addison-Wesley, 1968.

Dreier, Peter. "The Position of the Press in the U.S. Power Structure." *Social Problems* 29 (February 1982): 298–310.

Drury, Roger W. *Drury and St. Paul's: The Scars of a SchoolMaster.* Boston: Little, Brown, 1964.

Duncan, Otis Dudley. "A Socioeconomic Index for all Occupations." In *Occupations and Social Status,* edited by Albert J. Reiss, Jr. New York: Free Press, 1961.

References

Duncan, Otis Dudley; Featherman, David L.; and Duncan, Beverly. *Socioeconomic Background and Achievements*. New York: Seminar Press, 1972.

Durkheim, Emile. *Education and Sociology*. Translated by Sherwood D. Fox. New York: Free Press, 1956.

————. *Moral Education: A Study of the Theory and Application of the Sociology of Education*. Translated by Everett K. Wilson and Herman Schnurer. New York: Free Press, 1961.

————. *The Evolution of Educational Thought*. Translated by Peter Collins. Boston: Routledge & Kegan Paul, 1977.

Eckland, B. K., and Peterson, R. E. *The Exeter Study: Technical Report and Compendium of Findings*. Princeton, N.J.: Educational Testing Service, 1969.

Elkind, David. *The Hurried Child: Growing Up Too Fast Too Soon*. Reading, Mass.: Addison-Wesley, 1981.

Epstein, Joyce Levy. *The Quality of School Life*. Lexington, Mass.: Lexington Books, 1981.

Erikson, Erik H. *Childhood and Society*. 2d ed. New York: W. W. Norton, 1963.

Etzioni, Amitai, ed. *A Sociological Reader on Complex Organizations*. New York: Holt, Rinehart & Winston, 1965.

Evans, Florence. *The Headmaster*. London: Macmillan, 1979.

Falsey, Barbara, and Heyns, Barbara. "The College Channel: Private and Public Schools Reconsidered." *Sociology of Education* 57 (April 1984): 111–22.

Farnham, Nicholas, et al. "University Entrance Examinations and Performance Expectations, A Comparison of the Situation in the United States, Great Britain, France, and West Germany." ERIC document 227-102. Washington, D.C.: National Commission on Excellence in Education, 1982.

Feather, N. J. "Value Similarity and Value Systems in State and Independent Secondary Schools." *Australian Journal of Psychology* (December 1972): 305–15.

Finch, Janet. *Married to the Job: Wives' Incorporation in Men's Work*. London: Allen & Unwin, 1983.

Fiske, Edward B. "High Schools Stiffen Diploma Requirements." *New York Times*, 9 October 1983, 1, 68.

Fitzsimmons, William R., and Reed, Warren C. "Counselor Recommendations: Their Value in College Admissions." *College Board Review* 124 (Summer 1982): 7–9; 24–25.

Foucault, Michel. *Discipline and Punish*. Translated by Alan Sheridan. New York: Vintage, 1979.

Fraser, George MacDonald. *The World of the Public School*. New York: St. Martin's Press, 1977.

Fraser, W. R. *Residential Education*. Oxford: Pergamon Press, 1968.

Gaines, R. L. *The Finest Education Money Can Buy: A Concerned Look at America's Prestige Schools*. New York: Simon & Schuster, 1972.

Gathorne-Hardy, Jonathan. *The Old School Tie*. New York: Viking Press, 1978.

Gilligan, Carol. *In a Different Voice*. Cambridge, Mass.: Harvard University Press, 1982.

Glasberg, Davita Silfen. "Corporate Power and Control: The Case of Leasco Corporation versus Chemical Bank." *Social Problems* 29 (December 1981): 104–16.

Goffman, Erving. "Symbols of Class Status." *British Journal of Sociology* 2 (1951): 294–310.

————. *Asylums: Essays on the Social Situation of Mental Patients and Other Inmates*. New York: Anchor Books, 1961.

————. "The Characteristics of Total Institutions." In *Complex Organizations*, edited by Amitai Etzioni. New York: Holt, Rinehart & Winston, 1969.

Golding, William. *Lord of the Flies*. New York: Coward-McCann, 1962.

Goode, William J. "The Protection of the Inept." *American Sociological Review* 32 (February 1967): 5–19.

Gossage, Carolyn. *A Question of Privilege*. Toronto: Peter Martin, 1977.

Granovetter, Mark. "The Strength of Weak Ties." *American Journal of Sociology* 78 (May 1973): 1360–80.

————. "The Strength of Weak Ties: A Network Theory Revisited." In *Sociological Theory 1983*, edited by Randall Collins. San Francisco: Jossey-Bass Inc., 1983.

Gutwillig, Robert. "The Selective Seventeen: A Guide to Upper-Class Education." *Esquire*, November 1960, 162–63.

Halberstam, David. *The Best and the Brightest*. New York: Random House, 1969.

Halsey, A. H.; Heath, A. F.; and Ridge, J. M. *Origins and Destinations: Family, Class and Education in Modern Britain*. Oxford: Clarendon Press, 1980.

Hammack, Floyd M., and Cookson, Peter W., Jr. "Colleges Attended by Graduates of Elite Secondary Schools." *The Educational Forum* 44 (May 1980): 483–90.

The Handbook of Private Schools. Boston, Mass.: Porter Sargent, 1980, 1981, 1984.

Harp, John. "Social Inequalities in the Transmission of Knowledge: The Case Against the Schools." In *Structured Inequality in Canada,* edited by John Harp and John R. Hoffey. Scarborough: Prentice-Hall, 1980.

Harrington, John. "What has Happened to Our Product?" *Independent School Bulletin* 35 (December 1975): 64–65.

Harvard Educational Review. Socialization and Schools. Special Issue, reprint no. 1. Cambridge, Mass.: Harvard Educational Review, 1968.

Hawes, Gene R. *Hawes Comprehensive Guide to Colleges.* New York: New American Library, 1979.

Heald, Tim. *Old Boy Networks: Who We Know and How We Use Them.* New York: Ticknor & Fields, 1984.

Heckscher, August. *St. Paul's: The Life of a New England School.* New York: Charles Scribner's Sons, 1980.

Heintz, Peter. "Educational Code, Role Expectations and Information on the Social Structure: Some Theoretical Considerations." *Comparative Education Review* 19 (February 1975): 144–54.

Heyns, Barbara. "Social Selection and Stratification within Schools." *American Journal of Sociology* 79 (May 1974): 1434–51.

Hochschild, Adam. "True Prep: The Ties that Bond." *Mother Jones,* May 1982, 41–48.

Hoggart, Richard. *The Uses of Literacy.* London: Chatto and Windus, 1957.

Hopper, Earl. "Stratification, Education and Mobility in Industrial Societies." In *Readings in the Theory of Educational Systems,* edited by Earl Hopper. London: Hutchinson, 1971.

Jacoby, Susan. *Inside Soviet Schools.* New York: Schocken Books, 1975.

Jencks, Christopher. "Social Stratification and Higher Education." *Harvard Educational Review* 38 (Spring 1968): 277–316.

Jencks, Christopher, et al. *Inequality.* New York: Basic Books, 1972.

———. *Who Gets Ahead? Determinants of Economic Success in America.* New York: Basic Books, 1979.

Jencks, Christopher, and Brown, Marsha D. "Effects of High Schools on their Students." *Harvard Educational Review* 45 (August 1975): 273–324.

Jessop, Dorothy Jones. "Topic Variation in Levels of Agreement between Parents and Adolescents." *Public Opinion Quarterly* 46 (Winter 1982): 538–59.

———. "Family Relationships as Viewed by Parents and Adolescents: A Specification." *Journal of Marriage and the Family* 43 (February 1981): 95–107.

Kalton, G. *The Public Schools: A Factual Survey.* London: Longmans, 1966.

Kamens, David. "Colleges and Elite Formation: The Case of Prestigious American Colleges." *Sociology of Education* 47 (Summer 1974): 354–78.

Kanter, Rosabeth Moss. "Commitment and Social Organization: A Study of Commitment Mechanisms in Utopian Communities." *American Sociological Review* 33 (August 1968): 499–517.

———. *Commitment and Community: Communes and Utopias in Sociological Perspective.* Cambridge, Mass.: Harvard University Press, 1972.

Karabel, Jerome. "Status-Group Struggle, Organizational Interests, and the Limits of Institutional Autonomy: the Transformation of Harvard, Yale, and Princeton 1918–1940." *Theory and Society* (January 1984): 1–40.

Karabel, Jerome, and Astin, Alexander. "Social Class, Academic Ability, and College 'Quality.'" *Social Forces* 53 (March 1975): 381–98.

Karabel, Jerome, and Halsey, A. H. *Power and Ideology in Education.* New York: Oxford University Press, 1977.

Karen, David. "Who Gets into Harvard? Selection and Exclusion." Ph.D. diss., Department of Sociology, Harvard University, 1985.

Kavaler, Lucy. *The Private World of High Society.* New York: Douglas McKay, 1960.

Kelsall, R. K. *Graduates: The Sociology of an Elite.* London: Methuen, 1972.

Kerckhoff, Alan C. *Socialization and Social Class.* Englewood Cliffs, N.J.: Prentice-Hall, 1972.

———. "Stratification Processes and Outcomes in England and the United States." *American Sociological Review* 39 (December 1972): 789–801.

———. "Patterns of Educational Attainment in Great Britain." *American Journal of Sociology* 80 (May 1975): 1428–37.

Kerckhoff, Alan C.; Campbell, Richard T.; and Trott, Jerry M. "Educational and Occupational Attainment in Great Britain." *American Sociological Review* 47 (June 1982): 347–73.

References

Kett, Joseph F. *Rites of Passage: Adolescence in America 1790 to the Present.* New York: Basic Books, 1977.

Klitgaard, Robert. *Choosing Elites.* New York: Basic Books, 1985.

Knowles, John. *A Separate Peace.* New York: Macmillan, 1959.

Kohlberg, Lawrence. "Development of Moral Character and Moral Ideology." In *Child Development Research,* edited by M.L. Hoffman and L.W. Hoffman. New York: Russell Sage Foundation, 1964.

Kohn, Melvin L. *Class and Conformity: A Study in Values.* Homewood, Ill.: Dorsey Press, 1969.

———. "Social Class and Parental Values: Another Confirmation of the Relationship." *American Sociological Review* 41 (June 1976): 538–45.

Kohn, Melvin L., and Schooler, Carmi. "Job Conditions and Personality: A Longitudinal Assessment of their Reciprocal Effects." *American Journal of Sociology* 87 (May 1983): 1257–86.

Konolige, Kit, and Konolige, Frederica. *The Power of their Glory, America's Ruling Class: The Episcopalians.* New York: Wyden, 1978.

Kotz, David M. *Bank Control of Large Corporations in the United States.* Berkeley, Calif.: University of California Press, 1978.

Kraushaar, Otto F. *American Nonpublic Schools: Patterns of Diversity.* Baltimore: Johns Hopkins University Press, 1972.

———. *Private Schools: From the Puritans to the Present.* Bloomington, Ind.: Phi Delta Kappa Educational Foundation, 1976.

Krumpe, Elizabeth Chamberlin. "The Educational Ideas of the Clarendon Headmasters from 1860 to 1914 (England)." *Dissertation Abstracts International* 44 (1983): Sect. A, 1545.

Lambert, Royston. *The Hothouse Society.* London: Weidenfeld & Nicholson, 1968.

———. "The Public School Ethos." In *The Education of Elites,* edited by Madeleine MacDonald. Milton Keynes, England: Open University Press, 1977.

Lasch, Christopher. *The Culture of Narcissism.* New York: W. W. Norton, 1979.

Laski, Harold J. *The Danger of Being a Gentleman and Other Essays.* New York: Viking, 1940.

Lenski, Gerhard E. *Power and Privilege: A Theory of Social Stratification.* New York: McGraw-Hill, 1966.

Levine, Steven B. "The Rise of American Boarding Schools and the Development of a National Upper Class." *Social Problems* 28 (October 1980): 63–94.

Lewis, Lionel S., and Wanner, Richard A. "Private Schooling and the Status Attainment Process." *Sociology of Education* 52 (April 1979): 99–112.

Lightfoot, Sara Lawrence. *The Good High School: Portraits of Character and Culture.* New York: Basic Books, 1983.

Lortie, Dan. *School-Teacher.* Chicago: University of Chicago Press, 1975.

McArthur, C. "Personalities of Public and Private School Boys." *Harvard Educational Review* 24 (Fall 1954): 256–62.

McBeth, Sally J. "The Primer and the Hoe." *Natural History,* August 1984, 4–12.

Maccoby, Michael. *The Gamesman: The New Corporate Leaders.* New York: Simon & Schuster, 1976.

McDill, Edward L., and Rigsby, Leo C. *Structure and Process in Secondary Schools: The Academic Impact of Educational Climates.* Baltimore, Md.: Johns Hopkins University Press, 1973.

MacDonald, K. M. "The Persistence of an Elite: The Case of British Army Officer Cadets." *Sociological Review* 28 (August 1980): 635–40.

MacDonald, Madeleine, ed. *The Education of Elites.* Milton Keynes, England: Open University Press, 1977.

Machiavelli, Niccolò. *The Prince.* Translated by N. H. Thomson. Danbury, Conn.: Grolier Enterprises, 1981.

McLachlan, James. *American Boarding Schools: A Historical Study.* New York: Charles Scribner's Sons, 1970.

McPhee, John. *The Headmaster: Frank L. Boyden of Deerfield.* New York: Farrar, Straus and Giroux, 1966.

Maeroff, Gene I. "Top Eastern Colleges Report Unusual Rise in Applications." *New York Times,* 21 February 1984, A1, C10.

Malabre, Alfred L., Jr. "Drugs are Preying on the Prep Schools." *Wall Street Journal,* 19 May 1983, 34.

Mangan, J. A. *Athleticism in the Victorian and Edwardian Public School.* Cambridge, England: Cambridge University Press, 1981.

References

Mann, Thomas. *The Magic Mountain.* New York: Alfred J. Knopf, 1960.
Margolick, David. "Budding Lawyers on Wall Street Take New Approach to Tradition." *New York Times,* 30 November 1983, B1, B7.
Martindale-Hubbell Law Directory (annual). New York: Martindale-Hubbell, 1984.
Masemann, Vandra Lea. "Critical Ethnography in the Study of Comparative Education." *Comparative Education Review* 26 (February 1982): 1–15.
May, Rollo. *Power and Innocence.* New York: W. W. Norton, 1972.
Meader, Granville. "The State of the Arts." In *The State of the Arts and Corporate Support,* edited by Gideon Chagy. New York: Paul S. Eriksson, 1971.
Merton, Robert K. *Social Theory and Social Structure.* Rev. ed. New York: Free Press, 1968.
Meyer, John. "The Charter: Conditions of Diffuse Socialization in School." In *Social Processes and Social Structure,* edited by W. Richard Scott. New York: Holt, Rinehart & Winston, 1970.
———. "Education as an Institution." *American Journal of Sociology* 83 (July 1977): 55–77.
Miller, Karen; Kohn, Melvin L.; and Schooler, Carmi. "Educational Self-direction and the Cognitive Functioning of Students." *Social Forces* (forthcoming) 1985.
Mills, C. Wright. *The Power Elite.* London: Oxford University Press, 1959.
Mintz, Beth. "The President's Cabinet, 1897–1972: A Contribution to the Power Structure Debate." *Insurgent Sociologist* 5 (Spring 1975): 131–48.
Moore, Gwen. "The Structure of a National Elite Network." *American Sociological Review* 44 (October 1979): 673–92.
The National College Databank. Princeton, N.J.: Peterson's Guides, 1984. Bibliographic Retrieval Service electronic database.
National Commission on Excellence in Education. *A Nation at Risk: The Imperative for Educational Reform.* Washington, D.C.: U.S. Government Printing Office, 1983.
National Opinion Research Center. *Report to the National Center for Education Statistics Under Contract No. 300–78–0208.* Chicago: National Opinion Research Center, November 1980.
National Public Radio. "Days and Nights at the Round Table: How Dartmouth Admits Its Freshmen." *Chronicle of Higher Education* (20 April 1981): 9–10.
Neill, A. S. *Summerhill: A Radical Approach to Child Rearing.* New York: Hart Publishing, 1964.
New York Post, "Coke Scandal Rips Posh Prep School," 5 May 1984.
New York Times, "14 Choate Students Expelled in Inquiry Into Cocaine Arrest," 5 May 1984.
———. "Prep Schools in a Struggle to Curb Spread of Cocaine," 27 May 1984.
Nicklas, John M. "The Independent School's Headmaster: A Descriptive Study." *Dissertation Abstracts International* 45 (1982): Sect. A, P0713.
Offer, Daniel; Ostrov, Eric; and Howard, Kenneth I. *The Adolescent.* New York: Basic Books, 1981.
Orwell, George. *1984.* New York: New American Library, 1949.
Ostrander, Susan A. "Upper Class Women: Community Work as Holding-Action in the Class Structure of American Society." Paper presented at the American Sociological Association annual meeting, Chicago, Illinois, August 1977.
———. "Class Consciousness as Conduct and Meaning: The Case of Upper Class Women." *Insurgent Sociologist* 9 (Fall/Winter 1979–1980): 38–50.
———. *Women of the Upper Class.* Philadelphia: Temple University Press, 1984.
Paltridge, James Gilbert; Hurst, Julie; and Morgan, Anthony. *Boards of Trustees: Their Decision Patterns.* Berkeley, Calif.: University of California, Center for Research and Development in Higher Education, 1973.
Parkin, Frank. "Strategies of Social Closure and Class Formation." In *Social Analysis of Class Structure.* London: Tavistock Publications, 1974.
Parsons, Talcott. "The School Class as a Social System: Some of Its Functions in American Society." *Harvard Educational Review* 29 (Fall 1959): 297–318.
Persell, Caroline Hodges. *Education and Inequality.* New York: Free Press, 1977.
Persell, Caroline Hodges, and Cookson, Peter W., Jr. "The Effective Principal in Action." Reston, Va.: National Association of Secondary School Principals, 1982.
———. "Chartering and Bartering: Elite Education and Social Reproduction." Paper presented at the American Sociological Association annual meeting, Washington, D.C., August 1985.
Piaget, Jean. *The Moral Judgment of the Child.* New York: Harcourt Brace Jovanovich, 1932.
———. *The Psychology of Intelligence.* London: Routledge & Kegan Paul, 1950.
———. *The Construction of Reality in the Child.* New York: Basic Books, 1954.

References

Pierson, George W. *The Education of American Leaders.* New York: Frederick A. Praeger, 1969.

Plisko, Valena White. *The Condition of Education, 1984 Edition.* Washington, D.C.: U.S. Government Printing Office, 1984.

Prescott, Peter S. *A World of Our Own: Notes on Life and Learning in a Boys' Preparatory School.* New York: Coward-McCann, 1970.

Priest, T. B. "Education and Career among Corporate Chief Executive Officers: A Historical Note." *Social Science Quarterly* 66 (June 1982a): 342–49.

———. "A Note on Who's Who in America as a Biographical Data Source in Studies of Elites." *Sociological Methods & Research* 11 (August 1982b): 81–88.

Priest, T. B.; Sylves, Richard T.; and Scudder, David F. "Corporate Advice: Large Corporations and Federal Advisory Committees." *Social Science Quarterly* 65 (1984): 100–11.

Primack, Joel, and Hippel, Frank von. *Advice and Dissent: Scientists in the Political Arena.* New York: New American Library, 1974.

Private Independent Schools. Wallingford, Conn.: Bunting and Lyon, 1981.

Rae, Daphne. *A World Apart.* Guildford, England: Luiterworth Press, 1983.

Rae, John. *The Public School Revolution.* London: Faber & Faber, 1981.

Ratcliff, Richard E. "Banks and Corporate Lending: An Analysis of the Impact of the Internal Structure of the Capitalist Class on the Lending Behavior of Banks." *American Sociological Review* 45 (August 1980): 553–70.

Ravitch, Diane. *The Great School Wars.* New York: Basic Books, 1974.

Rehberg, Richard A., and Hotchkiss, Lawrence. "Educational Decision Makers: the School Guidance Counselor and Social Mobility." *Sociology of Education* 45 (Fall 1972): 339–61.

Rehberg, Richard A., and Rosenthal, Evelyn R. *Class and Merit in the American High School—An Assessment of the Revisionist and Meritocratic Arguments.* New York: Longman, 1978.

Riesman, David, with Nathan Glazer, and Reuel Denney. *The Lonely Crowd: A Study of the Changing American Character.* New Haven, Conn.: Yale University Press, 1960.

Roache, Beverly." The Private School as Total Institution: Parental Culture." *Delta* 15 (1974): 18–23.

Robinson, Robert V. "Reproducing Class Relations in Industrial Capitalism." *American Sociological Review* 49 (April 1984): 182–96.

Rodriguez, Richard. *Hunger of Memory.* New York: Bantam Books, 1982.

Rogers, Everett M., and Kincaid, D. Lawrence. *Communications Networks: Toward a New Paradigm for Research.* New York: Free Press, 1981.

Rogers, Everett M., and Larsen, Judith K. *Silicon Valley Fever: The Growth of High-Tech Culture.* New York: Basic Books, 1984.

Rothman, Stanley, and Lichter, S. Robert. "Media and Business Elites: Two Classes in Conflict?" *Public Interest* 69 (Fall 1982): 117–25.

Rousseau, Jean Jacques. *Emile: Or, On Education.* New York: Basic Books, 1979.

Salinger, J.D. *The Catcher in the Rye.* Boston: Little, Brown, 1951.

Salter, Brian, and Tapper, Ted. *Education, Politics and the State.* London: Grant McIntyre, 1981.

Saltonstall, William G. *Lewis Perry of Exeter.* New York: Atheneum, 1980.

Salzman, Harold, and Domhoff, G. William. "Corporations, Non-profit Groups and Government: Do They Interlock?" *Insurgent Sociologist* 9 (Fall/Winter, 1979–1980): 121–35.

Scott, John Finley. *Internalization of Norms.* Englewood Cliffs, N.J.: Prentice-Hall, 1971.

Secondary School Admissions Test Board. *Independent Secondary Schools: A Handbook.* Princeton, N.J.: Educational Testing Service, 1982.

Sewell, William H.; Hauser, Robert M.; and Featherman, David L. *Schooling and Achievement in American Society.* New York: Academic Press, 1976.

Shaw, J. "Finishing Schools—Some Implications of Sex-Segregated Education." In *Sexual Divisions and Society,* edited by D.L. Darker and S. Allen. London: Tavistock, 1976.

Sizer, Theodore R., ed. *The Age of The Academies.* New York: Bureau of Publications, Teachers College, Columbia University, 1964.

———. *Horace's Compromise: The Dilemma of the American High School.* Boston: Houghton Mifflin, 1984.

Smigel, Erwin. *The Wall Street Lawyer.* New York: Free Press, 1964.

The Social Register. New York: Social Register Association, 1984.

Spady, William G. "The Impact of School Resources on Students." In *Schooling and Achievement in American Society,* edited by William H. Sewell, Robert M. Hauser, and David L. Featherman. New York: Academic Press, 1976.

Spender, Dale. *Invisible Women: The School Scandal.* London: Writers and Readers Publishing Cooperative, 1982.

Stent, Angela. "The Prep School Boom." *Change,* August 1976, 16–18.

Stouffer, Samuel Andrew. *The American Soldier: Adjustment During Army Life.* Vol. 1; *The American Soldier: Combat and Its Aftermath.* Vol. 2. Princeton, N.J.: Princeton University Press, 1949.

Strong, William S. "New England Prep Schools—Are They Still the ULTIMATE?" *Town and Country,* August 1980, 65–72.

Talbot, Marjo. "The New Student Marketing Survey." Report, Committee on Boarding Schools, National Association of Independent Schools, Boston, Massachusetts, 1983.

Theroux, A. "The Pick of the Prep Schools." *Travel and Leisure,* November 1982, 24–28.

Thomas, Evan. "Choosing the Class of '83." *Time,* 9 April 1979, 73–74.

Tinto, Vincent. "College Origin and Patterns of Status Attainment." *Sociology of Work and Occupations* 7 (November 1980): 457–86.

Turner, Ralph H. "Sponsored and Contest Mobility and the School System." In *Class, Status and Power,* edited by Reinhard Bendix and Seymour Martin Lipset. 2d ed. New York: Free Press, 1966.

U.S. Bureau of the Census. *Statistical Abstract of the United States: 1982–83.* Washington, D.C.: U.S. Government Printing Office, 1982.

———. *Statistical Abstract of the United States: 1984.* Washington, D.C.: U.S. Government Printing Office, 1983.

———. *Statistical Abstract of the United States: 1985.* Washington, D.C.: U.S. Government Printing Office, 1984.

Useem, Michael. "The Social Organization of the American Business Elite." *American Sociological Review* 44 (August 1979): 553–72.

———. "Corporations and the Corporate Elite." *Annual Review of Sociology* 6 (1980): 41–77.

———. *The Inner Circle: Large Corporations and the Rise of Business Political Activity in the U.S. and U.K.* New York: Oxford University Press, 1984.

Useem, Michael, and Karabel, Jerome. "Educational Pathways Through Top Corporate Management: Patterns of Stratification Within Companies and Differences Among Companies." Paper presented at the American Sociological Association annual meeting, San Antonio, Texas, August 1984 (Revised November 1984).

Useem, Michael, and Miller, S. M. "Privilege and Domination: the Role of the Upper Class in American Higher Education." *Social Science Information* 14 (1975): 115–45.

Verdery, John D. *Partial Recall: The Afterthoughts of a Schoolmaster.* New York: Atheneum, 1981.

Wakeford, John. *The Cloistered Elite.* New York: Praeger, 1969.

Wald, Karen. *Children of Che: Childcare and Education in Cuba.* Palo Alto, Calif.: Ramparts Press, 1978.

Walford, Geoffrey. "Girls in Boys' Public Schools: A Prelude to Further Research." *British Journal of Sociology of Education* 4 (1983): 39–54.

Waller, Willard. *The Sociology of Teaching.* New York: John Wiley & Sons, 1965.

Weber, Max. "Types of Authority." In *Sociological Theory: A Book of Readings,* edited by Lewis A. Coser and Bernard Rosenberg. New York: Macmillan, 1976.

———. *Economy and Society.* Vol. 1. Translated by Ephraim Fischoff, et al. Berkeley, Calif.: University of California Press, 1976.

Weinberg, C., and Skager, R. "Social Status and Guidance Involvement." *Personnel and Guidance Journal* 44 (1966), 586–90.

Weinberg, Ian. "The Occupational Aspirations of British Public Schoolboys." *The School View* (Autumn 1966): 265–81.

———. *The English Public Schools: The Sociology of Elite Education.* New York: Atherton Press, 1967.

———. "Some Methodological and Field Problems of Social Research in Elite Secondary Schools." *Sociology of Education* 41 (Spring 1968): 141–55.

Weinzweig, Paul Alan. "Socialization and Subculture in Elite Education: A Study of a Canadian Boy's Private School." Ph.D. diss., University of Toronto, 1970.

Wessman, Alden E. "Scholastic and Psychological Effects of a Compensatory Education Program for Disadvantaged High School Students: Project ABC." In *Educating the Disadvantaged,* edited by E. Flaxman. New York: AMS Press, 1969.

Wheeler, Stanton. "The Structure of Formally Organized Socialization Settings." In *Socialization After Childhood,* edited by O. G. Brim and S. Wheeler. New York: John Wiley & Sons, 1966.

References

Who's Who in America. 43d ed. Chicago: Marquis Who's Who, 1984–85.

Wickenden, James W., Jr. "Letter to All Princeton Alumni." Princeton, N.J.: Princeton University, October 1979.

Wilensky, Harold L., and Lebeaux, Charles. *Industrial Society and Social Welfare.* New York: Free Press, 1958.

Wilkinson, R. *Gentlemanly Power.* London: Oxford University Press, 1964.

———. *Governing Elites.* London: Oxford University Press, 1969.

Winerip, Michael. "Moments of Truth Come by Mail for Seniors at Great Neck South." *New York Times,* 20 April 1984a, B1, B4.

———. "Hot Colleges and How They Get that Way." *New York Times Magazine,* 18 November 1984b, 68ff.

Winter, D. G.; Alpert, R.; and McClelland, D. C. "The Classic Personal Style." In *Learning in Social Settings,* edited by M.B. Miles and W. W. Charters, Jr. Boston: Allyn and Bacon, 1970.

Wober, Mallory. *English Girls' Boarding Schools.* London: Allen Lane, 1971.

Wright, Erik O.; Costello, Cynthia; Hachen, David; and Sprague, Joey. "The American Class Structure." *American Sociological Review* 47 (December 1982): 709–26.

Wrong, Dennis H. *Power: Its Forms, Bases, and Uses.* New York: Harper Colophon, 1979.

Yates, Richard. *A Good School.* New York: Delacorte Press, 1978.

School Bulletins Cited

The Bulletin of the Phillips Exeter Academy, January/February 1982.
The Choate-Rosemary Magazine, Fall 1981.
Cranbrook Schools, 1982–83.
Deerfield Life, 1982–83.
Groton School, 1981–82.
The Lawrenceville Experience, 1982–83.
The Midland School, 1983.
The Putney School, 1982.
Taft, 1981–82.
Verde Valley School, 1982–83.
Westtown School, 1982–83.

Index

Index